Grappling with Atrocity

Grappling with Atrocity

Guatemalan Theater in the 1990s

John Wesley Shillington

Madison • Teaneck
Fairleigh Dickinson University Press
London: Associated University Presses

© 2002 by Rosemont Publishing & Printing Corp.

All rights reserved. Authorization to photocopy items for internal or personal use, or the internal or personal use of specific clients, is granted by the copyright owner, provided that a base fee of $10.00, plus eight cents per page, per copy is paid directly to the Copyright Clearance Center, 222 Rosewood Drive, Danvers, Massachusetts 01923. [0-8386-3930-5/02 $10.00 + 8¢ pp, pc.]

Associated University Presses
440 Forsgate Drive
Cranbury, NJ 08512

Associated University Presses
16 Barter Street
London WC1A 2AH, England

Associated University Presses
P.O. Box 338, Port Credit
Mississauga, Ontario
Canada L5G 4L8

The paper used in this publication meets the requirements of the American National Standard for Permanence of Paper for Printed Library Materials Z30.48-1984.

Library of Congress Cataloging-in-Publication Data

Shillington, John.
    Grappling with atrocity : Guatemalan theater in the 1990s / John Wesley Shillington.
    p. cm.
    Includes bibliographical references and index.
    ISBN 0-8386-3930-5 (alk. paper)
    1. Guatemalan drama—20th century—History and criticism. 2. Guatemala—History—Civil War, 1960–1996—Literature and the war. I. Title.
PQ7493 .S45 2002
862'.64097281—dc21   2001040898

PRINTED IN THE UNITED STATES OF AMERICA

Contents

Acknowledgments	7
1. Introduction	11
2. History of Twentieth-Century Guatemalan Theater	35
3. Satiric Theater	77
4. Didactic Theater	113
5. Symbolic Theater	148
6. Conclusion	179
Notes	188
Bibliography	197
Index	205

Acknowledgments

I AM INDEBTED TO NUMEROUS PEOPLE FOR THEIR AID ON THIS PROject. I would like to thank the Guatemalan playwrights and artists for sharing their lives, work, and love of the theater with me. I also need to thank those people who helped me with the Spanish translations, including my dear friends Ginger Hooven, Patricia Campbell, and Hector Castro, all of whom live in Guatemala. I am grateful to Quique Mateo and Scott MacLauchlan, theater producers at *El Sitio* theater in Antigua, Guatemala, for their support on this project and for introducing me to Guatemalan artists. My sister, Sandra Shillington Lopez, and her husband, Toni Lopez, provided professional editing assistance in the final translations that was invaluable. I am grateful for the hours of conversation and guidance given to me by Dr. Oliver Gerland and Dr. Lee Potts. My partner, Elizabeth Webster Shillington, supported this project in innumerable ways from encouragement to hours of proofreading. And lastly, I thank my favorite Guatemalans, my children, Giancarlo and Maggie, for giving me the time and space to work on this lengthy project. I dedicate this study to them.

Grappling with Atrocity

1
Introduction

As I walked out of the bi-national institute IGA *(INSTITUTO Guatemalteco Americano)* in Guatemala City, where I had taught in the early 1990s, my head was swirling from three interviews that day with Guatemalan playwrights. I had forgotten the level of intense violence they wrote about and had experienced. One of the younger playwrights, Rubén Nájera, stated it clearly when he said, "Of course I write about the violence. I have never known a life outside of violence while living here in Guatemala." He was born in 1960, about the same time the civil war began. Another playwright that morning related to me how he had been tortured by the army during the repression of the 1970s. The third spoke about how he had lost his niece. She had "disappeared" during the "worst years," the early 1980s, because she was a student leader. All of them had been affected by the endless string of violence that occurred during the thirty-six years of civil war, which officially ended with the signing of the Peace Accord in 1996. Although the years of "peace" have been stressful and challenging, all three of them affirmed the statement by Luis Escobedo, an ex-guerrilla Guatemalan playwright: "A bad peace is better than a good war" (interview with Escobedo).

After those interviews my head was pounding from the effort of trying to adjust to the culture shock of being back in Guatemala. I needed a break. Heading toward the nearest Taco Bell, two blocks away, I turned the corner where I had often bought fruit on the street on my way to work at the IGA. I saw two men in their early twenties across the street in a heated conversation. The bigger one gave a sharp shove to the other. I stared in dull shock as the two started to fight with each other. Clearly the now-bloodied smaller one was going to lose the battle. A friend of the bigger one finally pulled him off and started to walk him away. The shorter man staggered to his feet, determined to make one last strike. He ran up, ready to attack with his right, when the larger man looked around, blocked the hit, and proceeded to pummel the bloodied man's face. At that point I moved on, wanting to escape from the escalating violence.

That fist fight might serve as an analogy for how the violence in Guatemala escalated to the level of a civil war. In 1960 a small group of soldiers rebelled against the corrupt government and military. This fight escalated as the soldiers organized a guerrilla peasant army. They demanded basic human rights and were brutally decimated over the course of thirty-six years. Using the fight I witnessed as an analogy, the mighty force of the stronger one represents the army and the smaller man's determination to fight for the shreds of his dignity, knowing he was probably going to lose, represents the rebels, or maybe the university students, professors, lawyers, leftists, peasants, priests, reporters, leaders of human rights groups, the frightened and angry urbanites who took up the guerrilla cause, the disappeared, those tortured by the army, or the decimated Mayan population. Perhaps the image could be useful in describing the persecution felt by the exiled or silenced directors, playwrights, and actors during the repression.

After a closer look, however, the analogy seems absurdly strained. No conflict of individuals can encompass the level of atrocity that left 200,000 dead between 1960 and 1996, or the acts of genocide against the country's Mayan population, including the 626 massacres (Lobe 1999). It does not begin to portray the thousands of "disappeared"; (39% of all "disappearances" throughout Latin America between 1966 and 1987 took place in Guatemala; Simon 1987, 14). The analogy is not able to capture the superlatives necessary to describe Guatemala: the worst figures in all Latin America on land distribution (Simon 1987, 20); the first to introduce the use of the word "disappearances" as a repressive tool in the Americas, following a technique used by the Nazis as a means of eliminating opposition without creating martyrs; the worst Health Care in Central America and, during the late 1970s, the second worst index of malnutrition in the world for children under the age of five (Trudeau 1993, 25); and the longest civil war in Latin America (Delli Sante 1996, 46), referred to in Guatemala simply as *la violencia* or *la situacion* [the situation]. All this in a country no bigger than my home state of Ohio.

The atrocities committed in the civil war have become a prominent subject in the theater in the 1990s. The theater in the 1990s has changed its emphasis from the provocative, revolutionary style characteristic of the late 1960s and 1970s. Instead, this theater seeks a balance between acknowledging the atrocities of the war and fostering a national reconciliation. The intense violence of the late 1970s and early 1980s effectively shut down the theater. National playwrights slowly began to portray social and political reality in Guatemala during the late 1980s and early 1990s. This movement has gathered momentum during the peace talks of the early 1990s with the culmination of the signing of the Peace Accord in 1996. Antiwar plays that use much factual history as well as plays that advocate a peaceful solution to the crisis have proliferated on the stage in the 1990s. This theatrical movement in Guatemala seeks to reconcile the present with the past by reflecting on the violence rather than laying blame for it. It foregrounds the turbulent past, reflecting on how violence begets violence, in order to find inspiration for the long road of forgiveness and healing. The purpose of this study is (1) to identify how the civil war as well as the change to civilian government in 1986, which culminated in the signing of the Peace Accord in 1996, has affected the form and content of the plays written in the 1990s; and (2) to examine the work of Guatemalan playwrights who have largely been ignored in Latin American theater studies.

In the chapters that follow I present plays written or produced in Guatemala City, the capital, in the 1990s that courageously grappled with the atrocities committed during the war as a means to help Guatemalans process their past and foster the national movement of reconciliation. I will trace the development of the middle-class mainstream *mestizo* [mixed European and native ancestry] theater in Guatemala in the twentieth century to present a context for understanding the plays of the 1990s. Within this historical overview, I highlight the "Golden Age" of Guatemalan theater in the 1960s and 1970s and its emphasis on protest plays. Latin American Theater Studies has identified a common international trend of protest plays written after the 1960s in Central and South America that directly challenges the Establishment; however, this dominant trend is no longer applicable to Guatemalan plays. The overview of twentieth-century plays in Guatemala suggests that a protest theatrical movement flourishes under dictatorships while a nationalistic theatre flourishes during the early stages of democracy.

Latin American scholar Judith Weiss defines national theatre as one that seeks to defuse potential conflict (1993, 6). However, a theater that seeks only to defuse potential conflict has no integrity. Reconciliation is meaningless unless the issues of the conflict are confronted and healing takes place on emotional, intellectual, and spiritual levels. My underlying assumption is that theater artists will inherently portray the reality of a nation's fears, aspirations, and significant cultural issues if censorship does not prevent them from doing so. The uppermost issue for Guatemalans is the wartime atrocity and how to avoid returning to the dark days of the late 1970s and early 1980s. Therefore, I believe the model of "theater of atrocity," which I will articulate with reference to the "theater of the Holocaust," describes Guatemalan theater most accurately in the 1990s. Atrocity is defined as overt violence on a large scale that produces communal shock, outrage, and condemnation of violence. Most of the plays in this study are communal condemnations of the violence and atrocities. However, the outrage is contained; the plays do not condemn the perpetrator nor suggest retribution. Rather, they suggest that understanding is the way to peace.

This argument raises three major questions, to be discussed in the conclusion: (1) What does this suggest about the purpose of theater in Guatemala at this time? (2) What are the limitations of this national theater movement which is promoted by both sides? and (3) How does this study challenge or enhance Latin American theater studies?

Balancing Theater of Atrocity and Theater of Reconciliation

The Truth Commission set up by the United Nations under the 1996 Peace Accord had asked that the information on the civil war be declassified in order to help with Guatemala's reconciliation process. The following excerpt from *The Economist* inspired my attempt to conceptualize this shift from revolutionary to reconciliatory themes:

> Roll over, General Pinochet. His Chilean regime's torturers and executioners were shown up as mere amateurs at their trade by the publication, last month, of a truth-commission study into the mass killings of the ghastly civil war in Guatemala. . . . Guatemala's truth commission was set up under the 1996 peace accords, which ended 36 years of fighting that had led, on its estimate, to 200,000 deaths, mostly of Amerindian Mayan peasants. To no one's surprise, the commission blamed the army for more than 90% of the torture, disappearances, murders and wholesale massacres. More surprisingly, it told the government the armed forces must be purged and reformed, and those guilty of genocide brought to justice. Genocide? The commission's use of the G-word has caused consternation—and tearful joy. (*The Economist*, March 13, 1999)

Thinking about theater and genocide brought up an obvious corollary: "theater of the Holocaust," which falls under the larger rubric of theater of atrocity. Theater of atrocity emphasizes abominable violent events in history in order to confront the individual and shock him/her out of complacency. A crisis occurs in the psyche of a nation when the historical events are too terrifying "to find meaningful expression through the culture's available symbols" (Langer 1995, 10). When a social-political crisis such as war or the act of genocide occurs, the people of that nation experience a moral, spiritual, and philosophical collapse and are forced to reassess their existence. Holocaust scholar Lawrence Langer writes, "Living in times of catastrophe shifts the rhythm of our imaginative efforts from creating the future—the challenge for our ancestors—to fighting a rearguard action against forces which menace us with annihilation" (Langer 1978, 2). Langer writes that after a traumatic national experience the artist, psychologist, and historian share the task of describing the catastrophe. "It is a ponderous, unappealing responsibility since it shifts our focus from renewal to decay; but the alternative is a blind insistence on the continuity of culture that contradicts the rhythm of mutual destruction which history has imposed on our time" (4). The great challenge for Guatemala is how to uncover meaningful symbols for the decay caused by the civil war without dismantling the fragile establishment of peace.

Most theorists of Latin American theater identify a trend of protest/political theater which provokes one to act on current social or political issues. However, the general movement in theater in Guatemala is no longer one of protest, blame, or revolution. It is rather one of reflection and reconciliation, an attempt to pour oil on the waters of the crisis and chaos. The country is worn out by violence and seeks a solution different from the one offered by the protest model of challenging authority. By the early 1990s the citizens, the guerrillas and those involved in the resistance movement, the army, and the governmental officials were aware that the civil war was a losing battle for everyone. It was a unique period when both those in power and those with the resistance movement sought to find a peaceful solution. It is as if the authorities came to realize that although institutionalized violence can destroy personal and communal resistance, it cannot establish political power. Although members of the resistance movement might never have arrived at the negotiation table if they had not sought to resist the violence, they seemed to realize that security, stability, and sanity could not be attained by perpetuating the conflict.

Langer, who coined the term "theater of atrocity," distinguishes between atrocity and violence. If violence is explicable in terms of cause and effect, then, Langer states, atrocity goes beyond apparent reason. Yet he acknowledges that facing atrocity in art may have transformative effects. He writes:

> If philosophy and religion and even literature have taught us in the past that human vision expands through discovery of the best, the history of atrocity has challenged us with an enlargement of consciousness through recognition of the worst. Who can say whether such insight will inspire men to transfigure the "worst" into a new "best"? (Langer 1978, 68)

Langer's definition of atrocity is tenuous at best since it is arguable whether the practice of genocide by massacring unarmed Mayan Indians was unreasonable, albeit abominable. The *American Heritage Dictionary* describes atrocity as "extremely evil," which is too subjective to be useful. I would argue that atrocity produces communal shock, outrage, and condemnation of violence. Although the definition is still subjective, it acknowledges that the standard for atrocity for one culture is not necessarily the standard for another. Most of the plays in this study are communal condemnations of the violence and atrocities. However, the outrage is contained; the plays do not condemn the perpetrator nor in any way suggest retribution.

Both "theater of atrocity" in Guatemala and "theater of the Holocaust" are tied to a specific historic, horrific, genocidal period and seek to draw lessons that will aid the healing process. Langer holds that these catastrophic events have "encouraged some men and nations to consider torture and inappropriate death as acceptable features of contemporary political reality" (1978, xiv). By confronting the spectator with the depth of the depravity, it seeks to shock him/her out of complacency. When the Guatemalan protest theater used aspects of theater of atrocity in the 1960s and early 1970s, it was for the purpose of inciting anger and challenging the perceived perpetrator. It was done at the same time as the atrocities were being committed. In the 1990s theater of atrocity is used in retrospect as a way to promote peace and stability.

During the late 1970s to late 1980s (the years of the most intense violence), Guatemalan playwrights and theater practitioners were completely barred from representing the current political-social reality. In the late 1980s and early 1990s, as the government progressively became more stable, culminating with the signing of the Peace treaty in 1996—the playwrights became more daring in confronting the issues of the violence once again. They included specific references to massacres, victims of political violence, and governmental misuse of power, which even in the late 1980s would have been impossible. Currently, most theater practitioners say there is very little censorship except when one attempts to burlesque the army. The question now for theater artists is not "Can I get away with this?" but "How am I going to attract an audience?" The audience's need for processing the war has fueled and directed the productions during the 1990s.

The motives of the Guatemalan playwrights, that is, enabling the people to process the war, resonate with Robert Skloot's theory of the motivation of playwrights of the theater of the Holocaust. He edits an anthology of Holocaust plays that, he theorizes, assisted people "struggling to come to terms with that awful time" (1982, 5). He states that playwrights enable spectators and artists alike to grapple with the huge questions of a time that has scarred the consciousness of a generation. Skloot suggests that atrocities, or "events of shattering and lasting effects on the lives of whole peoples," have caused nations to rethink the central questions of existence (3). He describes a world that is slowly and painfully having to come to grips with human depravity and human suffering in order to find deeper understanding of existence. The playwrights in Skloot's anthology struggle to make sense of the Holocaust experience by facing the troubling questions it raises. The central troubling question for a Guatemalan audience reflecting honestly on the atrocities is how to make sure the cycle of violence is not reignited. The major difference between the theater of atrocity in Guatemala and the theater of the Holocaust is that Guatemalan playwrights must find a means of confronting the horrible past without destroying the fragile peace that has been established.

Playwright Ariel Dorfman notes a similar balancing act in Chilean theater which is trying to cope with the devastation caused by the military dictatorship. He writes in the afterword of *Death and the Maiden* of his attempt to write an Aristotelian tragedy, "a work of art that might help a collective to purge itself, through pity and terror . . . to confront those predicaments that, if not brought into the light of day, could lead to their ruin" (1992, 78). In *Death and the Maiden* Dorfman seeks to find the fine line between political relevance and polemic writing. He posits that this crucial balance, however, raises numerous questions:

> How can those who tortured and those who were tortured coexist in the same land? How to heal a country that has been traumatized by repression if the fear to speak out is still omnipresent everywhere? And how do you reach the truth if lying has become a habit? How do we keep the past alive without becoming its prisoner? How do we forget it without risking its repetition in the future? Is it legitimate to sacrifice the truth to insure peace? And what are the consequences of suppressing that past and the truth it is whispering or howling to us? . . . And perhaps the greatest dilemma of them all: how to confront these issues without destroying the national consensus, which creates democratic stability? (1992, 78)

The balancing act Dorfman here describes—of needing to process the past while strengthening the reconciliatory progress—is at the heart of the majority of plays written in the 1990s in Guatemala. Therefore, a central question this study raises is whether the phenomenon of reconciliation is also promoted throughout the Latin American countries, especially the countries seeking more democratic government. The quote by Ariel Dorfman suggests that at least Chilean theater is experiencing a new emphasis on reconciliation.

Most of the studies done on Guatemalan theater have been written in Spanish. None of the plays written in Guatemala in this study have been translated into English. All translations, therefore, are my own.[1] Because of the language barrier, less study has been done in this area of theater than one would expect. Jane Westlake writes in her 1997 dissertation, *"Tierra Libre:* (Re)Visions of the Nation in Latin American Drama," that Latin American drama is studied almost exclusively in Spanish and Ibero-American Studies departments (15). She theorizes that scholars focusing more on literature than on performance rarely refer to the historical context. She does not mince words as to the reason for the neglect of Central American plays: "Latin American scholars generally ignore Central American drama because of the chauvinism of the wealthier and 'whiter' countries toward the poorer *mestizo* (mix of Mayan and European heritage) nations" (15). She laments that the few texts that do cover theater in Central America do it superficially and simply throw out "every name and play title on record without any depth" (16). She suggests that the new field of Latin American theater studies was overlooked in favor of the study of Spanish theater; she forcefully states that only recently has it "been deemed worthy of attention by European-American scholars" (16). Building on Westlake's argument, I believe Central American theater has been intentionally ignored for complex reasons, including Westlake's argument of racism. In the United States it is difficult to recognize our country's role in blatant post-colonial repression and to accept our role in supporting institutionalized violence. I believe there is a link between the lack of study of Central American theater and U.S. political involvement with these countries. Therefore I include some of the history of the United States' involvement in Guatemalan politics which suggests that the theatrical history has not merely been overlooked.

Challenges of Third-Worldism

As the failure of my opening analogy suggests, it is difficult to conceptualize the enormity of violence in Guatemala's past in a responsible and scholarly manner. I was asked by Guatemalan film director Sergio Valdez how I intended to avoid falling into the imperialist trap of coming down and analyzing the "poor little beaten-down country." He asked if it was possible to not judge the theater and country as inadequate from a position of authority and superiority supposedly conferred by my first-world status. Valdez suggested the problem was that there was no two-way communication. Foreigners come down (usually from the North) and create elaborate analytic paradigms which overshadow the Guatemalan's small voice. The voice is even more difficult to hear in theater since most of the plays are not published.

One of the clearest examples of the post-imperialist arrogance is found in Maxine Klein's article "A Country of Cruelty and Its Theater" written in 1968. She condemns Guatemala for its injustice and lambastes its theater festivals as a "desperate-comic attempt to identify with Europeans and North Americans" (166). Her patronization of the country and its theater is pervasive throughout the article. One example of this attitude is when she magnanimously acknowledges that the Guatemalans are beginning to head in the correct direction:

> We may say then that no matter how much the Guatemalan middle-class theaters may be faulted for their lack of daring and immediacy, the fact remains that through their recently implemented staging of native works, they are actively engaged in fostering a national theater art and, through it, a national artistic consciousness. (Klein 1968, 166)

Pascal Bruckner describes three common "Third-Worldisms" in his book *The Tears of the White Man: Compassion as Contempt:* judgment of the Bad Guys against the Good Guys; pity for the poor country; and idolizing the country or "Getting High on Paradise" (1983, 7). Klein's article manages to embody all three. It condemns the country and middle-class theater, while championing the indigenous theater for its ability to remain true to its "primitive" roots. She pities the "disgraceful and scandalous" situation in which the indigenous theater must "exist defensively against the cruelty of Spanish Guatemala" (Klein 1968, 167). She ends her article with the conclusion that "the people with the most money have the least art and the poorest people are the guardians of the earliest, greatest theater of the Americas" (170). Yet she never bothers to mention a single Guatemalan playwright from the middle class or to cite a single work. She vaguely states that the intellectuals and artists who produce the middle-class Guatemalan theatre "would like to do incendiary plays" but are unable to because it would put their lives in danger (165).

Klein's article displays a weakness from which many current books on Latin American theater studies suffer: generalizations lacking the support of in-depth research. Klein does not give the middle-class theater an opportunity to speak before she condemns it. The problem is exacerbated in studies dealing with Latin American theater generally. Scholars barely mention Guatemala, choosing rather to focus on the countries that have more plays published and the critics who document the work being done. With dismaying frequency they make sweeping generalizations about all twenty-five different countries without having done thorough research.

Bruckner suggests that the only way to avoid the pitfalls of the "Third-Worldist" attitude is to undertake an approach different from the "apathy of majority opinion and the masochism of Third World apologists" (1983, 7). He states that the more constructive attitude consists in recognizing the other as different, avoiding the confusion of guilt with responsibility, and adopting an attitude of receptivity to the contribution of the other. While the United States is certainly partly responsible for the atrocities committed in Guatemala, the emphasis needs to be on opening a channel to hear Guatemalans' contribution rather than taking on guilt for their suffering. In short, we need to solicit Guatemalan theater artists' views of what they do. This was the purpose of my research in Guatemala, and it lies at the foundation of this study.

The only way to avoid some of my cultural judgment is to be clear about my motivations. I am a foreigner to this country. At the same time I am profoundly connected to it. I am in the unique position of being both an outsider and a participant in Guatemala. I lived in Guatemala for three years, founded a theater group, and directed/participated in sixteen full-length productions (1994–99). I also have adopted two Guatemalan children. As a citizen of the United States, I have been slow to accept my responsibility (as opposed to guilt) for some of the violence in Guatemala. I would often bristle when I read the seemingly endless negative criticism of the United States in Guatemalan plays. I thought it had been written out of envy or lack of willingness on the Guatemalans' part to take responsibility for their problems. The more reading I did about the U.S. involvement in Guatemala, however, the more I came to recognize the justified anger in the plays.

Bill Clinton made an unprecedented acknowledgment and apology in March 1999 for the United States' involvement in Guatemala's political life:[2] "For the United States, it is important I state clearly that support for military forces and intelligence units which engaged in violence and widespread repression was wrong and the United States must not repeat that mistake" (quoted in Brodie 1999, 1). Ian Brodie elaborates on Clinton's apology:

> No president before has so directly admitted the U.S. role in the atrocities. In Washington, newly declassified intelligence documents added vivid details of the massacres, kidnappings, torture and other horrors committed by Guatemalan security forces who were trained and equipped by the CIA and U.S. army. (1)

At the risk of seeming overly idealistic, I believe this apology allows the U.S. a healthier relationship with Guatemala. Clinton's apology signals a new era in which we can listen to Guatemalans' perspectives on a war for which the U.S. shares responsibility. If the U.S. had not ousted democratically elected President Arbenz in 1954, the dissension between a military dictatorship and the people might have been avoided. This study focuses on the healing process occurring in the theatre today and how the warring parties are beginning to listen to one another. Now that our president has acknowledged remorse for our past intervention, perhaps a similar healing may occur between the U.S. and Guatemala through studies such as this one.

1: INTRODUCTION   23

LATIN AMERICAN THEATER STUDIES

Severino João Albuquerque posits that Latin Americans have a heightened sociopolitical consciousness, in large part because of the Cuban revolution. Diana Taylor, in her book, *Theatre of Crisis: Drama and Politics in Latin America,* notes that the Cuban revolution created a sense of national and international identity when twenty-five politically marginal, economically and culturally dependent countries began to perceive themselves as a "united, coherent entity" (Taylor 1991, 47). Although each country has its particular traditions and cultural images, they share a similar history of "conquest, colonization, economic and political instability and continuing sociopolitical and economic dependency" (8). This international identity is the underpinning for the plethora of books on Latin American theater in the second half of the twentieth century and is the cornerstone of the identified political-protest-oriented theatre which Latin American as well as North American scholars have identified. This growing field of both Latin American and international study focuses most of the research on comparing and contrasting the canonized works of Latin American playwrights from South America, highlighting the theme of repression and the effects of the last 500 years of colonialism and postcolonialism. Recent studies on Latin American theater have focused on the term "Popular Theater" or "New Theater." The concept continues the theme of repression, but is framed by the search for and achievement of breaking the bonds of servitude.

Violence is identified as the most prominent central theme in plays in Latin American theater studies. Albuquerque, the author of *Violent Acts: A Study of Contemporary Latin American Theater* (1991), focuses on the wide range of expression of violence in the plays written between the 1960s and the 1980s. Although he does not study Guatemala directly, he states that most of the countries in Latin America have a common history of guerrilla fighting against tyrants, of weak democratic and civilian rule, of lack of freedom of the press, of kidnappings, hijacks, holdups, and strikes and riots, as well as of poverty, illiteracy, disease, and hunger. One would have to admit that his list describes Guatemala's challenges fairly comprehensively. Like Guatemala, many of the countries discussed by Albuquerque suffer from a military that has been out of control, torturing and massacring its own people. He believes the political reality is essentially the same throughout the continent: "an unfair, rigid system that has historically been suitable for the perpetuation of the dominant class's control of the power machine . . . which excludes the less fortunate from the decision-making process" (14). He argues that the root of all violence is social injustice; official violence breeds unofficial violence, creating an endless cyclical effect.

Albuquerque's work is useful in understanding the "foreignness" of Latin American theater. He describes the difference in dramaturgy between Europe and Latin American countries in terms of a cosmological perspective. He theorizes that Europe came to believe in a world largely governed by irrationality, which led playwrights to reject dramatic realism and logical discourse and to favor a self-conscious, "highly gestural art form" (270). However, the development of theater in Latin America has "been tied to the consideration of urgent social, economic, and political inequalities, issues that inevitably lead to pervasive violence at all levels of life" (270).[3] He cites Europe's portrayal of violence as a vindication of the aggressive instinct inherent and fundamental in life. In Latin America violence is portrayed as state-institutionalized torture, geared to brutalize the dissenter and the innocent alike. He writes that the "victimization is officially sanctioned and its perpetrators tolerated and even rewarded" (270). The European model emphasizes individualized violence, the personal dark side of humanity. The Latin American model highlights the communal violence that was perpetrated by an institution. If Albuquerque's theory is correct it might help explain why Latin American theater's emphasis on institutional violence is not perceived to be "universal" and is even repulsive from a European/North American cosmological perspective of violence.

This subtle difference may help explain why our closest neighbors to the south are often ignored in terms of theater studies. Diana Taylor starts her book *Theater of Crisis* (1991), "Latin American theater is a relatively unknown field" (preface). Perhaps part of the reason for the apparent lack of interest in the field is that although we are geographically closer to

Latin America than to Europe, ideologically we are not easily compatible. Latin America is the embarrassing black sheep of the Americas family: poor, uneducated, and, worst of all, badly behaved because of its volatile expression of violence.

Judith Weiss's *Latin American Popular Theater* (1993) articulates a common political emphasis in Latin American plays. She explains that the *Nuevo Teatro Popular* [New Popular Theater] is part of an overarching project of radical social transformation which originated in university and workers' theaters and in Brechtian art theater. The term is in contrast to a "national" theater, which does not confront the political-social issues that question the existing hegemony (Weiss 1993, 6). She writes that "national" theater "served as 'unifying' value systems for projecting and reinforcing dominant national and class ideologies" (6). Weiss suggests that the interests of the marginalized are diametrically opposed to those of the middle and upper middle class. Her limited definition of national theatre as being designed to defuse potential conflict rather than confront a shared history does not permit the possibility that a national theater movement promoting peace might be able to unify and socially critique the status quo at the same time.

Diana Taylor's 1991 book contains the most encompassing approach in terms of contextualizing the theory, criticism, and history of Latin American theater. She echoes other Latin American scholars when she writes that the theater in the 1960s and 1970s sought to move from the passive consumer to an active participant. However, she identifies a trend in Latin American theater different from the one offered by her predecessors. She describes complex and contradictory theater of crisis, as opposed to the more instrumental revolutionary theater. She chooses plays written between 1965 and 1970, because after 1970 the theater had a stronger sense of mission, which excludes it from her definition of crisis theater. The playwrights of the 1970s were able to recognize the concrete causes of crisis and go beyond "crisis ideology." Crisis, in her view, is a turning point of disorientation, just before clarity has been reached, when the oppressor and the oppressed are not clearly differentiated and the path to take is not clear.

Taylor argues that the theater of the Holocaust and the theater of crisis have many similarities.[4] They both reflect the objective and subjective reality of crisis and subvert "the lines of demarcation traditionally used to distance the spectators . . . [implicating] them as accomplices in the onstage violence" (54). (Taylor uses Grieselda Gambaro's *The Camp* (1967) with its horror of Argentine fascism and death camps as an example of an overlap between the two categories.) She differentiates between the two classifications by stating that the theater of the Holocaust

> takes a step—temporally and ideologically—*beyond* crisis in that it isolates the problem and assumes a position in the face of it. And whereas the theater of the Holocaust fixes its attention on a historically limited and unique past, and protest theatre generally looks forward to a happier future, the theater of crisis is grounded in contradiction; it shapes undifferentiation. (54; Taylor's emphasis)

Taylor explains that the Holocaust writers have defined a moral commitment to speak which is linked to their clarity of direction. This clarity is absent in playwrights who write during the "disorienting moment of crisis" (121). Guatemalan playwrights of the 1990s also have this clarity of direction, even though the war has only recently ended. I argue that the theatre of atrocity in Guatemala fixes its attention on the civil war for the purpose of finding a happier future. This style of theater differs from Taylor's theater of crisis in that the mission is clear: the direction to take is toward healing, reconciliation, and peace.

Few of the texts on Latin American theater address Guatemala. There is only one detailed text about Guatemalan theatre before the 1960s, *Raíces del Teatro Guatemalteco [Roots of Guatemalan Theater]*, written in 1972 by René García Mejía. There are several articles detailing the history of Guatemala, such as Hugo Carrillo's *"Orígenes y desarrollo del teatro guatemalteco" [Origins and Development of Guatemalan Theatre] (1971)*. Both of these writings begin with the oldest theater forms in Guatemala, which date from the Maya-Quiché culture in the ballet-drama Rabinal Achí. This work is generally thought to be the only surviving pre-Columbian drama in Latin America. It is considered the best example of indigenous drama because it does not contain any of the late medieval Spanish stage conventions found in other extant pre-Columbian dramas, such as *Ollantay* of Peru (Leinaweaver 1968, 3).

The play, translated in 1862 by Charles Etienne Brasser, had been presented periodically over three centuries during the Spanish dominion in Guatemala.

Rabinal Achí focuses on a Rabinal warrior who has conquered a Quiché warrior. The Quiché warrior is told that he must appear before the governor and surrender. He refuses to humble himself and chooses sacrificial death instead. Guatemalan playwright Victor Hugo Cruz writes that the play, which had been successfully concealed from the conquerors for many years, is an expression of resistance against oppression. He suggests it is a seminal work in a long line of Guatemalan plays whose major function is social liberation. However, Cruz's description of theater as a long search for liberty does not incorporate the nationalistic plays promoting unity after the 1944 revolution and the democratic period which lasted ten years or this current period. I believe a more accurate overview of Guatemalan theater in this century would note a fluctuation between repression and openness, as I outline in chapter 2.

Cruz posits that the separation of the two strains of theater symbolically embody the central conflict of Guatemala as a country divided into two cultures: *"Idígenas por un lado, marginadas del mundo ... empobrecidas; y por otro, la Guatemala ladina, mestiza, occidental y burgués"* [Indigenous on one side—the marginalized in the world, ... and impoverished; and Guatemalan ladino on the other, mixed-raced, western and bourgeois.] (1988, 15). He believes that the theatre will always continue in Guatemala in spite of repression. It may be forced underground, but it will emerge again and again, addressing the inflammatory issue of racism. Likewise, playwright and theater scholar Hugo Carrillo stresses the need for *ladinos* [mixed indigenous and European heritage] to honor the indigenous blood that flows in their veins by celebrating the symbols and raging at the injustice created by the blatantly racist society cut off from its indigenous roots.

From these two perspectives one surmises that if a country's theater could be expressed as a general theme, modern Guatemalan theater would be about how the two different cultures in the blood of the *mestizo* [mixed European and native ancestry]have conflicted internally within the individual and externally in society. After 500 years the strife and conflict between the two different cultures finally came to an attempt at closure during the signing of the Peace Accord. If this moment of peace is not simply part of a repetitive cycle in an endless power struggle, then it might suggest an unprecedented change from the oppression model Cruz identifies. It is the beginning of a break with the endless struggle against opposing powers, protesting the blatant injustice and lack of power, with the only dignified option available being the self-sacrifice of the Quiché warrior. I would argue that the Guatemalan theater of the 1990s is seeking to find a less trodden path of fostering harmony between the two cultures.[5]

Personal Perspective

I understand on a personal level the desire to escape the effects of the civil war and political instability. While living in Guatemala I did not at first want to acknowledge the violence all around me. I was constricted with fear, trying desperately to be the proverbial ostrich with its head in the sand. It was only after living in Guatemala for three years that I began to have an inkling about the insidious violence, which creeps up on one living in such a volatile nation. There is no escape from it. This is why I believe Guatemalan theater is such an invaluable communal expression. It is a way for people to intellectually and emotionally process the civil war so they can move on with their lives.

My story with Guatemala began when my wife and I first went down there to adopt a child. We ended up adopting two children. We had planned to stay only three to six months. After I had lived with my son for three months and his adoption was finalized by the Guatemalan government, the U.S. embassy informed us that we would not be able to return with our son for two years because he possibly had a living father somewhere. Up until the point I decided to write this study, I intentionally knew little about Guatemala and its tumultuous history.

During my years in Guatemala I lived in a bubble and wanted to know nothing about the war or the violence. There were times when I could not avoid national events such as the coup d'etat in 1993 or the time a mob beat a foreign woman almost to death because some Guatemalans erroneously thought she was stealing children's body parts and stashing them in her backpack. The coup d'etat shook my faith in the stability of the government, but the story of the foreign woman had a more direct effect. After the beating incident we were warned by the U.S. embassy not to travel with our adopted children for fear a mob might think we were going to take the children back to the U.S. to be used for body parts. Yet, psychologically, I did not want to admit that the local situation was that different from growing up in the Midwest or acknowledge the violence that was all around us.

Only after I returned did I begin to realize how numerous my different experiences of violence in Guatemala were. While living in Antigua, I had known both Guatemalan and American women who were gang raped, and known people who had relatives kidnapped or involved in carjackings or had loved ones killed. Almost every foreigner we knew had been robbed or mugged at some point. One time my wife, Elizabeth, was walking down a street at noon and two teenage boys grabbed her from behind with a knife at her throat and stole her purse. She came home shaken while I panicked about how I was going to secure the house, since the key was in the purse. It was Holy Week and it would have been impossible to find someone to change the locks. Two minutes later I heard a knock on the door. It was my neighbor, Dennis Wheeler, who had witnessed the incident from a couple of blocks away. He had gone into his house for his gun, jumped on his motorcycle, caught the boys, and gotten Elizabeth's purse back.

Dennis had lived in Guatemala since the early 1960s. He theorized that people living in Guatemala develop a psychological protection from the violence. They believe the violence is directed toward others, the Guatemalans or other foreigners, and not toward oneself. His business partner and friend Michael DeVine had been kidnapped on June 8, 1990, by the army from a farm they shared together. DeVine's body was found the next day with his head partly severed by a machete. DeVine's case quickly came to dominate U.S. human rights policy toward Guatemala from 1994 to 1996 and caused the suspension of more than $14 million of military aid from the U.S. (D. Green 1992, 36). Dennis and DeVine's widow, Carol DeVine, had been trying to bring her husband's killers to justice. United States officials concluded that two Guatemalan presidents, two defense ministers, and high-ranking military officers paid by the Central Intelligence Agency (CIA) helped cover up the facts of his killing (Weiner 1999, 1). Captain Hugo Contraes, who had ordered the team to interrogate Michael DeVine and would have known about the involvement of other senior officials, escaped from prison in May 1993 on the day he was convicted and could not be located for questioning (J. Smith 1999, 2).

During the three years I lived in Guatemala I made a conscious choice never to ask Dennis about the progress of the trials or to enter into any kind of political conversation with him. Our interaction was purely social. He supported the theater where I worked and I cast him in a small role in one of the comedies I directed, poignantly entitled *The Search for Signs of Intelligent Life in the Universe*. It was during this production that I learned that the American couple who worked on the tech crew of my previous production, *Death of a Salesman*, had run off because someone had discovered they were on the FBI's Ten Most Wanted List and were hiding in Antigua, Guatemala. I simply continued in my bubble of security, directing nonpolitical, foreign plays. I was following a popular trend in Guatemalan theater to focus on romantic comedies. Throughout the 1990s, the popularity of the foreign comedies translated into Spanish has continued to expand. The bedroom farces often run for four to six months in the capital in dinner theaters, and the small theaters as well as in the National Theater. I have no doubt that the popularity of these productions as well as of my own stemmed from others seeking escape from the harsh political reality and the constant threat of violence throughout Guatemala. I wanted to create a secure, safe world. DeVine's widow often came to see my productions and attended several cast parties, but I never spoke to her about her husband's case. She had been publicly asking the CIA to explain why it paid Colonel Alpirez $44,000 when it was known he was helping to cover up the killing (Weiner 1999, 3). Somehow being around her made me feel uneasy, as if her reality might invade my own.

Although I kept my head in the sand, the Guatemalan theatre has made a saner choice. The national playwrights do not promote escaping reality. Escape may offer temporary respite, but it does not foster healing and acceptance of the current situation. They take on the harsh sociopolitical reality of the violence in order to attain a deeper level of reconciliation. They confront their fellow citizens with the atrocities committed during the war so they can begin to move forward as a nation.

Structure of the Chapters and Classification of the Plays

Chapter 2 will be an overview of the major events of the political history of Guatemala from the twentieth century, dovetailed with the history of Guatemalan theater. The ten years after the 1944 revolution in which the theater aided in forging a national identity is detailed in order to emphasize a similar movement in the 1990s. Both theatrical eras depict a country that had been riddled with injustice and violence in order to contrast it with the current national identity which is portrayed as more orderly and democratic. The most striking difference between these two periods is the portrayal of the antagonist. After the revolution, the enemy is positioned as outside Guatemala's borders. After the civil war, the enemy is found within the borders: Guatemalans' racial and class prejudice.

Between 1954 and 1986 the country was ruled by the military. The popular protest plays of the 1960s and 1970s from the "Golden Age" of Guatemalan theater will be described in order to highlight the distinction of the plays written in the 1990s. A common theme in many of these plays is harking back to the time of the conquest. The Establishment is placed in the role of the exploitative conquerors while the citizens are cast in the role of the angry victim. Using the memory of the conquest embedded in the psyche of a people is a provocative tool employed by some of the playwrights during this period to foster solidarity amongst the people.

Chapters 3, 4, and 5 focus on various plays produced or written in the 1990s. Each of these conclude with an analysis of how the plays discussed correspond to this theory on the balance between atrocity and reconciliation. In this analysis two questions are posed: (1) How do these plays encourage reflection on the atrocities of the civil war? (i.e., How do they frame ethical questions? What kind of emotional response does the work intend to elicit?); (2) How do these plays encourage reconciliation? (i.e., hope for a better future, promoting peace and forgiveness, healing the individual).

Only four playwrights from the "Golden Age" of Guatemalan theater continued to write in the nineties: Hugo Carrillo (who died in 1994), Victor Hugo Cruz, Fran Lepe, and Manuel Corleto. In the fall of 1999 I interviewed Cruz, Lepe, and Corleto, as well as Carrillo's nephew, Felipe Valenzuela, who is also a playwright and who was able to give me the two produced but unpublished scripts Carrillo wrote: one in the late 1980s and the other in the early 1990s. The four playwrights' previous work will be outlined before detailing their work in this period. Playwrights who began writing in the 1990s will also be included. The plays have been classified into three different groups: satiric, didactic, and symbolic. The satiric was the first to appear, testing the "political temperature" in a humorous manner. Didactic plays started to appear around the time of the signing of the Peace Accord and are the most daring in terms of presenting factual information. Symbolic plays are inherently more ambiguous and have appeared throughout the decade of the 1990s. The latter category tends to focus more on metaphysical concepts and universal archetypes.

The boundaries between didactic, satiric, and symbolic plays can be made with respect to the production as well as the text. The political satires are by far the most popular, lucrative, and longest running. The actors have been doing comedy throughout the 1990s and several have reached the level of celebrity status. The didactic plays often use untrained actors who enthusiastically take their message on tour in both rural and urban settings and play in untraditional theater spaces. The symbolic plays are usually performed by the traditional actors who do the classic and avant-garde pieces,[6] as well as works by more seasoned and serious Guatemalan playwrights (other than José Osorio's group discussed in chapter 5). They tend not to cross over to the satiric or didactic plays. One of these actors, who has been doing theater for thirty years, explained that he does not consider the political satires to be theater and would never sink to that level of crassness.

The following is a brief description of the categories that will be developed within the chapters 3, 4, and 5:

1. *Satiric plays* (chapter 3) emphasize a humorous, detached critique of the violence which enables audiences to approach

taboo subjects in a novel, safe way and to laugh at the political and social insanity of the violence. The political satires burlesque the politicians and institutions which had intentionally created the debilitating fear. The analogical satires (portraying a different situation in order to comment on the current social-political crisis) portray a world where there is no escape from the crisis. However, the lighthearted tone encourages the audience to grapple with the past. Both the political and analogical satires test the boundaries while asserting, in effect, "we're just joking!" The satires seem to be a release valve for the buildup of frustration in the society. Humor is both an outlet for hostility and an acceptable form for raising taboo topics such as the atrocities of the war. Both war and political violence are often portrayed with broad physical humor.

2. *Didactic plays* (chapter 4) focus on educating the audience on the specifics of the war; many are propaganda plays with blatant antiwar messages. George H. Szanto describes this type of theater as the "theater of agitation propaganda" (1978, 72). The purpose is to raise the audience's consciousness to a point where the social and political problems take on immediacy. However, these plays emphasize reconciliation over anger and avoid divisive issues. Both the victims and the perpetrators are portrayed sympathetically. This kind of play is the most overtly propeace and is probably the least accessible to non-Guatemalan spectators because of its emphasis on the factual history of the war. The more popular didactic plays allow a cathartic release for the atrocities committed during the war. These plays enable the audience to grieve the past. Most use psychological realism as a major stylistic choice in order to create a strong empathetic bond with the audience. The characters have become trapped in a cycle of violence and are struggling to end it. The violence tends to be portrayed realistically in terms of people being tortured, beaten or killed on stage.

3. *Symbolic plays* (chapter 5) tend to be more ambiguous, using analogies, archetypal characters, and symbols to create complex and contrasting perspectives. Most of these works are for an educated audience, challenging them to recognize the contradictions and complexities in the peace process. Whereas

the emphasis on the didactic plays is emotional healing, these plays depict the moral and philosophical collapse and raise issues of the spiritual crisis caused by the war. These plays often raise more questions than answers and offer less solace and resolution. Some continue the protest model identified in chapter 2, which is polemic and creates dissension because of the provocative style. The playwrights in this chapter relate their work directly to twentieth-century European postwar movements including Dadaism, Theater of the Absurd, and Existentialism. The violence is highly stylized, such as a ritual killing of Clytemnestra or throwing blood at actors' bare feet to represent Guatemala's violent history.

One example of this symbolic style of theater is Rubén Nájera's work. He told me of a play he was hoping to write based on news reports of the army raping some of the indigenous women whose husbands had left to fight with the guerrillas. After the husbands came back at the end of the war, the women preferred being with the men from the army. He was even hoping to use some of the actual interviews with the women. Clearly this could be "newspaper" theater which tells a factual, horrific story from the war. However, Nájera planned to treat the situation as an analogy for Guatemala being stuck in its postcolonial mindset, where the women would seek out the degradation offered by the soldiers rather than the love and respect offered by husbands.

There is a great deal of overlap between the classifications of satiric, didactic, and symbolic plays and their function. I am not equating the detached, witty satires only with the intellect, the cathartic, didactic plays only with the emotional, and the metaphysical, symbolic works only with the spiritual. All of these forms of theater encourage the spectator to grapple with the atrocities of the war on multiple levels. These categories are constructed to examine the plays in order to understand the theater's role in promoting national reconciliation through confrontation with atrocity.

2
History of Twentieth-Century Guatemalan Theater

GUATEMALAN THEATER AND ITS INTERACTION WITH POLITICS HAS always been very complex. Therefore I limit the historical study to the modern theater, its transition from a national emphasis on unity to a subversive, protest theater followed by its repression during the height of the violence in the 1980s when it almost vanished altogether. This chapter sets the stage for the theater's reemergence and the nationalistic reemphasis in the plays written in the 1990s. For clarity's sake I have divided the twentieth-century into six theatrical eras: (1) Elitist *costumbrista* (1900–30); (2) Dark Ages (1931–44); (3) Revolution and nationalist plays under elected governments (1944–54); (4) "Liberation" (1954); (5) "Golden Age" of Theater (1962–78); (6) Second Dark Ages (1978–86). (The nationalist plays promoting reconciliation written under democratically elected civilian governments (1990–2000) are discussed in the following chapters.) Nationalist plays are works that attempt to define the unique identity of a country where the people and the government are portrayed as working in tandem to promote unity. The nationalist unity and freedom of expression that characterized theater after the revolution of 1944 is similar to the emphasis on national unity from 1986 (the return to civilian government) to the present. Both National Theater movements follow periods of military repression during which the theater was virtually shut down. These theatrical trends illustrate an oppressive, conflictual past in order to emphasize a more orderly, just, and democratic nation. The major difference between these nationalistic expressions is in the depiction of the antagonist forces. After the revolution, the villains were portrayed as something other than "Guatemalans," that is, either the former dictatorships supported by the imperialist U.S. or the United States itself. After the civil war, the villains were portrayed as Guatemalans who refused to dialogue with each other.

Also in this chapter I highlight the contribution of three playwrights whose works trace the transformation from a National Theater to the protests of the "Golden Age" of theater: Manuel Galich, Hugo Carrillo, and Manuel José Arce.

Brief Overview of Guatemala's History and the Civil War

Guatemala is the northernmost nation of Central America and borders Mexico, El Salvador, Honduras, and Belize. Explored and conquered by Spain in 1524, it is one of two Latin American countries where more than 60 percent of the population is indigenous (Trudeau 1993, 1). The rest of the population is *mestizo*—of mixed European and native ancestry. The uneven distribution of power and the divisive racism leaving the majority indigenous population marginalized have persisted throughout centuries. This social inequity is the root cause of their civil war, Latin America's longest war in history. In the following paragraph is a brief account of the political history, presented in more detail throughout the chapter.

Following independence from Spain in 1821, which led to numerous dictatorships, in 1944 a student-led revolution ended the last reign of the official dictator, General Jorge Ubico. Democratically elected President Jacobo Arbenz was ousted in 1954 by a United States–supported force of mercenaries and the country was ruled by the military until 1986, when a civilian, democratically elected government returned. The guerrilla war began in Guatemala in 1960. It is usually described as a miniature cold war between extreme leftists who sought radical social reform and the extreme rightists who sought to maintain stability and the status quo. The leftists (guerrillas) are often linked with a communist/socialist ideology and sought governmental representation and/or revolution. The rightists are often portrayed as supporting a fascist dictatorship that merges military and business leadership. The war began when young soldiers who were inspired by the

Cuban revolution rebelled against the military government. The guerrillas were originally given support mostly by the peasants and Indian communities. The war ended officially with the signing of the Peace Accord in 1996.

1. *Elitist* Costumbrista *Theater (1900–30)*

Guatemala's theatrical history began before the Spanish Conquest with indigenous performance rituals and developed in two dramatic currents afterwards: one continued the indigenous tradition and the other, under the influence of the Spanish theatrical tradition, developed into the modern *mestizo* theater, which reflects the physical reality of the modern *ladino (mestizo)* social life. The indigenous theater continues, vigorous and uninterrupted into the present, but lies outside the scope of this work, except as contemporary Guatemalan playwrights appropriate symbols and images to remind Guatemalans of their common ancestry.

Middle-class *costumbrista* (a type of play that captures the customs, style, characters, and local color of a particular region) was the most popular form of theater in Guatemala between 1900 and 1930. *Costumbrista* began in Spain in the nineteenth century, and flourished in Spanish America in the early twentieth century. Carlos Solórzano, a Guatemalan-born playwright who after moving to Mexico quickly became a prominent figure in the intellectual and artistic world, writes at length about *costumbrista* theater in *Teatro Latinamericano del Siglo XX* (1961). He posits that it occurs when a country has developed a strong enough identity and desires to recognize itself in its own works. However, the style eventually becomes critical of social and political reality. Solórzano states that it is not possible to write about the problems of a certain region without eventually making allusions to the oppressive forces that have weighed on the people (11). He theorizes that this mostly apolitical form of *costumbrista* is a necessary step in the development of theater which inherently transforms into larger universal themes, nationalistic issues, or expressions of liberty. Mario Alberto Carrera states that the *costumbrista* transforms into a socialist theater beginning in 1944 (Carrera 1966, 29). Solórzano describes this stage of development as National Theater. However, this nationalist Guatemalan theater which supports the Establishment is followed by a "Dark Ages" of theater under the dictatorship of General Jorge Ubico, when even *costumbrista* was barely able to exist.

2. Ubico's Dictatorship—Dark Ages of Theater

General Jorge Ubico, in power from 1931 to 1944, was one of the most oppressive tyrants Guatemala has ever known. His autocratic rule and repression enabled the wealthy to become wealthier and forced the poor to become poorer (Landau 1993, 153). He was responsible for putting into effect his infamous *Ley Fuga* [Fugitive Decree].[1] After instituting this law he compared himself to Adolf Hitler, whom he greatly admired, boasting: "I am like Hitler. I execute first and ask questions later" (quoted in Perera 1993, 36). In 1934 Ubico created vagrancy laws which forced peasants owning less than two *hectares* of land to do manual labor for a minimum of 100 days a year. This assured wealthy plantation owners of vast numbers of migrant laborers.[2]

During Ubico's reign the theater completely avoided political or social critique. The dictator distrusted the theater and often imprisoned actors and directors. He occasionally sounded like a member of the Inquisition, describing the theater as bulging with diabolicism. Carrera explains the description of the devil: *"El diablo era todo aquello que atentara contra su gobierno"* [The devil was anything that attempted to be against the government] (1966, 22). Plays by Ibsen, Strindberg, and Pirandello as well as by other foreign playwrights with an emphasis on social critique were not known in Guatemala until after Ubico's regime. Carrera describes Ubico's influence as the dark curtain that separated Guatemala from the modern world (1966, 23).

After Ubico took power, he made it very difficult for nationals or visitors to mount plays. Through strong state censorship, his government would not allow historical, social, or political drama or anything reflecting national reality. He did not allow touring artistic companies to visit on the grounds that they would use up resources necessary to establish the economy (Fernández Molina 1982, 25).

One of the few exceptions of political-social plays was the *Huelga de dolores* held traditionally during Holy Week by the university students. Since 1898 these plays/skits had been performed annually and were essentially satirical jokes on political and social topics. They continued to be performed during Ubico's rule except in the last few years of his regime. (The only other time these traditional skits were banned was during the height of the violence in the early 1980s—which I refer to as the second Dark Ages.)

One of the most creative actors and directors of this period, Alberto Martínez Bernaldo, the creator of the *Sociedad Dramática Nacional*, was twice imprisoned during Ubico's rule. The first time was for the production of *Juan José*, a play about the problems of a worker, and the second was for writing *Los cuatro jinetes del Apocalipsis [The Four Horsemen of the Apocalypse]*, which was the title of a recently prohibited film in Guatemala critical of the German military (Peña Mancilla 1988, 22). Ubico, having great respect for the German military institution under Hitler's rule, accused the actor of denigrating it.

During World War II Ubico did not want to take action against the German plantation owners living in Guatemala because his government was doing significant amounts of coffee trade with them. He eventually seized their plantations in 1944. In part because of his support of Germany, he alienated the U.S. When the revolution of 1944 forced Ubico to resign, the U.S. government did nothing to stop the action (Westlake 1997, 26).

Modern Guatemalan Theater

3. Revolution of 1944—Nationalist Plays

René García Mejía writes in his book *Raíces del Teatro Guatemalteco [Roots of Guatemalan Theater]* (1972) that the modern theater is categorically different from the theater under independence (1821–1944): the revolution of 1944 *"rompe una cadena de sombrías dictaduras, abriendo las fronteras a nuevas corrientes de arte y cultura que los tiranos habían negado"* [breaks a chain of dark dictators, opening the borders to new waves of art and culture which the tyrants had suppressed] (11). In October 1944 a student-led rebellion staged a protest with thousands of people demonstrating in the streets to show their anger at Ubico. The coalition that emerged from the street protests announced that the next president of Guatemala would be chosen by free elections. Juan José Arevalo, a committed nationalist and believer in "spiritual socialism," was voted into office. He abolished Ubico's Vagrancy Law, introduced a social security system, and allowed for the legalization of unions and the Communist Workers' Party under the 1945 Constitution. Sixty percent of the workers, the highest number in Guatemala's history to date, were quickly unionized (Simon 1987, 21). Arevalo believed that Guatemala's destiny was to spread a series of reforms through Latin America (Landau 1993, 149).

The government founded several new cultural institutions, such as the General Office of Fine Arts and the Popular University. It also helped to establish schools for the study of theater, and theater festivals, and laid the groundwork for the construction of a National Theater. The theater was used as an instrument to gather popular support and to help further the reforms posed by the government. However, the theater was still an elitist institution (Carrera 1966, 25). It had simply shifted hands from the upper class to the middle-class citizens. The vast majority of the lower and lower middle class were not included until the 1970s.

Jane Westlake describes the 1944 coup as creating a political and cultural opening for "an era of national redefinition" (1997, 107). The theater was considered a viable instrument for bringing the government's message to the people. The feudal ideas of ethnic superiority that were supported by the army, church, and upper classes were challenged by the middle and lower classes. Guatemalan theater opened to currents of international influence. Grievances against monopolies, such as the vast United Fruit Company, arose.

The theater was slow to develop in terms of audience support. Manuel Fernández Molina states: "*Lo que la dictadura ubiquista había destruido en catorce años (1931–44), la costumbre de ir al teatro, no había podido ser reinstaurada en el hábito de los guatemaltecos*" [The habit of going to the theater, which Ubico's dictatorship had destroyed during his fourteen-year reign (1931–44), couldn't be reinstated quickly in the habits of Guatemalans] (1982, 29). (Likewise, after years of repression

[1978–86], it took four years before the public returned in large numbers to the theater.) Fortunately, immigrants from Europe and North America helped develop the theater. Spaniard Maria de Sellarés was appointed director of the Belén National Teacher's Institute.

Carrillo notes that the theater had a didactic character that de Sellarés helped to transform with music, painting, and poetry. Her students became the prominent theater directors of the future. One of her most successful productions was *Quiché Achí*. Inspired by *Rabinal Achí*, this indigenous theater played to packed houses in 1945 and toured Europe as well. The deliberate blending of indigenous theater with European training was the path of many future Guatemalan productions. Carrillo writes in *The World Encyclopedia of Contemporary Theatre:*

> The orientation that de Sellarés gave to the new theatre movement born at the Belén Institute—educational and socially rooted—would also be seen in the work of subsequent generations, who would later establish theatre schools, children's theatres, school theatres, puppet theatres, indigenous theatre research, university theatres and regional and national theatre festivals. (Carrillo 1996, 288)

In 1948 the *Teatro de Arte Universitario* (TAU) [University Art Theater] was created as part of the Faculty of Humanities of the University of San Carlos. That same year, Manuel Galich, a playwright who served as Minister of Public Education, began the state-supported *Teatro de Arte de Guatemala* (TAG) with the same core of people that de Sellarés had trained. TAG inaugurated its work with a season of plays by Guatemalan authors presented in conjunction with the Central American Olympic Games of 1950. TAU continued for two decades and established a school of theater art, created the country's first arena stage, encouraged other groups with technical and artistic advice, and participated in national festivals.

The theater continued to expand rapidly during the ten years following the revolution. In 1953 thirty-two new plays by contemporary European and U.S. authors were presented by Guatemala's twelve regularly producing groups (Carrillo 1996, 289). Some of these were subsidized by the state and others by the university. The Fine Arts Ministry subsidized a theater group to travel across the country performing plays by Cervantes, Lope de Vega, and Alejandro Casona under the direction of Ligia Bernal and Hugo Carrillo. But this touring theater ended quickly with the violent political shift of "liberation" in July 1954. Fernández Molina writes that the winds blew against artistic creation, especially in the rural environment (1988, 27). Although the group was not overtly political, the leader of the group in 1954, Carrillo, quickly decided to leave for Paris. Guatemala's most prominent playwright, Manuel Galich, left Guatemala in 1954 as well. Although he is considered the father of contemporary Guatemalan theater, he never returned to his native land. He lived in exile in Cuba, where he continued writing plays until his death in 1984.

Manuel Galich (1913–1984)

Manuel Galich was a prolific playwright as well as a left-wing professor and politician. His playwriting evolved from historical drama and *costumbristas* to nationalistic plays. Carrillo describes him as *"un dramaturgo de gran aliento latinoamericano"* [a playwright of great Latin American strength] (1992a, 95). Involved in the 1944 coup, he was appointed Minister of Education during President Jacobo Arbenz's democratic government. His play *Ida y vuelta [Roundtrip]*, a trilogy picturing the poverty and wars of nineteenth-century Guatemala, won the Central American Drama Competition of 1948. Willis Knapp Jones credits Galich for having shaken the theater of his country out of its rut of nineteenth-century romantic tragedies (1966, 449).

Galich began writing history plays for students to dramatize Guatemala's struggle for independence. In 1938 he wrote his first commercial play, *Papá Natas*, which focuses on a middle-class *mestizo* family and is considered the birth of modern Guatemalan theater. Although the play came out during Ubico's rule, the social criticism is very subtle and hidden by its moments of humor and its appearance of being an apolitical *costumbrista*. The character Marcos López, a ruthless exploiter, diplomat, and powerful politician, has vices similar to those of Ubico. Mario Alberto Carrera claims in his book *Ideas políticas en el teatro de Manuel Galich* (1966) that López is a veiled portrayal of Ubico. Carrera states that if Galich had tried to portray a more detailed portrait of a dictator (as Miguel Angel Asturias later did with *El Señor Presidente*), the playwright would have been killed (1966, 77).

Papá Natas became the first of an extraordinary trilogy which Galich wrote between 1938 and 1970. The three plays vividly portray three distinct eras in Guatemalan history: the tyranny of Ubico, the revolution of 1944, and the guerrilla movement of the 1960s–70s (Cruz, *Obra dramática de Manuel Galich*, 1991, 54). The trilogy chronicles the history of a fictional family, the Natases, and how they are affected by the thirty years of turbulent national political changes.

The first play, written under Ubico, is written in a kind of "code" that conceals its true political referent. The second play, *La Mugre [The Muck]* (1953), is written during the years of democracy. It highlights the challenge of balancing the rightist and leftist perspectives. His nationalist emphasis is transformed after Galich leaves, in exile, with the last installment of the trilogy, *El Cargo* (1970). It is an anti-Establishment, antimilitary play which supports the revolution. Carrera argues that the trilogy reflects Galich's personal transformation from a timid revolutionary in his first play to a clear Marxist sympathizer in the last, purposefully inciting people to revolt (1966, 54). Young people joining the guerrilla movement against the wishes of their family was a common phenomenon in Guatemala during the late 1960s and 1970s. The theme of a father being caught in a political struggle against his son is prevalent in Galich's *El tren amarillo [The Yellow Train]* as well as other Guatemalan modern plays reflecting the turbulent swings of a divided nation.

El tren amarillo, Galich's most prominent nationalistic play, took on the then current issue of the Boston-based United Fruit Company. The company owned all of the railroads and the only Atlantic port, Puerto Barrios, as well as large plantations. Ubico had supported the United Fruit Company and its practice of exploiting workers. Before Galich could produce the play, the CIA had organized and trained an army of Guatemalan dissidents who overthrew the Arbenz government in 1954. Galich went into exile and later joined the Cuban revolution in 1959. *El tren amarillo* premiered in Mexico City in 1957. It became a huge success in productions produced in Guatemala in 1959, 1973, and 1987.

Jane Westlake argues in her dissertation *"Tierra Libre:* (Re)-Visions of the Nation in Latin American Drama" (1997) that *El tren amarillo* was Galich's attempt to unite Guatemalans by creating a Guatemalan identity. The play focuses on Guatemala's history of economic and political domination by the United Fruit Company during the 1920s and 1930s. The company in the play is titled *La Bananera*. It oppresses the workers to the extent that starving people are executed in the field for stealing bananas to eat. The foreign boss calls the Guatemalans "communists" when they are starving and unable to work. At one point a woman with a sick child is told she cannot use the train to get to a doctor. This is in contrast to the image of the train in the first act being thought of as a help to the people. Westlake writes that "the Guatemalans seem better off without the constant reminder of the train whistle as it carries off their livelihood but cannot save their lives" (115).

The heinous actions of the foreigners are in strong contrast to those of the Guatemalans. The characters are from a wide range of ethnic backgrounds, which replaces the previous concept of Guatemalan as *criollo* (Europeans born in Latin America). Galich was seeking to portray Guatemalans as a diverse group and not just the *criollo* elite, and not even the *mestizo* who is the often appropriated symbol of the blending of *criollo* and indigenous people (Westlake 1997, 57). The attempt to identify "Guatemalans" as oppressed, ethnically diverse, working-class people continues to be embellished in plays written in the 1960s and 1970s. The play was also one of the first to be blatantly anti–North American in its strong anti-imperialistic stance, which became a prominent theme in Guatemalan theater during the "Golden Age" in the 1960s and 1970s.

I would argue that Galich's plays written during the democratic period of 1944–1954 are nationalist plays with a social-political critique. For ten years following the revolution Galich wrote plays that suggested solutions to problems that affirmed the current political structure, rather than advocating "revolutionary change." Westlake states that Galich's *costumbristas* were critical of the middle class while his nationalist dramas were critical of the obstacles to nation-building, such as the foreign capitalists who profited from foreign investment, racism, and classism. Clearly Galich's trilogy is critical of the middle class. Nevertheless, he depicts the characters who are faced with moral dilemmas sympathetically. After "liberation," he writes plays that support the resistance movement and are highly critical of the corruption in the government and the conservative middle class.

Carrera compares Galich's dramaturgy to Eugene O'Neill, Arthur Miller, and Edward Albee in his ability to combine the personal and the social (1966, 51). He theorizes that the constant theme of Guatemalan theater since 1944 has been social theater which critiques the social order and suggests solutions to the injustices. He cites Hugo Carrillo, Manuel José Arce, Manuel Corleto, and Víctor Hugo Cruz (the most popular playwrights of the 1960s and 1970s in Guatemala) as following Galich's example of socially relevant theater which seeks to revolutionize society. (He specifically cites Carrillo's *El corazón del espantapájaros* and Arce's *Delito, condena y ejecución de una gallina*, which will be discussed later in this chapter.) He argues that the major change with these playwrights is "following the fashion in Guatemala" in the 1970s of using allegory and farce rather than Galich's staunch realism (54). I disagree with Carrera's analysis. He does not acknowledge a major shift that occurs in the plays following the "liberation" that openly attack the military regimes. The playwrights of the "Golden Age" were writing anti-Establishment plays during the war (which Galich did as well in exile). The plays written after "liberation"[3] were socially relevant as Carrera suggests, but the solution they offered was to challenge and undermine authority.

4. *"Liberation"*—Beginning of Military Dictatorship

One of the major reasons the U.S. government overthrew the democratic government in 1954 in favor of a dictatorial regime was President Arbenz's challenge to the United Fruit Company and its monopoly. Arbenz's land reform demanded the expropriation of hundreds of thousands of acres which belonged to the United Fruit Company (UFC). He was planning on settling 100,000 people on the land. He offered the UFC the price it had declared the property was worth for tax purposes. The offer was refused. By this time, Arbenz had gained support from the middle class and was favored by the Communist Party. The U.S. received reports that communists were even being appointed to minor posts in the Guatemalan government. The U.S. perceived the appointments and the land reform as overt communist leaning and decided to intervene. After staging a coup, the U.S. denied involvement in the plot. Many of the most important artists left in exile and never returned. It was this point that marked the end of a short but intense and vital period in the development of Guatemala's nationalist theater.

The CIA handpicked Colonel Carlos Castillo Armas as the next president. He had been living in exile and was flown to Guatemala in the U.S. ambassador's plane. CIA officer Phil Roettenger notes that his main virtue as a leader was his "willingness to obey orders without question" (quoted in Landau, 1993, 159). This was the beginning of a military dictatorship and systematic repression which lasted until the civil elections of 1986. Armas returned the land to the United Fruit Company. In the process of dislodging the peasants from the land, thousands were killed (Landau 1993, 159). A postcolonial relationship between the controlling U.S. and dependent Guatemala has persisted throughout the years. Since "liberation," Guatemala has received millions of dollars in military aid from the U.S. Between 1957 and 1972 more than 2,000 Guatemalan army officers were trained in U.S. military schools while over 425 police officers received antiterrorist training in Washington, D.C. (Simon 1987, 24).

The government under Armas openly supported artistic activities but without the same democratic spirit of the revolutionary years. He pushed for a National Theater and helped establish a school. The number of foreign plays increased while the number of plays written by local playwrights decreased. The audience grew smaller, returning the art form to its previous elitist status as the plays focused more on artistic form than on socially relevant themes. Westlake argues that, after 1954, dramatists pursued national themes but did not make any direct political criticism. "Often the drama showed the effects of tyranny on the souls of its protagonists without directly criticizing the dictatorship itself" (Westlake 1997, 58). The imperative to support the hegemonic ideology was pervasive. Playwright Manuel José Arce writes of the political atmosphere of fear during those years:

> In 1954, immediately after the CIA-organized intervention, there was an exhibit of "proofs of Soviet penetration of Guate-

mala." It contained books, films, and records published in the U.S.S.R. and other countries on politics, science, art, and literature. Among them were books by Pavlov, Gogol, Dostoyevsky, Turgenev, Chekhov [...] Films of Eisenstein and of the Bolshoi ballets, "Swan Lake" and "Coppelia"; records of Kachaturian, Stravinsky, Tchaikovsky, Mussorgsky. [...] All this material was publicly burned, in an act that marked the beginning of the cultural era in which we now live.

Possession of any of those books, records, or films was sufficient reason to imprison the owner and subject him to interrogation and torture by the Committee for Defense Against Communism *[Comité de Defensa contra el Comunismo]*. I personally went to prison in 1955. From that time on, possession of works that could be considered "subversive material" was grounds for assassination. (Arce, quoted in Jonas, McCaughan, and Martinez 1984, 168)

Nevertheless, after the first five years of Armas's reign, theater activity grew again. The National Conservatory opened in 1957 and was the first state school dedicated to actors' training. TAU at the university and the National Conservatory were the only institutions in the country exclusively dedicated to the creation of a new generation of national artists. Both taught the Stanislavsky system with courses in fencing, stage design, art history, and directing. Manuel Fernández Molina writes that the productions created in the late 1950s were of better quality than had ever been seen in Guatemala (1998, 27).

The plays in the late 1950s and 1960s used analogies from the past to subtly criticize society and the government. Miguel Ángel Asturias, who won the Nobel Prize for literature in 1967, is the most famous modern novel writer from Guatemala. His writing often bemoans the fact that Guatemalans have lost touch with their Mayan roots. His renowned play *Soluna [Sunmoon]*, written in 1955, is a modern miracle play which blends ancient myths and modern life. *La audiencia de los confines [The Tribunal of the Frontier]* dramatized the struggles to prohibit slavery of the Indians, with the implication that Guatemalan Indians continue to be exploited (McMurray 1987, 273). His 1946 novel *El Señor Presidente* was dramatized by Hugo Carillo in 1974 and became the biggest box-office hit in Guatemalan history. The story focuses on the oppressive dictatorship of Estrada Cabrera during the 1890s. McMurray writes that it is a novel of "social protest anchored in historical reality, but its tense portrait of a society gripped by terror makes it a landmark in Spanish American fiction" (McMurray 1987, 21).

Fernández Molina writes that the government between 1958 and 63 under Miguel Ydígoras Fuentes advocated more democracy. The political climate showed more tolerance. Fernández cites the example that the press was given more freedom than it had ever had (1988, 28). Ydígoras often attended the orchestra concerts and occasionally attended the dance and theatrical functions as well. He chose Luis Domingo Valladares to head the Cultural and Bellas Artes which was still under the Ministry of Education. Valladares produced works by authors linked with the leftist regime of Jacobo Arbenz, such as Manuel Galich's *El tren amarillo* in 1959.

Hugo Carrillo (1928-1994)

Carrillo returned from Paris in 1958 with his new play *La calle del sexo verde [Red Light District]*, which was put in production the following year and was his first commercial success. Fernández writes that this play aroused a curiosity about the people who lived in the capital. It was experimental theater that used grotesque images and some Brechtian techniques. It was the first time on the Guatemalan stage that socially taboo issues such as abortion, homosexuality, pederasty, and street beggars were raised. One review from the magazine ESCENA writes, "*La obra de Carrillo es vigorosa y atrevida. Sin hipocresía ni doblesces denuncia crudamente algunos problemas humanos que antes han querido ser escondidos con pusilanimidad*" [Carrillo's play is vigorous and daring. Without hypocrisy or selling out, Carrillo crudely denounces human problems which previously have been shamefully hidden] (quoted in the First Festival of Guatemalan Theater magazine 1962). Carrillo's production and the foreign play *El diario de Anna Frank* by Francis Goodrich and Albert Hackett are credited with greatly increasing the size of audiences and revitalizing the theater (Fernández Molina 1988, 29).

In 1959 the National Conservatory organized a season of plays including Carrillo's *La calle del sexo verde* at a Theater Festival. This event helped define the way for Guatemalan theater in the 1960s and 1970s:

[p]lays of political and social criticism, a mixture of realistic elements with magical symbols, absurd, grotesque and poetic styles in the treatment of fables and myths, and especially the use of the *mestizo* and popular cultures in the permanent search for a national identity. (Carrillo 1996, 293)

Yet, because of the imposed military dictatorship, the search for a national identity was impossible in this divisive country. The search would only become more problematic as Guatemala became more polarized over the civil war.

5. *Protest Plays/"Golden Age" of Theater*

President Armas was assassinated in 1957 and Colonel Ydígoras Fuentes became president in an "electoral farce" (Landau 1993, 160). He and his successors undid the education and health reforms, begun by President Arbenz, that promoted literacy and minimum medical care. In 1960 forty-eight military officers organized a revolt to protest the corruption in the military and the Ydígoras government: this is considered to be the inciting incident of the civil war. The officers were also angry with Ydígoras because he did not inform them that their country was being used to train troops for the U.S. Bay of Pigs invasion; they felt betrayed because he supported the U.S. over another Latin American country. They stole large quantities of weapons and supplies and left the capital to go to the provinces where peasants joined with the rebels. In 1961 and 1962 the revolutionaries attacked police stations and remote army outposts. The guerrillas gained major victories throughout the 1960s. They were filled with optimism, thinking the Cuban situation might be repeated.

1962 was a memorable year for Guatemalan theater as well as politics. In March a political protest began when students rebelled in favor of the workers and the marginalized in society. The government was drastic in its repression, and was responsible for more than 120 deaths. In May 1962 Jean Anouilh's *Antigone* opened. The play's political content received a great deal of comment in the press but not many people attended the show (Fernández Molina 1988, 31).

In July, an unprecedented, daring, politically candid play opened: Carrillo's *El corazón del espantapájaros [The Heart of the Scarecrow]*. This potentially incendiary work portrays a "fictional" repressive government against its people. Furious, President Ydígoras interrogated the director of *Bellas Artes*, Domingo Valladares, who produced the work. Ydígoras was enraged, thinking the work was financially supported by the state because it was shown at the *Conservatorio Nacional* (Fernández Molina 1988, 31). However, because the play had been produced privately, the production not only continued its season, but also inaugurated the First Festival of Guatemalan Theater in the fall of 1962. The closing play of the festival was Galich's *El tren amarillo*. Both plays were great hits.

During the 1960s, numerous directors from other Latin American countries who were part of the Theater Festivals began to be invited to direct and give classes in Guatemala. The Festivals were created in part to foster the development of national playwrights. Plays such as *El corazón del espantapájaros* also played in other Latin American festivals and fostered the international political protest movement of *Nuevo Teatro Popular [New Popular Theater]*.

EL CORAZÓN DEL ESPANTAPÁJAROS

Carrillo's play proved to be not only artistically constructed and dangerously provocative, but also prophetic of the endless power struggle and violence that would plague Guatemala for the next thirty years. The center of the play is a play within a play. A group of circus performers are about to perform a comedy. Most of the actors play two roles: the character from the circus and the characters in a story of "long ago." The metatheatrical approach utilized in the drama enables the audience to see themselves as "double"—as an audience from the capital watching Carrillo's play and as a public from a small town watching a circus performance.

The play begins with the lead clown reminding the audience not to forget that when the clown laughs, it is because his soul is in pain. The "comedy" play within a play begins with women discussing the strike by the university students in the capital. One of the women states that some unknown person has been passing out anti-Establishment leaflets in their village. The women read one of the leaflets, which states:

2: HISTORY OF TWENTIETH-CENTURY GUATEMALAN THEATER 51

Ciudadano, despierta y mírate. Ha llegado el momento de pelear por tu libertad. El Gobierno prepara una farsa electoral para perpetuar en el poder a un tirano. ¿Vas a cruzarte de brazos y permitir en silencio la cadena que quieren imponerte? Ciudadano, ser hombre significa tener dignidad. Defiende la tuya con muerte si fuera necesario.

[Citizen, wake up and look at yourself. The moment has come to fight for your liberty. The government has prepared an electoral farce in order to continue the power of a tyrant. Are you going to cross your arms and silently permit the chain that they want to impose on you? Citizen, to be a man means to have dignity. Defend your dignity until death if it is necessary.] (97)

The following scene focuses on two pairs of lovers. Lucia is meeting with her fiancé Esteban, who is in the army. He complains that he cannot disobey the orders of his superior. He does not enjoy the daily grind of dragging the people from the roads, shooting them in the back, and then throwing them into the plantations, where they must die like scarecrows. He feels trapped knowing that if he protests, he will be shot as well. Domingo enters. He is a member of the visiting circus, meeting with his new girlfriend, Juana. She is a maid who is pregnant from having been raped by her employer (a common experience of Guatemalan maids). He leaves her with the anti-Establishment leaflets which he has been passing around.

Act Two begins with a man in the audience singing a protest song lamenting the lack of freedom of speech. This convention of having songs interspersed between acts by a singer in the audience or outside of the action became very common in political plays in the 1970s. Carrillo acknowledges that this structural convention originated in the *Huelga de dolores*, the performance of political satires and protest songs the university students have put on once a year since 1898 (Carrillo 1971, 47).

In the following scene Domingo speaks idealistically about the revolution with Juana: *"No sólo para botar al gobierno, Juana. Para cambiar la vida que llevamos. Para que todos los hombres tengamos derecho a vivir como seres humanos. Para despertar la conciencia de la gente"* [Not only to kick out the government, Juana. But to change the life we are leading. So that all of us have the right to live as humans. So that we might wake up our consciousness] (131). Domingo explains that he is not an enemy of the government, but an enemy of injustice and misery. He tells the story of his father being a revolutionary when he was a child. The military leader had incarcerated his father and taped up his mouth. The boy was forced to watch his father be beaten. The military promised they would stop hitting him if Domingo would show them where his father's weapons were hidden. Domingo, desperate to help his father, showed the police the hiding place. He thought he was helping his father but later realized he was actually responsible for his death. He states, *"A mi padre que era un buen hombre, lo mataron como a un perro. A mí que sólo era un niño, me obligaron a delatarlo. ¿Cómo creés que pueda vivir contento en un mundo donde la misma historia ocurre todos los días?"* [My father was a good man and they shot him like a dog. When I was just a boy they made me betray him. How could I live happily in a world where these same things happen every day?] (135).[4]

Ricardo's police force is played by the clowns who are portrayed as idiots speaking in an "indigenous Spanish" accent similar to characters in the Minstrels in North America.[5] In spite of their ineptitude, they finally capture Juana and Domingo. Ricardo tries to get them to confess, warning them that it is a thousand times preferable to be a murderer than to be an enemy of the government. He then tortures both Domingo and Juana, putting the woman in a cell with ten male criminals to be gang raped. Ricardo then discovers from Lucia and Esteban that she is innocent. Ricardo is about to let her go when he discovers that Domingo has been killed by overzealous torturers. Juana has lost her mind and is shot trying to escape. The mother of Ricardo enters with the great news that he has been named Head of Police in the capital. She hugs him in front of Domingo's corpse, assuring him that in a short time he will be the president. The "comedy" ends and the clown explains the moral of the story which is a barely veiled support of the resistance movement: *"homenaje a todos los que han enfrentado la adversidad con valor y heroísmo"* [a tribute to all those who have confronted adversity with courage and heroism] (170).

Carrillo's work proves to be historically significant; the play's inflammatory content serves as an example of the change of political climate. The play was a great hit in 1962 and marked a beginning of public acknowledgment of institutional violence. In 1978 a revival production was closed down because of death threats against the cast. The abrupt end of the revival marked the beginning of the repression of the theater.

Carrillo describes his play as a bitter comedy where love is smashed by violence (1971, 47). Mercedes F. Durán-Cogan states that the theme of the play is a conflict between tyrannical power and individuals unable to transform or affect the political process. These topics, accessible to both the elite and the masses, had never been dramatized as vividly before: the police torturing perceived subversives, the idealism of the young revolutionaries versus government corruption and fraudulent elections, exploitation of the working class, police brutality, dictators' misuse of power, lower army officials coerced into perpetrating violence on the civilians, the impoverished town caught between the government and the subversives, and the institutionalized murder of innocent people. This play is prophetic in that all of these issues touched on in 1962 become pervasive during the later years of the war. This play reads like a stereotype; it represents the international perception of Guatemala in the late 1970s and early 1980s.

Durán-Cogan argues that the play demythologizes the figure of the dictator by enabling the audience to recognize the bloody reality and oppression with which they live. Her analysis is useful in recognizing the depth of the metatheatrical techniques in creating simultaneous multiple realities. She writes: "We can see a profound subversion in everything which has been glorified, such as justice, faith, innocence or the truth whose appearance is in tragic contrast with injustice, cruelty, violence and the bitterness of a society without hope" (Durán-Cogan 1993, 98).

She notes that when the clown tells the public they must be silent, the following sound is the brutal noise of torture. This is an example of when the public is simultaneously a victim, a witness, and an accomplice to the violence in Guatemala. The play accentuates the complicity of the public in the violence while at the same time getting them to look at barely veiled references and the political reality. The play ironically illustrates that in Guatemala the truth can only be expressed by people who are mad (Juana) or fools (the clowns).

Carrillo writes that in 1962 there was a shift to more political theater with the opening of *El corazón de espantapájaros*

(1992a, 96). It was followed by other political-social works by Manuel José Arce, Víctor Hugo Cruz, and others. This era became known as the "Golden Age" of theater. However, Fernández Molina points out that the early commercial successes of Carrillo and Galich during the late 1950s and early 1960s do not accurately reflect Guatemala's openness at this time. The *mestizo* theater served only one percent of the population—the middle class living in or near the capital. Therefore, Fernández argues that the government did not have a need to censor or repress the theatrical creations. This is the reason the liberal theater was able to continue in Guatemala until the 1970s when the audience numbers increased significantly.

In the early years of the war the major cities were not greatly affected. The decade's violence was concentrated in the rural areas in the beginning of the 1960s, but by the later years the repression was felt throughout Guatemala. Between 1966 and 1970 around 10,000 people were killed in the effort to assassinate an estimated 300–500 guerrillas (Simon 1987, 25). The death squads began in the mid-1960s as a joint effort between the Guatemalan military and the National Liberation Movement. These killers who were working with the military and police called their organization *Mano Blanco [White Hand]* and systematically assassinated labor leaders, radical professors, and students. They would terrorize the entire population, especially the political sector of Guatemala. Anyone suspected of engaging in subversive activities received an announcement on their door: a white hand inside a red circle (Landau 1993, 165). Then the accused would be kidnapped and tortured. Later, the mutilated corpse would turn up and be widely publicized in order to scare the entire Guatemalan population. By 1967 there were around twenty death squads in operation in Guatemala City proclaiming they would "eradicate national renegades and traitors to the fatherland" (quoted in Simon 1987, 24). Ironically, it was this type of out-of-hand institutionalized violence, originally intended to control the violence, which created stronger resistance in the people and thereby increased the number of recruits for the guerrillas. Resistance and social protest were expressed in numerous ways, most notably in the *mestizo* theater which continued to grow in popularity in the late 1960s and 1970s and eventually became a force to be reckoned with.

Carrillo writes in 1971 that the *mestizo* theater is an expression of social protest that reflects the drama of a people in rebellion (1971, 47). He describes this theater as actively taking part in the struggle by seeking to unite the people through their social reality and common Mayan heritage. He exacerbates the conflict between the government and the people by tapping into the anger over the Spanish Conquest which is imbedded in the psyche of the Guatemalans. He draws a parallel between the fascist government with the Spanish conquerors and the people as the persecuted Mayans.

Carrillo argues that theater liberates people from the idea that they have no control of their destiny and empowers them to confront the crisis. He believes the theater can give them strength by reminding them of who they were, reflecting on who they are, and inspiring them to think about who they might become. He writes:

> And our popular theatre, full of reminiscences, mysteries, traditions and strange religious fervor is the root, the talent and the source which we playwrights should recognize and use to reinterpret our myths. We should merge our myths with the current reality in order to define the truthful lines of our identity as a community that searches for its own solutions, vehemently yearning for liberty, for authenticity ... with the pride and dignity of its roots. (1971, 48)

EL SEÑOR PRESIDENTE

In 1974 Carrillo's adaptation of Miguel Asturias's novel *El Señor Presidente* opened during the Twelfth Festival of Guatemalan Theater. Up to this point plays generally were shown on weekends for about two months. *El Señor Presidente* sold out for ten consecutive months and attracted audiences across the various social sectors. It later toured other regions and major cities in other parts of Central America. More than 50,000 people saw it in total (Levenson 1989, 291). However, Carrillo became very particular about how the play should be staged and became enraged when a production in El Salvador changed a few scenes (interview with Margarita Kénefic, student of Carrillo, who wrote the English version for Joseph Papp). Years later, he withdrew the play from the New York Latin American

Festival in 1987 when he had a public disagreement with Joseph Papp over casting (Dreyer 1994, 186).

Although the play is about a dictator's repression of his people at the turn of the 1900s, the analogy with modern experience is clear. Carrillo states that he is proud that the theater continued in spite of the fear. He writes, "The theatre was an island surrounded by collective terror, persecutions, disappearances, people in exile or dead by the thousands who maintained their voice and expression unscathed" (1992a, 96). Theater producer and director Dick Smith (a U.S. citizen married to a Guatemalan) writes that Carrillo's play was the zenith of the "Golden Age" of theater. Although it was only to last four more years, it was a time when a playwright was able to reach all sectors of society and create an outlet for the people where they could dare to voice their reality, their repulsion and rage at the injustice, and their hope for reform. Smith describes the excitement caused by the theater:

> It was extraordinary what Arce and Carrillo and Morales (the director of the aforementioned playwrights' work) contributed to Guatemala. The Golden Age of Theatre—fed by their productions—fed the Golden Age of Ballet, which fed the Golden Age of Concerts, which fed the Golden Age of Painting, which all together fed, nourished, and informed the public's disgust with the Brass Age of Authority. . . . . The UP's (*Universidad Popular*) production of *El Señor Presidente* was the talk of the town—and deservedly so. Bursting onto the dangerous Cold War scene with Hugo Carrillo's scathing script and Rubén Morales's vivid, broad-stroked directing, it brought home to all Guatemalans a fact, which their Paris-ensconced Nobel Prize winner (Miguel Austurias) was demonstrating only to an elite: that Guatemalans from every walk of life are capable of creating world-class, relevant works of art. (Smith 1997, 3)

The play broke all box office records in Central America and received all the awards from diverse cultural associations. Carrillo writes that the public once broke the doors of the entrance to the theater where it was playing from the excitement of wanting to see the play (1992, 97). Unfortunately, the government also paid attention. Carrillo, fearful of the political repercussions of writing the adaptation, at first did not take credit for writing the play. At the opening he asked Dreyer's cousin to dress in costume as the "playwright" so he could release photos of "Franz Metz" meeting with director Rubén Morales (Dreyer 1994, 185). Members of the secret police came to the theater demanding Miguel Ángel Asturias's address, "which at the time happened to be the National Cemetery" (Dreyer 1994, 186).

Carrillo writes that the government slowly took action because of the success. They paid closer attention to the previews of the plays starting in 1975. The spectacular success of Carrillo's adaptation awakened government officials to the potential of theater as an instrument for raising social consciousness. The numerous collective creations were becoming more critical and antagonistic to the system and the repression for which no one was being held accountable. New playwrights such as Manuel José Arce were gaining prestige in their open defiance of the government.

Manuel José Arce (1935–1985)

Manuel José Arce was the most overtly anti-Establishment playwright, representing the voice of the people who felt disenfranchised and powerless (which in Guatemala is the vast majority). Galich focused on the conflicts of the middle class, but he was forced to leave before he could reach the lower classes. Carrillo took the next step. He opened the doors to the masses and sought to raise their consciousness about the rampant injustice and oppression. But it was Arce's leadership in political theater that deliberately incited the people to anger and action. Smith describes Arce and Carrillo as the prolific leaders of the political theater movement, but he states that Arce "was born to be Guatemala's Václav Havel—the talent, the following, and the classic villains were all in place—but, alas, he was much too sensible to fulfill such promise" (Smith 1997, 3). (He left the country in exile before he could be killed or imprisoned.) René Acuña describes the playwright as one of the champions who shook up the system through his forceful expression in poetry and drama (1975, 65). He states that new artists such as Arce challenged the elite in the country who were fearful of the new ideological and esthetic currents. Acuña theorizes that the theater was a didactic tool that had been co-opted by the government. He believes that the government was trying to create a National Theater, which was impossible in a divided country such as Guatemala. A National Theater could not be supported by the government in a military state and at the same time represent the people and their collective voice.

According to Acuña, most of the playwrights before the 1970s avoided overt political themes and left that to the foreign plays. The playwrights did not believe themselves to be powerful enough to survive in a military state. However, by the 1970s, artists like Arce were starting to break the molds of social convention (Acuña 1975, 65).

Arce wrote ¡Viva Sandino! which details the history of Nicaragua up to the birth of Sandino. The play suggests that Nicaragua needed a liberator such as Augusto Sandino. The implication was that Guatemala also needed a leader to liberate it from the fascist government.[6]

Delito, condena y ejecución de una gallina [Crime, Punishment and Execution of a Chicken] (1970) is Arce's most famous play. The play deals with class struggles between the chickens (actors dressed as chickens), the farmers, and the buyers. The buyers exploit the farmers, who in turn seek to exploit the chickens. The chickens try to unionize to protest the recent decision by the farmers to give them nutritionless feed. The analogy was provocative in a country where any attempt at unionizing or requesting basic rights was perceived as a communist threat.

As in *El corazón de espantapájaros*, there is a person singing protest songs from the audience between the scenes. As a communal act of rebellion, the starving chickens eat their own eggs. Although they consider it an abomination, they have no other leverage. One chicken proclaims, *"Lo único que nos queda es destruir todos los huevos que pongamos!"* [The only thing left to do is destroy all the eggs that we lay!] (122).

The wife of the farmer, recognizing that the chickens are brighter than anyone had previously thought, demands that the beak of the ringleader be burnt in front of the other chickens. At the end of this scene, slides are projected of Ubico and various other dictators in Guatemala's past. (Arce states in the stage directions that the production can choose any repressive politician for that particular country [127].) The wife demands that the farmers kill a chicken in front of the others. At this point in the play, the actor playing one of the chickens is replaced by a real chicken. The actor states that this is the moment when the farce becomes reality. *"Ahora, cuando los símbolos dejan de ser símbolos y la sangre comienza a ser sangre verdadera"* [Now is when the symbols stop being symbols and the blood begins to be real blood] (137). There is a mock trial during which the chicken proclaims that this is the moment when the son will rebel against his father (à la Galich), the soldier against its general, the servants against their masters. The final scene is memorable. With the chickens screaming "Don't kill her! Assassin!," the chicken is slowly and ritually killed, actual blood spurting everywhere on the stage. The chorus falls silent. The silence remains until long after the chicken has stopped moving (146). The play ends with the actors playing chickens chanting in unison, "In the struggle until the end!" They walk amidst the public, encouraging the audience to repeat the phrase as well.

Dick Smith acknowledges Arce's bold and daring confrontation with the Establishment, but criticizes his writing as using

> ever-expanding shock waves, the most singular of which was the on-stage decapitation of some surprised chickens who found themselves caught up in Arce's attempts to bring political realities home to roost in the minds of Guatemalan audiences. As a dramatist he was pure Danton: "Audacity, more audacity, and still more audacity!" . . . Heavy-handed simplistic didacticism. Another playwright's [Carrillo's] highly successful adaptation of Asturias's *El Señor Presidente* had set the style here:
>
>> Good guy meets evil guy.
>> Evil guy sadistically delights in crushing good guy,
>> Good guy goes to martyr hills.
>> His pals predict the Second Coming.
>
> Sound familiar? The difference on Guatemalan stages is that this plot focuses on the villain. His sadistic crushing of the good guy constitutes the overwhelming bulk of the drama. The producers and audiences who relished these productions were not too different from the Romans who got their kicks matching Christians with lions. (D. Smith 1992, 34)

Although Smith criticizes Arce's melodramatic style, this period of social and political crisis fostered extreme measures and polemic reactions which portrayed their reality as having clearly delineated good guys and bad guys. Although through a "North American lens" this writing appears melodramatic, this style accurately portrayed the audience's perception of reality and tapped into their feelings of outrage at the injustice perpetrated daily by the military. The theater became a place to vent one's rage as well as create a sense of solidarity.

Arce was well known for writing anti-Establishment poetry, newspaper articles, and drama that eventually caused him to receive death threats. In spite of the odds, he was out on the front line until he left the country for France, fearing for his life. When Arce writes in exile in 1984 (the year before his death), he acknowledges that the protest theater had reached an impasse; the army would no longer tolerate their subversive accusations. He writes:

> I left my country because of threats against me and the impossibility of self-expression as a writer and as a citizen. The campaign of extermination against my colleagues made me decide to survive outside my country. I know now that the existence of the present army is incompatible with the existence of freedom of thought. (Arce, quoted in Jonas et al. 1984, 169)

Proliferation of Political Theatre

Numerous theater artists asked me why I did not want to write solely on the "Golden Age" of theater, the political theater of the 1960s and 1970s. It was described as a time when theater was purposeful, powerful, and passionate. The problem is that many of the plays were not scripted and cannot be documented. The second problem is many of the ones that were written tended to be agitprop (agitation propaganda) plays.

Dick Smith writes about the era of the 1960s and 1970s in theater in his unpublished story on Guatemalan theater, "Hawks and Handsaws" (1992).[7] Although he is highly critical of this style of theater and its dubious relationship with the Establishment, his perspective is unique as an outsider who was not caught in the gathering snowball effect of idealism, righteousness, and rage. He writes in a tongue-in-cheek, detached style to describe the political dynamic: "A string of military presidents gave protesters their perfect foil. It was the Brass Age of politicians and the Steel Age of the protest play" (26).

Smith's perspective is refreshing after reading numerous idealistic accounts of how the "Golden Age" of political theater is "real theater." One grows weary of reading accounts where artists like Acuña accuse "apolitical" theater artists who "hide behind Mayan folklore" of being cowards and lacking artistic integrity (1975, 64). I quote Smith at length because he acknowledges this was a significant movement in theater and is able to vividly describe the atmosphere of the time. Yet, he seems less prone to exaggeration in terms of the overall impact theater had on the political reality. He is also the only writer to offer an explanation as to why the theater was given so much leeway. Smith writes:

> When my life really started centering around theater, in the late sixties and early seventies, the fad of politicizing from the Guatemalan stage and of theatrically belling Big Cats was all the rage. Up to ninety productions a year were being produced for Guatemala City's small theaters during the decade which ended with the '76 earthquake. Many of these plays were original; nearly all of them, politically inspired. Angry young men and women were writing and appropriating anti-Establishment themes as fast as they could be mounted. An impressive elective affinity bonded artists from all the disciplines. Painters, dancers, musicians, writers, actors, united as seldom before or since. An extraordinary woman, Eunice Lima, headed the governmental department which supported the arts, and usually she was able to convince the military that having artists dissent openly from stages and galleries, was much better policy than forcing them underground. One can only imagine the cabinet debates which this philosophy must have provoked, but on the whole, probably because of the military's basic indifference towards matters artistic, she generally managed to promulgate tolerance and organize festivals. (D. Smith 1992, 25)

Smith realizes that most politicians did not pay much attention to the theater and points out the self-inflating temptation an artist can fall prey to when (s)he believes the theater profoundly changes the world rather than reflects life. He writes:

> I doubt if any politician ever deigned to sit in our theaters or visit the art galleries, but nowhere was the Guatemalan político being examined so relentlessly—and so warily. It mattered to be an artist

> in those days. Every changeling looked in the mirror and saw an artist. Every artist looked in the mirror and saw someone who evoked change. And no matter how technically incompetent any artists might be, they could be confident that one camp or another in the Cold War's all-inclusive battlefield would pamper recruits and absolve shortcomings.
>
> Experimenting with novel approaches (that is, rediscovering avant-garde) was especially rampant. . . . In Dadaistic gibberish, Guatemalan artists discovered a highly useful tool: they could express dangerous things more or less safely. No mind that most audiences and prospective recruits were as mystified as government *orejas* [spies] by their double-talk. (D. Smith 1992, 26)

Likewise, Adolfo Hernández Solís writes in his article on the Guatemalan political theater in the 1970s of the abundance of quantity but often lack of quality. He cites several groups, such as *Teatro Centro*, as capable of maintaining artistic integrity with their political interpretations but says they were the exception. He writes: "Working in the theatre was always seen by the puritans as synonymous with a bohemian lifestyle and scandal. It was seen as a dangerous instrument for politicians. And the common man regarded it as somewhat inconvenient and a pastime of little worth" (1988, 48).

Numerous groups sprang up during the 1970s. *El Teatro Vivo* was created in Guatemala under the direction of Francisco García Muñoz in 1977. It incorporated dance and mime into its presentations. It sought to take the theater out of the buildings and into places where it generally never went (Espinosa 1982, 122). The work was collective; the group members of *El Teatro Vivo* would propose a theme and initiate improvisations until it formed into a whole. The group worked to unite unions and the towns. However, in 1980, the assassinations of actors Miguel Angel González and Gustavo Hernández led them to the decision to leave the country and work a foreign campaign of solidarity. Likewise, Roberto Díaz Gomar created a theatre group, XX, that did work similar to *Teatro Vivo* in seeking to take the work to the streets (interview with Díaz). XX is the term used for the unidentified dead and was used to protest the disappearances. However, Díaz Gomar had to leave the group one night when someone tried to assassinate him in 1978. The killers shot and killed Díaz Gomar's brother thinking it was him. He left the next morning for Spain and did not return until 1998 to live in Guatemala, where he continues to do theater.

6. Repression—Second Dark Ages

After the earthquake of 1976, which left over 27,000 dead and hundreds of thousands of people homeless (Perera 1993, 11), the climate of terror increased, creating a worse political and social crisis. In 1978, Romeo Lucas García took office in an election the *Washington Post* called "a fraud . . . so transparent that nobody could expect to get away with it" (quoted in Simon 1987, 71). His government is generally considered the extreme in terms of state violence. There were widespread massacres of Indian villages suspected of supporting the insurgency as well as numerous assassinations of political rivals.

A restaging of *El corazón del espantapájaros* in 1978 brought about anonymous telephone calls to the Popular University's theater with death threats for the director and cast if they did not immediately cancel the season. Carrillo had already left the country for Mexico in fear of his life. The theater staff called him in Mexico to explain the situation and the director and playwright decided to close the show.

In 1978, *Teatro Centro*, under the direction of Alfredo Porras Smith, had tried to incorporate more political ideology in their theater, which up to that point had staged mostly classics or avant-garde formalism (interview with Smith). They had produced Shakespeare's *Julio César* using slides of previous dictators during the play. They had thought to do *Fuente Ovejuna* [The Sheep Well] by Lope de Vega but decided against it. They were afraid that a play that deals with a town's uprising and violent beheading of an authority figure would be too inflammatory at the time. Instead they chose the patriotic play with minor political overtones *Es mi bella Guatemala un gran país* [It Is My Beautiful Guatemala, a Great Country]. Although it was a great success in 1978, the government of Lucas closed the theater. The government had recently begun a bloody repression.

On October 20, 1978, numerous student leaders were assassinated following the disappearances of syndicate leaders, professors, and thousands of peasants. This marked the beginning of a massive repression with at least 5,000 extrajudicial killings in Lucas's first eighteen months in office (Simon 1987, 72). Saul Landau uses the image of Alfred Jarry's King Ubu to describe the Lucas politics in 1978 (1993, 177). Ubu is a military man who becomes king after destroying his opponents and stealing all the nation's wealth. Lucas was notorious for his corruption and for killing members of opposing political parties. In 1980, hundreds of teachers, lawyers, priests, reporters, and students were murdered by government forces simply because they had shown sympathy for peasant or labor organizations. Death squads routinely patrolled the streets. In the same year, 1,000 unionists were assassinated. Three hundred members of the university were killed between 1980 and 1981. One student describes the oppression: "No one admitted to being an USAC (University of San Carlos) student. We were all scraping the USAC decals off our fenders, and hiding our student I.D.s inside our shoes" (quoted in Simon 1987, 76). Landau writes that "anti-military rule, anti-repression became the call of all the civilized people" (1993, 179).

Many theater groups were forced to close because of death threats in the form of "mortuary" gifts such as small coffins, wreaths, and tombstones. Some theater artists were kidnapped or assassinated, while some went into exile (Carrillo 1996, 295). However, the 1979 Festival was held and dedicated to the work of Manuel José Arce. Arce writes in exile:

> Threats have prevented the staging of many theatre works when not directly prohibited by the government. The National Theatre Festival of 1979, which carried my name and was dedicated to me as a tribute from the theater workers' union, was expressly prohibited from presenting any of my works. (Arce, quoted in Jonas et al. 1984, 169)

Robert Trudeau writes that January 31, 1980, has come to symbolize the brutality of the Guatemalan government. A group of thirty people (mostly Indians) entered and occupied the Spanish embassy. The Spanish ambassador, who was sympathetic to the Indians' plight, negotiated a peaceful solution. The ambassador went to the doorway and demanded that the building's sanctuary be respected since a solution had been negotiated. The police opened fire on the embassy. The hostages and all of the Guatemalans were burned to death except for the ambassador because he was in the doorway and one Guatemalan who had been buried under a pile of bodies (Trudeau 1993, 5). The Spanish embassy incident is mentioned in several plays in the 1990s. Some of the actors from *XX* had joined with the peasants at the Spanish embassy where they lost their lives during the massacre.

Panic spread throughout the theater community. Actress Juanita Loza de Molina was imprisoned in an insane asylum for having publicly demanded to see the slain body of her son. When the police broke into the Cultural Center University during a meeting with theater artists in 1981, the panic spread, the theater artists disbanded, and the groups retreated. *Las muestras de Teatro Departamental* patrons quickly canceled its seasons in 1980 and 1981 and programmed the season for children's theater and collective works without any social or political content. The *Festival Guatemalteco de Teatro* continued but with theater that was apolitical.

The most prominent theater groups in the country began to produce only traditional plays, foreign comedies, musicals, or adaptations of classical Latin American novels. Arce writes, "Following the courageous flowering of a theatre that dealt with reality, today in Guatemala there are only costume comedies and 'boulevard theater' " (quoted in Jonas et al. 1984, 169). There was a cultural "curfew" throughout the country which continued until 1986, when a civilian government was restored. Carrillo describes the events:

> *Tácitamente y por consenso general los teatristas se impusieron una autocensura que aún está vigente hasta el momento. El viraje fue radical. De la noche a la mañana todos los grupos teatrales se dedicaron a presental a un público cada vez mayor, a raíz de El señor presidente, vodeviles o comedias sin ningún contendido que despertara la menor sospecha de las autoridades. La época de oro del teatro guatemalteco de autores precipitadamente se acabó. Arce se fue al exilio a Francia y falleció a los 50 años en Albi. Galich desapareció de las carteleras teatrales por muchos años y falleció en Cuba. Asturias no volvió a presentarse en escena. Se callaron también las voces de Víctor Hugo Cruz . . . y otros autores.*

> [Tacitly and with general consensus the theater artists imposed a self-censorship which is still in effect at this moment (written in 1992). The change was radical. Suddenly vaudeville shows and

comedies, whose content would not make authorities suspicious, were presented to larger audiences by all the theater groups which had dedicated themselves to presenting works even better than their common roots of *El Señor Presidente*. The Golden Age of Theater with fearless authors had suddenly ended. Arce was exiled to France and died at age 50 in Albi. Galich disappeared from the theater billboards for many years and died in Cuba. Asturias did not return to the stage. The voices of Víctor Hugo Cruz . . . and others also were silenced.] (1992, 97–98)

Four student actors from the *Universidad Popular* were killed in diverse incidents. Fernández suggests that one of the most shocking moments to the theater community was the machine-gunning of a building which was part of the theatre of the *Arte Universitario* on January 29, 1981. The actress Zoila Portillo was gravely wounded and one administrator was killed. It was reminiscent of the police assault of the Spanish embassy. Ironically, a tribute for people who had died during the embassy assault had been held in the same building that was machine-gunned. Fernández describes the psychological effect on the theater community:

[e]s cierto que en un contexto de terror la racionalidad fría deja de existir y da paso a la psicosis de guerra; Así, aunque el ametrallamiento no hubiese sido destinado a reprimir la actividad escénica, lo cierto es que inhibió mucho a los artistas, dado que se dio en un edificio que era sede de un teatro y por el hecho de haber sido gravemente herida una actriz.

[I]t is certain that in the context of terror, cold rationality stops working and the psychosis of war begins. Although the machine-gunning had not been destined to repress the theatrical activity, it is certain that it inhibited many artists, given that it happened in a building that was the headquarters of the theater and the fact that an actress had been gravely wounded.] (1988, 36)

Smith describes the fearful atmosphere and the "mysterious fire" of the Popular University's theater:

Terrorism in Guatemala turns indiscriminate. Shoeshine boys are as likely to be blown up as businessmen and student activists. . . . And the *Universidad Popular*—home to political shows so vibrant with conviction that the whole community talked about them—mysteriously goes up in flames one night. . . . Anti-Establishment chaps approach Rubén Morales Monroy, the director of *Teatro de la Universidad Popular*, and demand to know why he no longer uses his now charred and canvas-topped theater to promote social change. He reminds them his job is to teach theater arts, not to change society, and he produces *La tía de Carlos [Charlie's Aunt]*. This is the way Golden Ages end. Sometimes with a bang, just as often with a whimper. (D. Smith 1992a, 35)

The Guatemalan army had become the deadliest and most effective counterinsurgency force in Central America by 1982 (Perera 1993, 108). Even President Reagan's administration, which had supported Lucas's regime in 1978, was finding it difficult to provide military aid because of the extreme human rights violations, referring to Lucas's government as "a bunch of thugs" (Trudeau 1993, 44). Lucas's response to every crisis was to escalate state terrorism which only created more economic problems for the country. In 1982 there was a coup d'état led by young military officers. The major objective was to improve the international image of Guatemala in order to help the economy. The officers installed retired General Efraín Ríos Montt. He had become an evangelical Christian after retiring from the army. He referred to his being chosen leader of the country as an act of God. One of his first declarations was that there would be no more assassinations. However, the number of rural massacres soared after he took power. He changed the law to say that the government could "kill legally," rationalizing that it was "preferable that it be known that people were shot, and not just twenty bodies have appeared beside the road" (quoted in Simon 1987, 111). By late 1982 death-squad vehicles appeared again. The newspapers published innumerable graphic photos of dead Indian peasants. Simon describes a small portion of the horror:

In San Francisco Nentón, Huehuetenango, some 350 villagers were massacred—(that same month) villagers from Plan de Sánchez, Rabinal, Baja Verapaz, were killed after the army raped every woman, except one who escaped and lived to tell the story; on September 13, in the village of Agua Fría, Rabinal, army soldiers burned to death over six dozen villagers. Even Ríos Montt sometimes admitted army culpability: after learning of the Nentón massacre, he ordered a full investigation, which concluded that the army had been responsible. No one was punished. (1987, 110)

Ríos Montt could have made the artistic climate extremely negative, given his fanaticism with the evangelical fundamentalists. However, because his wife had done theater with María de Sellarés and had personally known the professional ability of Norma Padilla who was the General Director of Bellas Artes, he did not have a negative impact on the artistic life in Guatemala (Fernández Molina 1982, 36). Nevertheless, Padilla died in 1984 by a "mysterious" hit-and-run car accident (some of the people I interviewed, who asked to remain anonymous, believed it was because of her interaction with student leftists).

The reign of President Ríos Montt who stated often that he was "sent by God" was brief: 1982–84. However, he made a profound impression because of his religious fanaticism mixed with merciless brutality. There have been several plays written about him in the 1990s which I discuss in chapters 3 and 4. Ríos Montt was replaced by Huberto Mejía Victores who reorganized the politics, enabling Christian Democrat Vinicio Cerezo to win the popular election in 1986. Molina writes that the transitional government of Mejía Victores did not bring about major changes for the theater even though terror was on a decline.

The small independent theaters continued with foreign commercial works. The university programs produced plays about Guatemala's history before 1900 as well as Greek and Roman classics. The actors did not have confidence in the political stability and the new constitution (the fourth in Guatemala since 1945). Fernández states that the theater community continued to be haunted by the violence: "(because of) the scars of totally indiscriminate terror by Lucas's dictatorship, the artists have barely begun to feel the new theatrical freedom which had characterized Guatemala for such a long time" (1988, 37). However, he does note that in 1988 there was a movement that supported the international politics of propeace work. Unfortunately, the successes achieved have been less than modest. He notes that there are three major strains of theater in 1988: the Popular University which does comic realistic theater, the theater of Dick Smith who uses the National Theater to produce copies of Broadway-type plays, and *Teatro Centro* which returned to its roots of esthetic apolitical experiments in comedy of the absurd or the classic Greek plays (Fernández Molina 1988, 37).

Productions During the Repression

The theater remained apolitical with very few plays produced by Guatemalan writers. Ricardo Mendizábal's theater group, *Grupo Diez,* was fairly unaffected by the violence. He felt that "the oppression by the military was exaggerated" since no one was really sure who set fire to the Popular University's theater (interview with Mendizábal). *Grupo Diez* had been founded in 1971 and was considered one of the most significant artistic theaters in Guatemala (Meléndez de Alonzo, "*Importancia del Grupo Diez en el teatro Guatemalteco contemporáneo,*" 1996 5). It continued doing foreign plays and apolitical national plays until the late 1980s. One production in the early 1980s called for a character to be dressed as a general in the army. A military man came to the theater and told Mendizábal to reconsider doing the play. The charismatic Mendizábal was able to convince the man that it was not offensive to the military and produced the play. *Grupo Diez* wrote a collective creation in 1983 called *Con el dedo en el fosforito (O los superhéroes) [With the Finger in the Flame (Or the Superheros)].* Mendizábal describes the play as focusing on Guatemalan problems. However, the comedy focuses more on the interpersonal dynamic between the superheros, such as Batman and Superman, and barely mentions the economic crisis "Gotham City" was experiencing during the early 1980s.

Two of the most popular seemingly apolitical plays produced in the early 1980s by a Guatemalan playwright were *Electro show [The Electric Show]* and *La consigma [The Slogan]*, both written by Jorge Godínez. He published them in the 1990s under the title *Qué lindo ser feo! [How Lovely to Be So Ugly]*, referring to Guatemala's self-image as pathetic and impotent.

The plays appeared to be innocuous enough to be produced at this time. Either the subversive edges were sufficiently muted not to cause concern for the Establishment or the plays fostered a detached, paralyzed reaction to the terror which the army rubber-stamped. Both plays center around characters who feel impotent in an insane world and are seeking to forget the past. *La Consigna* is a comedy which takes place in a bar filled with whining, self-loathing drunks. A drunk professor tries to talk his drunk student out of killing himself. The student complains that he can't stand the pain and he plans to kill himself. The professor tells him he must accept reality—and not to worry since there are many years ahead of the student in which to drink. They make a pact for a double suicide and plan to leave the bar. In the following dialogue, they make only slight reference to the political reality of the numerous disappeared:

> *Tomás. Espérese un cacho Profe, sólo voy a ver si cargo mis papeles.* [Wait a minute, Prof, I want to see if I have my papers/I.D.]
> *Profesor. Papeles?* [Papers?]
> *Tomás. Si, para que no me entierren como XX.* [Yes, so that they don't bury me as unidentified.]
> *Profesor. Tiene razón, hay mucho cadáver indocumentado.* [You're right, there are so many unidentified cadavers.]
>
> (200)

Electro show takes place in an insane asylum. Several of the inmates are obsessed with the idea of erasing the problems in the world. They continually fantasize about erasing money, hunger, guns that make war, and time. The male nurse, who according to the stage directions has a mustache like Hitler's, is telling the inmates of the exciting "electric show" they are all going to go see. He takes them one by one to get electroshock treatment (a common torture device used by the military). The nurse eventually kills one of the inmates who had amnesia, but, unfortunately, was not capable of forgetting everything. The inmates ask the dead man's closest friend and fellow inmate why he was killed; he responds that his friend died from the futility of trying to erase the past:

> *Querer borrar la maldad es una utopía que no conduce a nada, porque no podemos presindir de los opuestos. El hombre necesita conocer lo malo para sentirle el sabor a lo bueno; y al conocer lo bueno, ergo tendrá que sentir el dolor, el dolor, el dolor, el dolor.*

[The desire to erase the evil is a utopia that does not lead anywhere because we cannot do without opposites. Man needs to know evil in order to taste good; and once he knows good, he will have to feel pain, the pain, the pain, the pain.] (85)

These two plays reflect a theme that would be repeated often in the 1990s. There is a strong desire for people to escape the past, escape pain and retreat into apathy, insanity, or drunkenness. The only cure suggested by the plays is to confront reality and feel the pain. This remedy is spelled out even more succinctly in plays discussed in the following chapters.

Return to Civilian Government— Theater Tests the Political Waters

In 1985 the military allowed the election of a civilian government. In 1986 Christian Democrat Vinicio Cerezo Arévo took office and promised to end military impunity. However, throughout his five-year term, the security forces continued to kill and torture their perceived opponents without punishment.

Nevertheless, there were hopeful signs for a rebirth of socially relevant theater. In 1986 the country paid homage posthumously to Manuel José Arce (1933–85) with a staging of his play *Sebastián va de compras [Sebastian Goes Shopping]*. The Popular University presented several of Manuel Galich's plays in its tent theater. Carrillo writes that during the administration of Arévo the works of national playwrights were timidly mounted again, but "the plays passed a prudent self-censorship before being mounted" (1992a, 98). Although the Ministry of Culture in 1985 supported developing, protecting, and promoting the arts, Carrillo writes that they were not able to reach their objectives. He wrote in 1992 that still there was no protection for the Guatemalan theater artists.

One of the first overtly political productions was Galich's *El tren amarillo* in 1987, directed by Rubén Morales Monroy. Although the play seeks to unify Guatemalans against the imperialism of the United States, which is a fairly safe scapegoat, the play still promotes a perilous critique of oppressive power. One reviewer responds that the revival production challenges one to look at difficult choices in life: "There is a shrieking sound of silence in the search for the corner where the road forks in sacrifice for dignity or the broken jaw after being hit brutally with the butt of a rifle and recoiling from the powerful one" (Eloy Amado Herrera, quoted in *"Once espectáculos para la memoria,"* Pérez Coterillo 1988, 43).

Víctor Hugo Cruz's *El benemérito pueblo de Villanueva [The Worthy Town of Villanueva]*, a farce dealing with fraudulent elections, was remounted and had more than 100 presentations (Carrillo 1992, 98). (This play was remounted in 1999 at the National Theater and will be discussed in chapter 3).

Most of the plays did not openly confront the military, but skirted around the topic of the war. Olga Armírez's *Domingo [Sunday]* opened in 1988 and is one of the first plays to mention the war after the repression. Rather than focus on the height of the violence, the play begins with the early skirmishes of the war. More factual than inflammatory, Armírez writes that it is an autobiographical story about when the army started to fight with the guerrillas, an actuality that first began in her village on Sunday, November 13, 1960. She was trying to document how the people had no idea what was happening and to shake people out of their apathy (interview with Armírez). The characters are a group *"marginado de las decisions políticas y económicas del país"* [alienated from the country's political and economic decisions] (1). The family is only concerned with the problems of daily life. The people wish to stay ignorant about the rebels and their struggle. Their worries center on the rising cost of food rather than the onslaught of troops. After they hear that the war has started, they continue with their activities. A song from the radio is interrupted by a shocking announcement that meetings of more than four persons are prohibited and that there will be a curfew and other restrictions caused by the state of emergency.

Carrillo continued to write antimilitary protest plays but could no longer find an interested audience. He wrote *Cuando las putas se vestian de papel crepe [When the Whores Dress Themselves in Crepe Paper]* in 1988. The play centers around a Madame of a brothel who feels she has "sold out," continuing to sell herself to the army officers and rich North American businessmen. The theme of forgetting the past is prominent in this play as well. Her son is a "criminal" who is hunted by the police. However, the conflict between the son and the army is never made explicit. The son's position is deliberately left ambiguous. When the army tries to carry away her wounded and dying son, she attacks the army official by asking if their business is to exploit the world. When the commander calls her a whore, she responds that he is a worse whore than she is because the army *"vive de fornicar muertos"* ["lives by fornicating with corpses"] (42). She shouts that they can kill her too if they want to but it will do no good. *"Sólo así podrán gobernar tranquilos este cementerio. . . . Pero sobre su voluntad está la voluntad del pueblo"* [Only (if you kill me) will you be able to quietly govern this cemetery. . . . But above your will is the will of the people!] (43). Almost immediately after this statement one of the prostitutes stabs the commander.

This play stands out in its abhorrence of the military. It is one of the last plays to suggest meeting the violence of the military with violence. Perhaps this is a mixture of fear and the realization that blaming is not going to move the issue further. Whatever the case may be, there is a thematic difference in the plays written in the 1990s. This play was not popular with audiences and had a very short run (interview with Felipe Valenzuela, playwright and nephew of the deceased Carrillo). Although it is an intriguing play, the era of angry oppositional political theater was over and could not be resuscitated even by Carrillo.[8]

Grassroots political theater began popping up again after 1986. Although direct repression of the theater mostly disappears in the late 1980s, violence against some political theater continued. In 1989 José Rolando, an actor in the union theater company *Dos Que Tres*, was tortured and killed. *Dos Que Tres* was the only working-class theater group to have existed in Guatemalan theater in the past thirty-five years and it disbanded after Rolando's death (Levenson 1989, 4). It had grown out of the conflict between the Workers Union and the Coca-Cola plant, where eight workers were assassinated and dozens jailed and beaten. The plant was going to shut down in 1984 when the workers took it over and occupied the premises. The occupation lasted a year. During that year they put on the show *El gran robo [The Great Robbery]* to dramatize how Coca-Cola's owners faked bankruptcy in order to destroy the union. In 1986 the group decided to tour and gave over 200 presentations with the financial backing of the union. Levenson writes:

The plots of each [of the plays] were clearly not comic, but the manner in which *Dos Que Tres* portrayed politicians, plantation-owners, functionaries and military officers was hilarious—breaking the paralyzing effect of thinking them sacrosanct. (Levenson 1989, 4)

One of the actors whose brother had been "disappeared" explained that it had a healing effect to speak of political violence through this comic approach and "not to hide from what has pained me so deeply" (4). Levenson argues that the group not only has an explicit political message but an implicit one as well; the workers have the ability to make culture and therefore challenge the hegemony.

Several members had received death threats but continued performing until Rolando's death. Levenson posits that his death did not spark the outcry which would have resulted if he had been a middle-class artist or well-known union leader. She writes:

If the middle class has faced violent repression for its attempts to communicate intellectually and artistically, the urban poor have had far greater problems. Besides the violence, they have been denied the tools, from literacy to the wages to buy a decent paint brush. They have no socially sanctioned space in which to be creative. . . . To be an artist in these circumstances requires tremendous will. (Levenson 1989, 5)

THE POLITICAL ENVIRONMENT IN THE EARLY 1990s

Director Rubén Morales Monroy, when interviewed in 1990 by *ARTEATRO,* acknowledged that there were very few playwrights in the early 1990s who wrote about Guatemalan reality. He believes that the *Universidad Popular* was attacked because of the work they had done to expose the problems of Guatemalans. "The truth is that Guatemala is a country where the public is eminently religious and eminently political, and the playwrights who now have a conscience when writing about the daily life of the Guatemalans, produce a social-political play" (Hernández Solís 1991, 5). Unfortunately, the director and the actors suffer the consequences when they put the work on the stage. Morales explains that the self-censorship is caused because of the past violence and the playwright not wishing to return to those times. He states that one must not put the institution or the people who participate in the plays in danger of the repercussions.

Dick Smith was interviewed in the early 1990s by Pedro Bravo-Elizondo, a theater professor from Wichita State University. Bravo-Elizondo states that the Guatemalan theater scene is depressing since the politically relevant plays have disappeared. He asks if bedroom farce and commercial theater is Smith's legacy and if he has corrupted the development of a truly Guatemalan theater. Smith concedes this point, but pleads innocent of evil intent. He acknowledges that "the relevance of politics just about disappeared in (Guatemalan theater). As far as relevant theater's concerned, it's just that you've hit a low season" (Smith 1992, 235).

Conclusion

The "low season" that Smith identifies changes quickly in the 1990s. Guatemalan theater has survived numerous political upheavals and challenges during the twentieth century. Hugo Carrillo states that the *ladinos* had no theater of their own until the revolution in 1944. He theorizes that the revolution opened up new horizons for humanistic expressions and developed a powerful, educated middle class (1971, 44). Carrillo posits that contemporary theater began after the revolution and has continued to become more socially relevant up until the repression in the late 1970s. Before the revolution, theatrical expression was either in the form of indigenous dances for indigenous people or in the form of European-influenced plays for the elite. However, playwright Víctor Hugo Cruz argues that the European-influenced works produced during the nineteenth and early twentieth centuries are authentic expressions of *mestizo* theater. According to Cruz, both the indigenous and the *mestizo* theater have been trapped in the context of making art under repression and alienation (1993, 3). He argues that a continual theme in *mestizo* theater is the cry for political freedom. I believe that Cruz and Carrillo, both internationally recognized playwrights of the protest movement, are describing the overview of theater from the tenets of the "Golden Age" philosophy which perceives the theater to be a tool to challenge the Establishment. However, Cruz's description of the *mestizo* theater as a long search for liberty and Carrillo's perception of the theater as becoming continually more socially relevant do not incorporate the ten years of unprecedented freedom when the arts flourished after the revolution. I suggest that a more accurate overview of Guatemalan theater in this century is the fluctuation between repression and openness.

The theater experienced two dark periods during which self-representation was politically dangerous: 1931–44 under Ubico and 1978–86 during the worst years of the violence. After both these periods, a nationwide determination to support a democratic, peaceful stability arises; likewise, a theater emerges that seeks to define the nation again, reflect on a turbulent past, and unify the people and offer hope. The political theater that developed after "liberation" in the 1960s and 1970s protests the lack of voice the people have in political decisions. The "Golden Age" reflects a time when there was a wide chasm between the people and an oppressive governmental body, and tends to set these two groups against each other obviously privileging the righteous, honest citizens. This dramatic commonplace is transformed during the 1990s into a reconciliatory, reflective theater during the decade of the Peace Accord. This new theater is in strong contrast to the protest plays of the "Golden Age" and will be detailed in the following chapters.

The major difference between the national theater c.1945 and c.1986 is that World War II exposed Guatemalans to international conflict while the civil war exposed them to the depths of their own domestic strife. The National Theater after 1945 defined the villains outside of their borders, especially the U.S. It began to unify the indigenous with the *ladino* as "Guatemalans." The National Theater which slowly emerges after 1986 does not strive as hard to identify the villain with outside powers as with Guatemalans themselves. They acknowledge responsibility for their violent past and blatant racism, while respecting their desire for a more unified, stable nation.

3
Satiric Theater

SATIRE HAS A WIDE RANGE OF EXPRESSION: FROM ANGRY POLITICAL protest that attacks specific political and social institutions through irony, wit, and sarcasm to a more generic burlesquing of human vice or folly. This range can be noted in the university political protest satires of the *Huelga de dolores [Strike of Complaints]* to the more gentle *mestizo* commercial satires in the 1990s. This chapter will focus on two major strains of satire in mainstream, commercial Guatemalan theater of the 1990s: political satire and analogical satire. (It will also describe the precursor of the satiric forms: *Huelga de dolores*.)

Political satire refers to specific historic events and burlesques past/present politicians. The political satirists Jorge Ramírez and Douglas González and their work as a team and separately will be discussed in this chapter. Their form of satire stems directly from the political protest satires of the *Huelga de dolores*. However, the *Huelga de dolores* leans toward subversive protest while the commercial strain leans toward conformity and comedy. Although both make critical comments about society, the commercial theater disguises its anger in the form of light humor. A good example of the difference between these two styles of theater is the treatment of the same political figure, General Ríos Montt. This chapter details the variety of lampooning in both the political protest satires *(Huelga de dolores)* and the political satires that focus on the iconic figure of Ríos Montt.

The second category is one of my own. Analogical satire portrays a situation in the past, in a different location, or in a fictional situation that is analogous to the current social-political situation. While all satire is based upon "discernible, historically authentic particulars" (Rosenheim 1963, 317), the analogical variety offers more distance than usual from the current political-social issues. Nevertheless, parallels are made obvious by the playwrights in order for the Guatemalans to laugh at their own chaotic, upside-down world. The analogical satires of William Lemus and Víctor Hugo Cruz will be discussed, as well as the political parallels they depict.

The purpose of both strains of the middle-class commercial satires (political and analogical) is not as much to provoke people into action as to get them to begin to look at Guatemala's painful divisive civil war through the enticement of humor. The middle-class audiences are laughing at themselves, not at a more privileged class. This differs from the protest-oriented *Huelga de dolores,* which is a satire by people who feel they have been ignored by the government. Although the rage and call for revolution of the *Huelga* plays are more similar to the "Golden Age" plays discussed in chapter 2, I include them in this chapter for two reasons: (1) to show the development of satire; and (2) to highlight the difference between the fringe protest plays and the commercial theater of the 1990s.

The first significant theatrical depiction of the social-political reality after the repressive 1980s is satiric. Dustin Griffin argues in his book *Satire: A Critical Reintroduction* that the conditions for satire are more favorable under censorship than in extremely open political climates. He states that the most inventive satire arises when "the artist is seeking simultaneously to take risks and escape punishment for his boldness, and is never quite certain himself whether he will be acclaimed or punished" (Griffin 1993, 139). He explains that when the conditions of danger are removed, the satire becomes arbitrary and attracts writers of less spirit. In Guatemala, satire emerges during the period after the darkest repression and censorship. Plays of this kind test and push the boundary line of censorship, which in turn opens the path to the more explicit, direct works discussed in the following chapters.

Satire

Leonard Feinberg states that satire "is such a protean species of art that no two scholars use the same definition or the same outline of ingredients" (1967, vii). The most common ingredients are humor and criticism, but the innumerable blends of the two ingredients account for the numerous definitions. Theatre scholar Edgar Johnson explains that plays need both humor and criticism to qualify for the definition of satire: humor has a specific purpose of "laughing-at, not merely irresponsible laughing" (quoted in Petro 1982, 6). David Worcester argues in *The Art of Satire* that the content of satire is criticism (1960, 16). However, the art of satire is the concealment of the anger. Worcester posits that anger is a natural reaction to painful situations. However, because it is the most repellent emotion, humor is necessary to turn a painful situation into a ludicrous one. Although satire may be inspired by rage, the writer must detach him/herself from the material in order to effectively communicate the idea.

The spectator's interpretation of the purpose will therefore determine the category into which it falls. One person's satire is the next person's comedy if one sees social critique where the other does not. The potentially subversive intent hiding behind the humor creates a mystique of daring by appearing to challenge the status quo. This mystique is in large part responsible for the overwhelming popularity of commercial satire in the early 1990s in Guatemala. Yet, it appears more daring than it actually is; the criticism is quite mild in the commercial theater. The mainstream playwrights emphasize humor over critique. The impetus for writing the satires is probably anger and frustration. However, the commercial satires end with containment of the satiric energy, projecting a positive, serious message of national unity.

In most of the satiric commercial plays of the period, the writers are portraying a world that middle-class Guatemalans cannot control. Situations are insane and resistance makes no sense. Protest would be a waste of energy—one might as well just give in and laugh at the insanity. This form of theater creates a solidarity among people needing to move beyond fear. The recent history is deeply painful to assimilate and the first approach to confronting the past is through laughter. The laughter creates community, offering camaraderie and the sense that they all have gone through this insane political upheaval together.[1] It also serves as a communal fantasy. The politicians and institutions that incited deep fear are burlesqued. Powerful political leaders such as President Ríos Montt are demythologized. Genocide, massacres, coups, and corruption are openly portrayed for the first time since the repression of the 1970s-1980s under the least threatening guise: humor.

HUELGA DE DOLORES

The tradition of satire in Guatemala begins with the university plays during the *Huelga de dolores* which began in 1898. Most current playwrights started out writing these protest scripts. The list of ex–*Huelga de dolores* writers includes the aforementioned playwrights Manuel José Arce, Manuel Corleto, Luis Escobedo, Víctor Hugo Cruz, and Miguel Ángel Asturias. (As noted in chapter 2, Hugo Carrillo styled some of his plays on the *Huelga de dolores* structure.) This form of theater is "political protest satire" which functions as a release valve for expressing pent-up anger. It is a carnavalesque fantasy where everything is topsy-turvy—where those without power, the students, are given the opportunity to burlesque those that have power, the government. The plays blame those at the top of the hierarchy for the problems in Guatemala. The students' scripts claim the moral high ground by creating a them/us model that is a basic tenet of protest theater. These plays cite current political events and have an inherently short life span because of the specific topical references and the venue. The villains change depending upon who is in office that particular year and the national and international issues of the moment.

The *Huelga de dolores* celebration has continued every year with a new script and is presented during the Easter holiday (except for a few years in the early 1940s during General Ubico's regime and a few years in the early 1980s during the height of the repression). On Good Friday of Holy Week the students march in the streets in a crowded parade, often wearing hoods or grotesque masks to hide their identity. They demand money from people. If they do not receive what they demand, they often do something offensive, for example, a minor physical assault on a citizen. It is similar to Halloween except that the participants are not children but young adults, and the "tricks" frequently get out of hand: the activity is notorious for causing minor riots. After the parade, the students perform plays written especially for that political year. Usually the author(s) do not claim credit for the work in case of repercussions from the authorities.

The plays tend to be crude, risqué, sarcastic, and completely irreverent. Favorite targets are politicians, religion, indigenous leaders, the army, and ex-guerrillas. A traditional target is the United States government. The students burn *papier-mâché* dolls in the image of the various politicians, burn flags from the United States, carry protest signs, and shout slogans in front of the National Palace. The stated purpose is "an escape for the people in order to forget the economic problems and the insecurity of the citizens" (*Celebran Centenario* 1999, 1). Its propaganda states that this is the voice of the people and offers the illusion that they have power. For example, when the participants chose the *"Rey Feo" [ugly king]* of the ceremony, *Eligio Lustrabotas [The Chosen Bootshiner]* in the 1998 *Huelga de dolores*, he made this proclamation to the gathered audience:

> This [celebration] has not been a hundred years of strike, they are a hundred years of struggle for the people that have been repressed, but now they are going to rise. We put President Arzu there where he presently reigns; therefore, he is our servant and has to do what we tell him even if he doesn't want to. (*Celebran Centenario* 1999, 2)

The *Huelga de dolores* satires are around forty-five minutes to an hour in length and feature protest songs with politicized lyrics and popular tunes interspersed. The plays often have short scenes connected by that year's theme. The plays usually end with a song of solidarity between the students, workers, and peasants. The characters are often a mixture of current political figures put in a different time period. For example, the plays will have biblical characters with the last name of one of the presidents being parodied, for example, Judas Arana or Caín Castillo Armas. In the *Huelga de dolores Vida, pasión y muerte de un pueblo [Life, Passion and Death of a People]* (1974), written in the mid-1970s, the *Maestro* [teacher] uses the structure of the Sermon on the Mount but changes the words to "Blessed are those who rebel, because they will make reforms; blessed are those who are persecuted, because they will persevere; blessed are those that do not vote for President Arana, because they will have a tranquil conscience" (González Dubón 1998, 96). *El hombre sin mancha [The Man with Honor]* (1978) is another *Huelga de dolores*. It is a parody of *The Man of La Mancha*. Don Quixote struggles against *"dantesco desfile"* [Dante's parade]—all the death that has plagued the country during the war. Don Quixote seeks to challenge the government, end injustice, and stop the repression. He seeks to stop Guatedulce (Guatemala) from being the U.S.'s whore and to purify her again. He defies the structures of the old windmills that cut off the heads of the men who oppose the direction of the current political wind. (A Coca-Cola windmill is in the background, symbolizing the protest against the U.S.)

The gallows humor is forcefully crude. The plays are structured as burlesques of horrific current political issues, such as the massacres, interspersed with a great deal of earthy sexual humor, as well as jokes from local TV commercials. Nothing is sacred or exempt from attack/critique. The students will use as grist for their mill current topics as varied as the murder of Bishop Gerardi in 1998 and Monica Lewinsky.

During the years of the most intense violence, the *Huelga* plays satirized the brutality. In the past five years, with less incendiary political material to work with, the plays have focused more on sexual lewdness for shock value. *La Creación*, written in 1999, focuses on numerous jokes about Viagra and the sexual appetites of Saint Peter interspersed with current events, such as the creation of the new highway through Guatemala. They traditionally use current "hot button" themes: 1999's issue was adoption and the problem of stolen babies mixed with sex jokes and national figures. An example of the jokes is a boy selling newspapers who shouts the headlines: "The latest news. Test tube baby born pregnant! They kidnapped a baby, but it was still inside the mother. The wife of Umaña [political official] offers boys and girls for adoption but they are still inside the reproductive organs of their parents" (*Huelga de dolores* 1999, 469).

Huelga de dolores influenced the grassroots satirical movement as well as the *mestizo* commercial theater. Grassroots satirical political protest began to make a reappearance in 1990 and has continued up until the present. The audience is made up of mostly lower-class workers and farmers. The plays are a less abrasive style of satire than the *Huelga de dolores*. Andrew

Sofer, a United States citizen and member of the association of Artists for Guatemala, describes his experience at a joint performance of two grassroots theater groups in Guatemala City. *Grupo Teatral Fantasía* was founded in 1990 by the inhabitants of a shantytown. *Tortilla con Sal [Tortilla with Salt]*, which became an official theater group in 1989, is made up of university students. The name of their group derives from what the common people always ask for: salt with their tortilla. They claim to present "satirical-comical-musical theater" which makes current political jokes. For example, they poked innocuous fun at the current president by stating that he had no head (D. Green 1992, 48). They have performed throughout all of Guatemala as well as in San Salvador and Managua. Sofer writes, "Some politicized Guatemalan theatre groups appear to have earned a tenuous and temporary?—amnesty from explicit political intimidation" (quoted in D. Green 1992, 49). 1990 was also the year the commercial political satires of Jorge Ramírez and Douglas González began their domination of the theater scene. Whereas the temporary carnavalesque world of the political protest focused on provocation, the commercial satire ended with a serious message that encouraged a more permanent national solidarity. Ramírez's and González's comic approach not only revitalized the mainstream theater, it paved the way for theater that could address the atrocities committed during the war.

Commercial Political Satires

Jorge Ramírez and Douglas González both started their playwriting careers in *Huelga de dolores* during the 1970s and 1980s when they were at the university. In 1990 they spent one weekend drafting the satire *La epopeya de las Indias españolas [The Odyssey of the Spanish Indians]* as a social commentary on the upcoming 500 year celebration of Christopher Columbus. Unexpectedly, the play was a phenomenal commercial success which ran for most of the year. The actors became minor celebrities in Guatemala. They toured with the play and are planning a revival of the play to open their new theater in 2000 (interview with Ramírez).[2]

La epopeya de las Indias españolas (1990) is the story of the

Conquest and takes place 500 years ago. However, the story is inverted; the Guatemalans who speak in Spanish accents sail over to Spain to conquer the Spaniards who speak in Indian accents. This inversion of power challenged people to recognize the colonized perspective of the celebration. As in the satire tradition from *Huelga de dolores*, there is still plenty of sexual innuendo. But the language has been cleaned up enough to be acceptable for middle-class families. The play was the first major theatrical success since the repression, marking the rebirth of theater in Guatemala. People were again recognizing that the theater had potential to change Guatemala.

In the play, the "Guatemalans" talk about their expansionist empire and their successful battles. The leader laments that his country has been caught on a treadmill where continued expansion is necessary for the political-military empire to survive. One of the Guatemalans' assistants points out the irony of a country thinking it has the God-given right to invade other countries. He states: *"Hemos sido formados para vencer y no para ser vencidos, entonces cuestiono a su majestad: ¿cómo vamos a vivir en la paz, si la guerra es un negocio?"* [We have been taught to conquer and not to be conquered. Therefore, I ask your majesty, how could we ever live in peace if war is a business?] (3). Understandably, the "Spanish" are angry and wonder what right the "Guatemalans" have to invade their land. But the conquering leader defends his aggression, explaining that he raids other countries in order for progress to be made. They try to assuage the "Spaniards" by convincing them that through conquest, nobody stays behind. Neither the "Spaniards" nor the Guatemalan audience are persuaded. The play ends as actors spell out the moral and comment in chorus on the inversion: *"Así no fue, pero si así hubiera sido, a ver si España lo celebraría"* [It wasn't like that, but if it had been, who knows if Spain would celebrate it] (16).

Ramírez and González used the same actors in their following plays, including *Sopa de cebollas [Onion Soup]* (1993) which was another big hit. It satirized former president Serrano (1990–93) who was facing charges of corruption and abuse of presidential power. Instead of allowing his case to go to trial, he dissolved the Congress and the Supreme Court, censored the press, suspended part of the constitution, and resolved to rule by decree. After his "auto-coup," which is referred to in the satire as "*Serrano's famoso serranazo*," the U.S. and many European countries suspended all aid. Rigoberta Menchú and other popular leaders and thousands of supporters protested in the streets until he left office.[3] All of these scandals were lampooned with comic mastery by Ramírez and González.

In 1994 the sequel, *Sopa de cebollas II [Onion Soup II]*, opened. They lampooned President León Carpio, who was considered the fearless human rights ombudsman before he was elected. The play begins with great hope for the new president. He enters in a Superman costume. Faced with the "kryptonite" of current issues, however, he slowly becomes weaker. I was fortunate enough to get a ticket to the sold-out run of this production. The house was packed and the audience was in hysterics seeing their president portrayed in this fun-loving manner.

Each of Ramírez's and González's political plays met with great success. They began to pump out at least one political satire a year, each one becoming a bit more shocking and novel. The audience of middle-class to upper-middle-class people came to the theater in part because they were shocked at how far the playwrights would go (interview with René Molino, theater director). These playwrights hail from the same social level as the audiences. In this case and generally, the commercial theatre is written and produced by theatre artists who have a strong influence in society.

González, who is from a well-connected family, stated that he claims he is not afraid of anyone in Guatemala (interview with González). When I first met him, I had read several of his *Huelga de dolores* which were especially critical of the United States and capitalism (he is credited with having written the aforementioned *El hombre sin mancha*). I expected to find a radical leftist ex-guerrilla. However, in our first meeting he explained that he wrote plays to get people to laugh rather than to push a political agenda.[4] He did not consider himself an artist (he repeated this three times), but a businessman. He was proud of the fact that he made more money on his first commercial success than Carlos Peña (one of Guatemala's most famous and often employed actors) had made in his entire theatrical career. As Griffin suggests, a satirist often claims to be apolitical. The satirist's primary goal is not to declare a political principle but to respond to a particular occasion. Griffin posits that they are usually not motivated by a clearly articulated political ideology or principles (Griffin 1993, 149).

Dick Smith claims that the epochal conversion of Guatemalan theatre to an economically prosperous profession was accomplished by writers Jorge Ramírez and Douglas González.

> For those artists who could put a comic spin on political protest, the box office responded so splendidly that revived pioneers of the genre might have wondered if supercomics Mónica Sarmientos and Rafael Pineda (members of their acting troupe), and prodigious dramatists Jorge Ramírez and Douglas González weren't satirizing one of the Cold War's most sacred notions: that somehow it is obscene to make lots of money. (D. Smith 1992, 26)

Although Smith refers to Ramírez's and González's plays as political protest, a better description is political satire. These playwrights emphasized the strain from the *Huelga de dolores* that used current or recent topics and burlesqued national leaders and situations. Their tone was self-effacing rather than abrasive and sarcastic. Whereas *Huelga* plays emphasize polemic political content, Ramírez and González focused on comic timing while the political situation served as a drawing card for audiences.

Douglas González and Jorge Ramírez broke up their partnership in 1995, but both continued to write popular satires using their formula of inverted power positions. Ramírez wrote *Señora Presidente* about how the country would change if a woman became president. González wrote *Adan y Eva* as a romance which switched the traditional roles in the male and female relationship. In 1995 Ramírez wrote his first political satire dealing with the war and the controversial General Efraín Ríos Montt, *El General no tiene quien lo inscriba [The General Doesn't Have Anyone Who Can Register Him* (to be a candidate for president)*]*.

Background on General Ríos Montt

Ríos Montt has left an indelible mark on the country: numerous plays outline his impact on Guatemala. He remains a controversial figure with many followers and many enemies. He has not been permitted to run for president because of an amendment to the constitution, Article 186, which stated that anyone participating in a coup cannot run for president (written specifically to stop him from running for office). However, he adopted the practice of including his name in the propaganda for the presidential candidates running with his party (innumerable posters papering the main streets and TV/radio ads), suggesting that the candidate supports Ríos Montt's position. His party won the presidential election in 1991. Millions of *ladinos* and Mayans who have been disenchanted with the government's broken promises long for Ríos Montt's leadership: his devotion to God and honor, his parental authoritarianism, and his stance against crime and corruption. Victor Perera describes his charismatic appeal in his book *Unfinished Conquest: The Guatemalan Tragedy*:[5]

> The downtrodden ladinos recognize in Ríos Montt a fellow sufferer who transforms defeat and humiliation into an irresistible will to power. And Pentecostals welcome his fiery-eyed, eschatological pronouncements as signs that he is indeed the Chosen One to carry out God's design. (1993, 331)

Ríos Montt presided over massacres of peasants in 1973 when he was Chief of Staff. He ran for president under the Christian-Democrat Party in 1974 and received the most electoral votes. However, the "official results," in a case of electoral fraud, gave General Kjell Laugerud the victory. In 1978 Ríos Montt decided to become an evangelical minister and retired from the military. When he returned to the political work he merged his newly found commitment to God and his military training in modern counterinsurgency. After his evangelical Christian conversion, he became an enigmatic mixture of "ascetic self-abnegation and arrogant self-assertiveness" which is seen in his contradictory roles as philanthropic evangelical and ruthless anticommunist general (Perera 1993, 330).

Ríos Montt participated in the coup on March 23, 1982, along with 900 dissident officers of the armed forces. Tanks and cannons were placed next to the fountains in the central plaza and aimed at President Lucas's office. On June 9, Ríos Montt dissolved the *junta* and declared himself president. He continued Lucas's brutal massacring of villagers and capturing "subversives" in the cities. Ríos Montt differed from Lucas in that his actions were motivated by divine visions, believing he was preparing for the Apocalypse. Trained in counterinsurgency at the Interamerican Defense College in Washington, he promised his avid supporter President Ronald Reagan that he would clean up Guatemala's human rights image after taking office.

Ríos Montt was disciplined and dedicated to his calling as one of Christ's servants. He held a strong anticorruption stance and was very strict against crime. He fought against police abuse and demanded that the Guatemalan soldiers carry a copy of the conduct code. The symbol he used for his party slogan was three blue fingers against a white background imprinted with the words, "I don't steal, lie or abuse power." The generals who preceded Ríos Montt in the office of the presidency had received enormous salaries and used their position to acquire private companies and large landholdings, and in some cases, established their own banks to increase their economic interests. The strength behind the corruption which began in 1954 could not be challenged easily. However, Ríos Montt, who loved and honored the military, perceived the internal corruption as a threat to the institution. He challenged the military oligarchy in order to strengthen it.

Ríos Montt's government forced the peasants to choose political allegiance through a program called *Fusiles y frijoles* [Rifles and Beans] in order to defeat communism and promote Christian values. The poor peasants would receive food and arms if they would fight against the communists. He began the *patrullas de autodefensa civil (PAC)* [civil self-defense patrols] program which according to Simon "obligated almost every rural male to act as the army's eyes and ears and, at times, as its cannon fodder" (Simon 1987, 118). If they refused membership they would be killed. It became the most extensive civil defense program in the world.

He challenged the citizens to be more disciplined and dedicated to God as well. Every Sunday night he appeared on television in civil dress and sermonized about the need for patriotism. Following the U.S.-based Moral Majority, Ríos Montt became a strong authoritarian figure, depicting himself as the father of the country who demanded unquestioned obedience. He encouraged the people to pray as a way to stop violence. He states in one of his sermons/addresses on TV:

There will be no more murdered people on the roadsides; anyone who acts against the law shall be executed. Let's not have any more murders. We want to respect human rights and defend them. It is the only way to live democratically. (quoted in Landau 1993, 189)

Ríos Montt's extremes of mixing religion and the military are in part why he makes such enticing material for burlesque as well as drama. Few other dictators have inspired such creative depictions.

Parodies and Portrayals of General Ríos Montt

Ríos Montt's authoritarianism established enough stability that the capital city's commercial theater could open its doors again under his regime. Dick Smith writes that Ríos Montt made Guatemala "dangerous for some notorious hypocrites and safe again for stage actors" (1992, 152). Smith's production of Thornton Wilder's *La casamentera [The Matchmaker]* in 1983 included a daring scene that parodied the military leader. One of Wilder's minor characters in the play is drunk and finds a wallet. The character sermonizes to the audience about how they should not steal. Halfway through the speech, the actor changes his voice to imitate General Ríos Montt's Sunday-night sermons. Smith writes:

> But on the night when Salomón Gómez (actor playing the drunk) first satirized the Sunday night sermonizer, nobody knew beans about Guatemala's upstart Lord High Executioner; nobody knew how he might react to such impertinence. Nor, indeed, how his friends and enemies might react. . . . No few members of the cast thought we were fools to even consider ridiculing Ríos Montt. . . . When the audience realized what he was doing with his monologue, there was a collective gasp of recognition. Then, roaring into the amazed night, came the same convulsive, helpless laughter that the cast had experienced first in Salomón's unforgettable rehearsal. . . . What a grand discharge of existential nausea was thereby made by some in the audience! What a grand catharsis of fear was experienced by others! The packed audience who left the theatre that opening night, went home healthier, happier people—saner, in their chronically-abused democracy, than they had been

earlier in the evening. Such sanity is no small accomplishment for Theatre in a banana republic. (Smith 1992, 158)

Smith claims that audience members came a second time just to see this speech. He notes that no one ever objected to the imitative monologue and states that the play could have played through the next century. "And if I read Ríos Montt right, and I think I do, I doubt if his government would have stifled such parody" (Smith 1992, 159).

Smith identifies the healing impact this harmless burlesque had on the people. The political satires of Ramírez and González in the 1990s which were to become so popular served this same purpose, to enable the people to laugh at the government—that volatile beast that had terrified everyone into silence for the past decade. Robin Andrew Haig, a medical doctor, argues that comedy is physiologically good for the individual as well as the community. He describes psychoanalytic theories on humor which suggest that the lifting of repressions regarding aggression and taboo subjects results in surplus "energy" being available for laughter (Haig 1988, 10). Haig stresses the social aspect of comedy which brings people together, changes the tension, and reduces anxiety. He writes that humor is an acceptable outlet for hostility, pushing forward problems of denial, repression, and suppression which leads one to acceptance of one's situation. In accordance with this theory, I believe that comic satire is a vital first step for the theater in enabling Guatemalans to begin to process the recent turbulent past.

The actor's gentle parody in Smith's production is in stark contrast to the acrid portrayal of Ríos Montt in the *Huelga de dolores* entitled *El paquete tributario* which was also presented in 1983. The play holds the government, and especially the president, responsible for the massacres and raises questions about recent incidents of disappeared university students. The script satirizes specific deaths, such as those of a Mariachi band killed because the army spotted them out past the curfew and thought they were planning a coup. The play ridicules Ríos Montt, his new taxes, and his Sunday sermons. The character of Ríos Montt states in his Sunday sermon that he is happy to sacrifice 95 percent of the population in order to implement his new tax. He continues:

Mi Dios, que también es suyo, en un orgasmo de locura me ha iluminado proporcionándome los lineamientos técnicos y Pseudo-religiosos para implantar el paquete tributario y como ustedes ya saben, el impuesto del timbre era en cascada, este en cambio tendrá el carácter de cagada.

[My God, who also is yours, in an orgasm of insanity has illuminated me, giving me the technical expertise and pseudo-religiosity for the purpose of implanting the new tax program and as you already know, the tax stamp which was the ever increasing step, which in exchange will now have the character of shit]. (*Huelga de dolores* 1999, 234)

Later the character speaks of his program *"FFF—Frijoles y fusiles a fusiles y más fusiles"* [Beans and rifles and rifles and more rifles] as well as *"MMM Masacres y Más Masacres"* [MMM—Massacres and More Massacres] (*Huelga de dolores* 1999, 236). These jokes are similar in tone to the jokes in Ramírez's commercial satire in 1995. The difference is that the *Huelga de dolores* was done during Ríos Montt's regime by some of the people who felt his repression directly. Ramírez's satire has less edge in part because it was done twelve years after the general was in power.

There were serious works as well which covertly portray Ríos Montt's regime. An opera written with Mayan music, *En los cerros de ilóm*, by J. Orellana, was produced in 1992 at the National Theater. It features the story of a religious fanatic general who is on a mission to clean up the land and burn all the communists. There is also an indigenous woman similar to Rigoberto Menchú in her protestations. The producers were going to take the play overseas but were informed that if they left the country with this production, they would not be able to return (interview with Raul Lorka, member of cast). Whether the Establishment was more concerned about their international image concerning the Ríos Montt character or the Rigoberto Menchú character (Rigoberto Menchú won the Nobel Peace Prize the same year this production was mounted and caused great embarrassment for the government because the international community unequivocally supported the indigenous struggle in this manner) or simply wanted to contain the negative representation is debatable. Whatever the case, the tour was canceled.

Los Herejes [The Heretics] written by Miguel Angel Chavarria Pareds won first prize in a national drama contest in 1994. The serious drama is set during the Dark Ages of the fourteenth century and centers on a religious fanatic determined to bring the people into line. He massacres them in the name of God in order to ferret out the heretics. The head of the state, Umanoff, sermonizes in tones similar to Ríos Montt. The character is confronted with his contradictions and hypocrisies and in the end is eventually destroyed.

Satirist Jorge Ramírez wrote, produced, and acted in *El General no tiene quien lo inscriba [The General Doesn't Have Anyone Who Will Register Him* (to be a candidate for President)*]* in 1995 in the smaller, 400-seat house of the National Theater. This daring work sold out for the time it was running, but Ramírez felt it was too provocative to continue and decided to close it (interview with Ramírez).[6]

The play begins in Ramírez's usual slick, almost Las Vegas style with a flashy dance number scene set in a cemetery and reminiscent of Michael Jackson's *Thriller* (stage directions in script 1). The play begins with Don Chus trying to sell tombstones during "Happy hour" on November 1st, the Day of the Dead. He is offering two deaths for the price of one, *"estamos echando los occisos por la ventana"* [we are throwing the murdered ones through the window] (1). Two of his friends come in and confront him about his capitalist attitude toward the dead in a broad, slap-stick manner complete with a "Three Stooges" type of banter. Chus complains that it is a difficult time since there are fewer corpses these days:

> *Refugio. Para usted que volvieran los tiempos de la dura repre, cuando se daban por manojo y costaladas los muertos.* [It would be better for you if the times of the strong repression returned, when the deaths came by the sackful.]
> *Chus. ¡Malaya los tiempos del indio Lucas!* [Boy, those were the times during Indian Lucas!]
> *Remedios. ¡Sacrilego! ¡Hereje! Hijo de Belcebú, quinto jinete del Apocalipsis. No mencione ese nombre y menos en el cemeterio.* [Sacrilege! Heretic! Son of the Devil, fifth horseman of the Apocalypse. Don't mention that name, especially in the cemetery.]
> *Chus. Pero si yo sólo trato de decirle que cuando el general Romeo Lucas . . .* [But I was only saying that when General Romero Lucas . . .]

3: SATIRIC THEATER 93

Remedios. Cállese, ciudadano de Sodoma, fanático del chupamirto descendiente de la dinastía de Transilvania, Hijo del conde Dracula! [Shut up, citizen of Sodom, fanatic bloodsucker descended from the dynasty of Transylvania, Son of Count Dracula!]
Chus. Discúlpeme doña Remedios, no lo vuelvo a hacer. El Señor es contigo. [Sorry, Mrs. Remedios, let's not go there again (litany of names). The Lord is with you.]
Remedios. Y con su espíritu. [And also with you.]
Refugio. Ahora ya sabe don Chus: en este país, por seguridad siempre se habla bajito bajito. [Now you know, Chus, in this country, for security, we always speak in a low voice.]
Chus. Claro y después de 500 años se va uno acostumbrando. [Of course I know that. After 500 years one grows accustomed to doing it.]

(2)

They decide to remind Don Chuz of the history of the early 1980s, beginning with the coup. The following scene is in President Lucas's office when the cannons are pointing at his window. Broad jokes are made about the leader's Parkinson's disease, disappeared students and unionists, his notorious corruption, and his passion for blood. He is just about to suck the neck of his assistant when the military breaks in to inform him he must leave.

The Militar. Debe comprender varias cosas. El pueblo no acepta el fraude, la oposición crece, el conflicto interno se agudiza, continua la crisis . . . la situación es insostenible. [You have to understand some things. The people don't accept fraud, the opposition is growing, the internal conflict is out of control, the crisis continues . . . the situation is unbearable!]
Lucas. Pero dáme una razón de peso para que yo me vaya. [But give me one good reason that I should have to leave.]
Militar. Hay tanquetas apostadas al frente del palacio. [There are tanks stationed in front of the palace.]
Lucas. ¡Ha bueno! . . . así por las buenas quien no. Estos mis patojos, hombre. 'Ta bueno pues, si la institucion castrense pide que me vaya, pues me voy. [Ah, right. Well, for that reason, who wouldn't? Those are my children, you know. Well, good-bye. I always say if the military institution asks me to go, well then I go.]

(3)

The scene returns to the cemetery and the characters set up the next "vaudevillian joke" as they talk about the promising future for the Guatemalans after Lucas: "The next to arrive to power is . . . another General" (4). The play then becomes a game show which has been dedicated completely to the coup of 1982. The contestants have to answer questions about the event in order to win a free plot in a cemetery. The game host mimics Ríos Montt's mannerisms and asks the contestants whom he is imitating. They cannot remember. The next game is introduced with mock enthusiasm:

> Model 1. *Ahora sea usted juez y parte, en donde se juega la vida uno de nuestros ciudadanos.* [Now, you be judge and participate in the game of the life of one of our citizens.]
> Model 2. *Y lo más impresionante del concurso es que es sin jurado, sin testigos, ni proceso legal!* [And the most impressive of the contest is the one without jury, without witness, and without a legal process!]
>
> (7)

They do a mock trial ceremony and decide to shoot one of the contestants.

Game Host. "*Correcto y volvió a ganar, ganó un embalsamiento completo cortesía de cloroformo Inc. Don Pablo le damos el honor de gritar la orden de fuego al pelotón de fusilamiento.*" [Correct! You win again. You win a complete embalming courtesy of Chloroform, Inc. Mr. Pablo will do us the honor of shouting the order to the firing squad!] The contestant is shot. They continue to make jokes about PAC as *"patrullas de auto defensa Civil del Capitán Crunch"* [the Defense Patrol of Captain Crunch], jokes about *frijoles y fusiles* [beans and rifles] and *tierra arrasada* [wretched land (to refer to the villages that were burned to the ground)], *XX* [disappeared], and a joke that one cannot win with the word *libertad* [liberty]. The last game is introduced as follows: *"La final es muy sencilla. Si está en contra de nuestro sistema y se mata, usted gana el nicho. Así es concurso de la ruleta rusa"* [The last round is very simple. If you are against our system and you are killed, you will win a grave plot. This is the contest of Russian Roulette] (9). One of the contestants asks to be shot. The host offers him U.S. $2,000 and exile, but he insists on being shot.

The play continues to make jokes about Article 186 in the Constitution, which states that no one can run for president who has been involved in a coup. One actor does a caricature of Ríos Montt and his Sunday-night sermons: *"Usted es Guatemala. Yo soy Guatemala y usted y yo somos uno y yo ya no sé quien soy yo y ahí está el detalle"* [You are Guatemala. I am Guatemala and you and I are one and I don't know who I am but this is an insignificant detail] (14).

The second half of the play centers on Ríos Montt's failed attempt to become president again through his organization FRG. The message of the play is that the Guatemalans need to look carefully at Ríos Montt's past performance before they consider supporting him for office. Don Chus makes the three-fingered FRG salute with his hand; the others react as if they are vampires in front of a cross. Chus has decided he wants to help the general become registered. He defends the general, saying he serves the *"muy leal necropolis de Guatemala"* [very faithful "metropolis/necropolis" of Guatemala] (22).[7] Don Chus explains that he wants a government that does not rob, lie, or abuse. Remedios simply reminds him, *"Pero no se le olvide de su historia, de la historia del país. Pues el que actúa sin conocer la verdad, es un ignorante. ¡¡ Pero el que sabiéndola, la oculta: es un criminal!!"* [But don't forget the history of the country. He who acts without knowing the truth, is ignorant. But he who knows the truth, and ignores/hides it: he is a criminal!!] (23). He argues that anyone who has the smallest spot on his record shouldn't be able to be president. *"Y eso incluye a los culpables del genocidio"* [And that includes those guilty of genocide] (25). Ramírez's message is the oft-heard argument that people who fantasize about Ríos Montt being president again are deluded about the past and not confronting reality.

The play ends with the general threatening to return to power through the FFG some day in the future. An actress changes the date on the roulette wheel, indicating that the FRG is going to return to power in 1995, then in 1999, 2003 . . . Then he asks the people to raise their hands in support for him. His party lost the election the year the play was presented in 1995. I left Guatemala on the day of the 1999 election when the country was littered with propaganda with Ríos Montt's name on it. The following day his party, the FRG, won the presidency by a large margin which enabled Ríos Montt to become the head of Congress.

Romeo Subuyuj and *Julieta Pirir*—
Advocacy for the Peace Accord

Just after the signing of the Peace Accord, González Dubón wrote a parody of Shakespeare's *Romeo and Juliet* using the civil war as the battle that raged between the two households. His contemporary version with numerous topical references and names of officials focuses on a pair of star-crossed indigenous lovers. Julieta comes from the Pirir household, a rightest indigenous family that were officials in PAC, the patrols that ruled over other indigenous families and guarded against communist infiltration in the community. Romeo comes from the Subuyuj household, a leftist indigenous family. There are numerous lines translated straight from Shakespeare interspersed with others that show González's humorous twist.

Patrice Pavis describes this style of theater as a parody, which consists of a parodying text and the text parodied. The irony is emphasized by contrasting the two texts. "It quotes the original by distorting it, and constantly calls on the reader or spectator to reconstruct it" (Pavis 1998, 250). He writes that the parody replaces respect with disrespect and seriousness with mockery. However, this parody written in the year of the Peace Accord, 1996, has intentions as noble as Shakespeare's original. Although the play vacillates between travesty and drama, the underlying themes of peace, the challenge of forgiveness, and the necessity of not passing past hatreds on to future generations are clearly delineated. This modern interpretation/parody honors the play and brings new poignancy to Shakespeare's lines: "Two households, both alike in dignity / In fair Verona, where we lay our scene / From ancient grudge break to new mutiny / Where civil blood makes civil hands unclean" (*Romeo and Juliet*, prologue).

González mirrors this prologue in his opening. He explains the civil war conflict and how old vendettas continue to threaten the country's existence:

> *Eran dos casas, ambas de la misma estirpe, las dos del mismo origen. Una de estas casas se lanzó en armas contra la opresión y por la construcción de una utopía, la otra casa sin saber que era lo que defendía o a que se oponía, luchó cruelmente por la destrucción del sueño y arrazó [arrasó] la tierra y aldeas; el holocausto fue gigante.*

3: SATIRIC THEATER

La otra casa, la primera mencionada, también aportó llanto y muerte. Los viejos rancores se renovaron con furia. . . . Por sus odios mutuos durante 36 años se pagó con inculpada sangre, algunos aún hoy desean que la muerte con su guadaña, absurdamente cante nuevas y crueles victorias. La sangre derramada ensució las manos de ambas casas y a ambas la historia las tiene señaladas. Sus inocentes hijos pagaron también la pena de estos rencores, léase REHMI, la reconstrucción de la memoria histórica. Rencores que trajeron la muerte y el fin de muchos hijos e hijas, como los que hoy recordamos. Atended el enredo y suplireis con vuestro conocimiento y entendimiento, lo que falte tanto a la tragedia como a la comedia.

[Two households, both alike in lineage, both from the same origin. One of the houses hurled themselves in arms against the oppression and for the construction of a utopia. The other house, without knowing what it was that they defended or what they were against, fought cruelly for the destruction of the dream and raided the towns and villages; the holocaust was immense. The other house, the first mentioned, also contributed weeping and death. The old people's hatred was rejuvenated with fury. Because of your mutual hatred during thirty-six years of fighting with innocent blood, today some of you still desire death with the Grim Reaper, absurdly sing new and cruel victories. The spilt blood dirtied the hands of both households and the history has been demonstrated to both households. The innocent children also paid the price for that hatred. Read REHMI; the reconstruction of the historical memory. (REHMI is the Reconstruction of Historic Memory of the struggle Bishop Gerardi documented with a list of 500 crimes committed during the war before he was bludgeoned to death.) The hatred brought death and the end of many sons and daughters such as those we remember today. Join the plot and you will suffer with your knowledge and understanding, what is missing in both tragedy and comedy.] (1–2)

The play takes place just before the signing of the Peace Accord. More than just parodying the text, the play seeks to bring an entertaining perspective to the challenge of healing past wounds. González burlesques the fears and the seriousness surrounding the Peace Accord. For example, a newspaper boy shouts the headline that states that the people are going to be living in peace . . . immediately! The boy makes comment on the guerrilla leaders "risking" their lives in five-star hotels and the heroic military valiantly lifting their cups of whiskey before both sides sign the agreement.

The play goes back and forth between broad parody and the serious topic of the civil war. The parodic emphasis is noticed in the opening fight which takes place on a city street between a leftist and a rightist:

Chepe. Sacá tu machete pues, qui no quiero qui tu sangre me salga regalada, y la necesito para firmar la paz. [Take out your machete. I don't want your blood given to me as a gift. I need it in order to sign the peace.]
Juan. Encomendate a tus santos: al Arcangel San Lenín y a San Carlos Marx, por qui vas a pasar al otro potrero y sin pasaporto y carente de visa norteamericana. [Send regards to your saints: The Archangel Saint Lenin and Saint Karl Marx because you're going to pass to the other side without a passport and lacking a North American visa.] *[They fight until Chepe cuts open Juan's shirt and marks him with a Z. Juan responds, "Hijue tu nana! Ya me chingaste la NAUTICA!" (Son of a bitch! You fucked my NAUTICA shirt!]*

(3)

There is a fistfight between the two family matriarchs. When Romeo's mother asks why Julieta's family has been so antagonistic toward them, Julieta's mother responds, *"La puritita verdá, es que no estoy muy clara, piro mi casa representa a las PAC y defendemos prácticamente los intereses de los hijos de los hijos de Don Pegre de Alvarado. Puras ironías de la historia"* [The very truth is that I'm not really sure, but my house represents PAC and we defend practically all the interests of the sons of the sons of Don Pedro Alvarado. Pure ironies of history] (5). PAC was a group of armed indigenous people who patrolled other indigenous people in their area. González's line comments on the irony of PAC's postcolonial attitude upholding the "conquerors" position 500 years later.

However, the humor turns on a dime when the prince chastises them for fighting in public:

Rebeldes, enemigos de la paz, derramadores de sangre humana! No quereís oír, chafas y subversivas criaturas, que apagáis en la frente sangrienta vuestras vidas, el ardor de vuestras iras. Arrojad en seguida al suelo las armas fraticidas y escuchad mi sentencia. Mil millones de veces por absurdas quimeras y crueles motivos, habéis ensangrentado las calles de toda la nación haciendo a sus habi-

tantes los más graves atentados, empuñad los machetes y descarguen el hierro sus manos por la paz.

[Rebels, enemies of the peace, spillers of human blood. You subversive rightists and leftists don't want to hear that you have extinguished the bloody essence of your lives through the ardor of your rage. Throw down your fratricidal arms this minute and listen to my decree. Hundreds of thousands of times your absurd quarrels and cruel motives have bloodied the streets of all the nation making the most serious assaults on its inhabitants, grab the machetes and attack with the steel in the name of peace.] (8)

The play shifts again to camp humor with plenty of sexual innuendo in the scenes with Romeyo and Julieta:

Julieta. Oh Romeo, Romeo, dónde ponés el caite qui no te veo? (Oh Romeo, Romeo, where do you put your sandals at night? I can't see you.]
Romeyo. Qui hago, seguir oyéndola, o encaramármele. [Shall I hear more, or shall I jump her bones?]
(30)

When González wrote this play in 1996, there was great apprehension about the Peace Accord and fears raised over which side would dominate in the negotiation, as well as worries of impending changes in a society accustomed to war. González makes the point that most people were upset about the Peace Accord from hearsay rather than from having studied the agreement. In one scene the characters whine about how boring the peace agreement is going to be. Paris worries that he might have to work too hard to follow the tenets of the peace agreement. Julieta's father, Antony Pirir, assures him it will not be as terrible as he supposes:

Antony Pirir. ¿A ver decime, vos has leído los tales Acuerdos? [Tell me, have you read the details of the Peace Accord?]
Paris. ¡Nel! [No!]
Antony Pirir. Ya ves, y si les preguntáramos a toda la caitada, incluyendo a los ladinos igualados si los conocen, todos dirían la misma respuesta: Ni un palabra. [You see, and if we ask the entire mob, including equally the *ladinos* if they know the details, they will all say the same answer: Not one word.]
(12)

The offspring have been encouraged to adopt their parents' hatred, but Romeyo resists the pressure:

Mercutio. Pero si tus tattas son de las guerrilles subversives. [But your parents are on the side of the guerrilla subversives.]
Romeyo. Ellos sirán lo qui les de la gana, yo practico la neutralidad activa. Tipo suizo. [They will do what pleases them, I practice an active neutrality. The Swiss type.]

(10)

Romeyo's mother accuses him of having been with the enemy when he explains his love for Julieta. He informs her that they are her enemies and not his. Julieta has taken a sleeping potion in order to avoid having to marry Paris. Romeyo comes to her and she wakes from her "dead" sleep and the play ends with them alive and in love. Romeyo brings home the message of the play through the parody of "a rose by any other name" speech which he addresses to the audience:

Romeyo: Total usté y yo semos iguales, porqui aquí, todos semos iguales, solo qui algunos semos má iguales qui otros. Si usté se dejara ue llamar ladino y yo me dejara de llamar indígena, todos nos llamaríamos guatemaltecos. Solo nos diferencia el traje y el hablado. [You and I are both equal, everyone is equal. Around here it's just that some are more equal than others. If you stopped calling yourself *ladino* and I stopped calling myself indigenous, all of us would be called Guatemalans. The only difference is the clothes and how we speak.]

(36)

Previous political satires from the early 1990s make light of political authorities and endless political turmoil, and tack a moral on at the end. In this play, González is burlesquing the political changes as well as Shakespeare's play. But the purpose is more clear throughout—to promote a positive reflection on the Peace Accord and to challenge people to let go of their old grudges. This play is a transitional play between the political satires and the more direct didactic plays in the following chapter.

Analogical Satires—Ironies of Insanity and Injustice

The analogical satires in Guatemala emphasize the ludicrous level of chaos into which the country has fallen in order to draw attention to the profound state of spiritual, political, and social crisis. The writers use analogies with other eras and settings to comment on the current social-political situation. Some plays make up fictional histories set in remote places, such as the Wild West of the U.S. or countries that prize corruption. Others in this category use parallels to past crisis situations, such as the French Revolution and the struggle between the rightists and the leftists, to highlight the current instability caused by the war. Characters, other than the lone protagonist, are oblivious to the level of insanity and injustice around them. The plays do not offer a solution. There is total lack of faith that any social system can govern with equanimity or that any spiritual institution, from the church to the family unit, can offer solace. In these plays there is no escape from the dysfunctional state of the world. The situation may be incurable, but the writer's lighthearted tone keeps the plays from becoming too pessimistic. Although most of the plays end happily, the world of the play is still impersonal and chaotic. The playwrights simply distort the social situation and so enable the audience to laugh at it.

William Lemus and Víctor Hugo Cruz are both playwrights who have been writing since before the repression until the present. They have a long history of writing analogical satires. Throughout the years the world they portray has become more chaotic and deranged, teetering on the brink of destruction. These plays enable audience members to acknowledge the depth of crisis they are experiencing while at the same time offering the comfort that they are not facing it alone.

Víctor Hugo Cruz

Víctor Hugo Cruz is the most well known living playwright in Guatemala and has been writing satires since the early 1970s. His plays all have a light comic touch with a clear social-political moral. The plays do not focus on the psychological realism of characters but on the social situation in which the protagonists fight against a corrupt system. His plays tend to be mild (in comparison with Arce or Carrillo) intellectual protest satires. For example, Cruz's *La Pastelería [The Pastry Shop]* (1974) is a protest against classism which encourages unionism among the workers. The focus of the play is Juan's desire to be able to afford a pastry in a fancy pastry shop. This leads to his seeking higher wages for all his co-workers, a move combated by exploitative bosses. The play ends in a song of resistance which states that someday the workers will overcome oppressive authorities. This style of play is representative of the protest plays during the "Golden Age" of theater.

El benemérito pueblo de Villa Buena [The Worthy Town of Villa Buena] is a parody of a Western film about cowboys and Indians from the U.S., focusing on a community that destroys itself because of corruption. Cruz's play has been revived four times since the original production in 1974. It deals with fraudulent elections and tends to be produced just before elections. Whereas Arce and Carrillo plays are not frequently repeated, this one is a perennial favorite. It played twice in the 1990s (hence its inclusion in this study). The play is set in a fictional U.S. Western town and makes frequent reference to Indians who had to be slaughtered for the settlement. The powers in the town, including the richest man, the newspaper man, and the minister, conspire to make sure that their candidate for sheriff, the hired gun Peter Gun, is elected. They use their influence to manipulate the press, the parishioners, and the employees to do their bidding. They want to elect someone of whom everyone is afraid so that they can control the town. Evident throughout the play is the parallel between an elected hired gun and the fraudulently elected line of dictator presidents controlled by the wealthy citizens (and the U.S.) who threaten the populace into obedience. One of the lyrics from a song in the play makes this plain: *"Aparenta el Sheriff ser mandamás, el que tiene a todo el mundo como en Alcatraz, pero en verdad es una marioneta a quien controlan con hilos desde atrás"* [It seems the sheriff is in control, he that holds everyone as if they were in Alcatraz, but the truth is that he is a marionette who is controlled with strings from behind] (20).

Johnny Land, an honest man fighting for the people and land reform,[8] who wears a white hat, decides to run in the fraudulent election, but loses. The "bad guys," the corrupt rich man, newspaper man, and minister, have manipulated the Indian vote through promises they do not intend to keep. After the hired gun has been elected, a shot rings out, killing the new sheriff. All the townspeople join in the shoot-out, which leaves everyone dead except the woman who shot the sheriff. It turns out that she was the hired gun's estranged wife. An officer from the cavalry who discovers the massacre states that the responsibility lies in the hatred of the two warring sides. The officers in the cavalry decide to blame the deaths on the Indians. *"Así tendremos razones para exterminarlos totalmente"* [In that way we will have reasons to completely exterminate them all (the Indians)] (72). The stated moral of this play is that it was the hatred that won the elections. The play ends in a song: *"Villa Buena fué un pueblito que realmente no exisitó pero todo lo que vieron si sucede y sucedió! Y a quién le venga el guante si quiere que se lo palante"* [Villa Buena was a town that really didn't exist but everything you have seen happens and happened. And if this play applies to you, then admit it].

Although it was originally written as a protest against the fraudulent elections and dictatorships, today the message has changed. In the revival production I saw in 1999, in the 2,500-seat main auditorium of the National Theater,[9] the play was about how blind hatred between warring factions had created great destruction for both sides. The songs in the play were updated and reminiscent of the numerous upbeat jingles on the radio commenting on the war and advocating "peace between brothers."

Cruz wrote *"Vicente Nario"—O cómo la Revolución puede ser un juego [*"Vincent Nario"* (title is a play on words—sounds like the name of an Indian as well as *"Bicentennial")—Or How the Revolution Can Be a Game]* in 1989 and published it in 1994. It is a very layered play which raises themes of postcolonialism, dominance, and violence.[10] This satire emphasizes the similar political climate of unbearable oppression under the French monarchy during the revolution with the Guatemalan military dictatorship. The play takes place in present-day Guatemala at the French embassy where a troupe of inept actors are staging an amateur drama for the French ambassador and the embassy workers. Most of the comedy in Cruz's play is broad and comes from the actors' lack of rehearsal and interpersonality conflicts. The inept, egotistic actors miss their cues, make disparaging comments on the characters they are playing, argue about their interpretation of the roles, and complain about their makeshift costumes. The history play is entitled "Liberty, Equality and Brotherhood" and focuses on the

French Revolution. At the end of the history play, Vicente Nario, an Indian stagehand and minor actor who has been bossed around by the other members of the production, pulls out a gun and takes over the embassy. This metatheatrical moment highlights the comparison of the French Revolution with the recent history of insurrection and massacre in the Spanish embassy (discussed in chapter 2).

On the title page, Cruz includes the following quotes:

> *"La democracia es una gran mentira"* [Democracy is a great lie], Adolph Hitler;
> *"El año 1789 será borrado de la historia"* [The year 1789 will be erased from history], Joseph Goebbels (assistant to Hitler).

The fascist perspective is shown to be as misguided and short-sighted as the French monarchy under Louis the Fourteenth, the Nazi party under Hitler, and the Guatemalan dictatorship. The play suggests that governments are doomed to failure until they become a democracy and learn to listen to the people. Dictatorship, whether in the form of a tyrannical monarchy or a fascist military state, leads to conflict and horrible destruction. The corollary between the Guatemalan civil war and the French Revolution is made in the first scene: the director of the play tells the "embassy" audience that they are commemorating the French Revolution, an event that changed the course of history. He states, *"La gloriosa y terrible Revolución Francesa, producto de la insensatez de la clase dominante que dió fin a la paciencia del pueblo debibo a la injusticia, desorden legislativo y económico, demagogia, corrupción administrativa.... En fin, ¡caos social!"* [The glorious and terrible French Revolution, a product of the insensitivity of the dominant class, put an end to the people's patience due to injustice, legislative and economic disorder, demagogues (leaders who make use of popular prejudices, false claims and promises in order to gain power), administrative corruption, ... which ends in social chaos!] (15).

Cruz draws numerous parallels between the current state of affairs in Guatemala and the French Revolution, for example, both the dictatorship in Guatemala and the French monarchy are out of touch with the people, and both countries experienced an economic crisis and mass starvation. The European community's stance against the monarchy reflects the international community's pressure on Guatemala to find a more equitable solution. Other obvious similarities are the *"descamisados"* ["shirtless ones"] threatening the aristocrats and bourgeoisie who are not willing to equalize the riches, the numerous assassinations of officials to gain political advantage, the endless fighting between leftists and rightists, and the church and government's complicit relationship.

The history play within the play portrays how the French wrote the Declaration of the Rights of Man and Citizen and how they denounced despotism. A repeated theme in the play and the history play within the play is *"¡El odio nos destruirá a todos!"* [Hatred will destroy us all!] (50) (which was also Cruz's central message in *El benemérito pueblo de Villa Nueva*). The hatred escalates in the history play until the rightists perceive the need to create a war to exterminate the people:

> *Pitt. Que debemos ir a una guerra de exterminio.* [We must go to war to exterminate them.]
> *Bouille. ¡Es indudable! O los exterminamos a ellos, o ellos a nosotros.* [Undoubtedly! Either we exterminate them or they will exterminate us.]
>
> (32)

Cruz's metatheatrical structure highlights the numerous levels of hierarchy and oppression. For example, the actors raise the issue of the injustice done to Indians through dialogue such as the following between the director and an actor as they discuss cowboy films:

> *El Agregado. Todas las películas de vaqueros de ustedes son iguales. Siempre pierden los indios.* [All your cowboy films are the same. The Indians always lose.]
> *Don Touch. La ley del más fuerte y del más inteligente.* [It's the law of the strongest and most intelligent.]
>
> (10)

Abusive dominance is prevalent in "the law of the strongest." It is portrayed in the relationships of the characters in both the play and play-within-the play (for example, the relationship between the dictatorial director and the cast and especially Vicente Nario, and the relationship between the French monarchy and the people, and later, in the history play, in the betrayals of the rebels on both the right and left side). As the power swings between the rightists and the leftists, both sides are seen as corrupt. If they cannot find a peaceful sharing of power, they will return to the oppressive monarchy, which is where the play begins. The narrator announces Napoleon's military coup in 1799 as *"[u]na nueva monarquía, despótica y militar, había nacido"* [a new monarchy, despot and military was born] (57) when Vicente Nario takes over the embassy. He shouts that this was the only action he could take to make the people listen. Indisputably, history will repeat itself until humanity finds a more democratic way to solve its problems.

WILLIAM LEMUS

William Lemus is a medical doctor who has written five adult plays and three plays for children. In 1982, when most theaters changed their seasons to children's theater, Lemus wrote the children's play *El gran tití [The Great Puppet]* which has been remounted numerous times since 1982. It is unabashedly antiwar/propeace. In this work for youth, Lemus is overtly optimistic and didactic, an approach that completely changes in his full-length satires. It is amazing that this provocative children's play was produced during the height of the violence in Guatemala: it contains a message that could not be spoken in the adult theater for another decade.

There are two characters: a boy, who is obsessed with trying to get more power, and a clown. The clown tells him, *"No te confundas, niño, en la guerra nadie gana . . . perdemos todos. Los que sobreviven han perdido a sus amigos, familiares. La victoria es otra farsa"* [Don't be confused, child, in the war nobody wins . . . we all lose. Those that survive have lost their friends and families. Victory is another kind of farce] (3). When the boy pretends to blow up the world, the clown grieves for the world: *"Pobres habitantes del mundo: Todos somos esclavos de la violencia, del dolor y el llanto"* [Poor inhabitants of the world: We are all slaves of the violence of pain and tears] (3). The boy retorts that he is the richest and the most powerful in the world. The clown responds that he will never find happiness: *"Porque afortunadamente el poder y la riqueza que devienen de la guerra no dan felicidad. . . . Cuando el mundo está llorando de dolor porque han perdido a sus familiares y a sus amigos y han perdido la libertad . . . nadie puede ser feliz* [Because luckily the power and the riches that come from the war don't offer happiness. . . . When the world is crying of pain because it has lost its family and its friends and has lost liberty . . . nobody can be happy] (5). The final moral message the clown imparts to the child is that children can change the world and end war.

Lemus's moralistic, positive style changes completely when he writes satires for adults.[11] In 1983 he wrote *Pánico en la cocina [Panic in the Kitchen]* which won first place in the national annual theater contest *Juegos Florales de Quetzaltenango*. This full-length black comedy centers around a housewife who is confronted with the violent death of her father, which slowly awakens her to the violence all around her. If Joe Orton had written a script for "I Love Lucy," it would end up similar to this play. In this broad comedy the woman is the only sane voice in a whirlwind of violence. Her father has been found decapitated, missing one arm, and hanging from a wire. When she hears about the death she screams—"This is the end of the world. The Four Horsemen of the Apocalypse!" The rest of the family remains oblivious to her pain. Her desensitized daughter plays with her doll, laughing about how funny it is that they killed her grandfather in the same way her doll's head fell off. Her inept husband informs her that no one will go to the funeral because of death threats against anyone who attends. Throughout this trauma the television blares commercials in the background, suggesting a disjointed world in denial of the social crisis: *"Cótex Liberté: Mayor seguridad en esos días críticos"* [Kotex Frees You: security in those critical days . . .] (66). She tries to wake the people up to the insanity of the violence. She becomes hysterical, shouting *"Todo el mundo es una larga cadena de sufrimemientos y tristezas"* [All the world is a large chain of suffering and sadness] (71). Her family ostracizes her for her hysterical reaction. The play ends happily in that the father is discovered to be alive; the police made a clerical error. Sardonic humor about people's lack of awareness and sensitivity to others runs thoughout the play, such as *"Los familiares han enterrado cadáveres ajenos que después aparecen vivos, y vice versa. Familias que han vivido con un cadáver toda la vida"* [Families have buried some cadavers that later appear alive and vice versa. There are families that have lived all of their lives with a cadaver] (72). Lemus satirically points out that people have become deadened to the violence and social chaos.

Lemus continues his theme of individuals against an upside-down world in his full-length satire *Frente al Palacio Nacional [In Front of the National Palace]* (1993). The play takes place in the plaza in front of a palace in the fictional world of *Corruptaluña* [Corruptville]. Everything is inverted in this world. Homer, the blind Greek poet, is the central character, barely surviving in the central plaza as a street cleaner. He is the only one who sees the perversion and depravity. He shouts to the heavens, *"¡Los dioses nos protejan!"* [Gods protect us!] (3). The hot dog seller responds, *"¡Aquí los únicos dioses son los del ejército!"* [Here the only gods are the army!]. At that moment some soldiers try to stage a coup but stop when they hear God's voice saying that today is not a good day for this activity. The voice tells them that he will advise them when the correct time will be. The mayor comes out and explains that the cause of coups is misinformation. Therefore, he has come up with the idea of closing all the schools from preschool to the university. He concludes in this way that the citizens will be happy. He states, *"He cerrado museos, bibliotecas, escuelas de teatro y estamos decididos a dinamitar todo aquello que se oponga a la ignorancia. . . . Amigos, viva la ignorancia!"* [I have closed the museums, libraries, theater schools and we have decided to destroy everything that opposes ignorance. . . . Friends, long live ignorance!] (6). He later explains that the advanced system of government will do anything to avoid coups which belong to an outdated caveman era. The people cheer when they hear the mayor say he plans to close the university when he is president. They all shout *"¡Corrupción total! ¡Corrupción para todos!"* [Total corruption! Corruption for all!] and begin to sing *Corrupción* as if it were a war hymn. An interviewer asks him: *"Y respecto a los derechos humanos?"* [And in regard to human rights?]. He responds, *"Todo ciudadano tiene derecho a ser fusilado en la vía pública sin juicio"* [All citizens have the right to be shot in public without judicial trial] (28).

Unionists who come to protest in front of the palace are massacred. The reporters from the television come in and take pictures and film the scene. The president defends the action stating: *"Les habla su Presidente amigo. El Presidente de Unidad Nacional, me preocupa que aún hayan grupos que no se acostumbren a vivir en corrupción. La corrupción, amigos, es un sistema ideal de gobierno y de vida. La corrupción abarca la mordida, el fraude, el despilfarro"* [Your president speaks to you as a friend. As President of the United Nations, it worries me that there are still groups that are not accustomed to living in corruption. Corruption, my friends, is an ideal system of government and of life. Corruption encompasses bribery, fraud, and reckless spending] (17). He reminds the people of the advantages of living in such an evolved, sophisticated political system: *"En un sistema corrupto todo es válido. Siempre hay grupúsculos enemigos de la corrupción, que en las pasadas elecciones no pudieron hacer fraude. ¡Está claro que el fraude es la única forma de hacer gobierno!"* [In a corrupt system everything is valid. There are always enemy splinter groups of corruption, that in the past elections (unfortunately) couldn't commit fraud. It's clear that fraud is the only form of governing!] (18). The sweepers come along whistling and singing, shouting obscenities as they clean up the dead bodies.

Numerous different groups come to strike in front of the palace. The last group is a Madame and her prostitutes who argue that the tax is too high, especially since they give employment to 90 percent of the population. In protest against the high taxes, they decide to give their services for free until the government falls. The corruption throughout the city has robbed life of any meaning. Homer philosophizes as he sweeps: *"¿Las huelgas vienen, las huelgas se van y qué queda? Basura. Nada más. Los hombres y las mujeres convertidos en basura"* [The strikes come and the strikes go and what remains? Trash. Nothing more. The men and the women are converted into trash] (59).

The Virgin Mother Mary enters the plaza to strike against the people who have lost their faith. Homer commiserates with her, saying that the people have lost faith in philosophy and rationality as well. She suggests she could create a miracle of blood shooting out of the fountain. He tells her not to do this since there has been enough blood flowing in this country already. He tries to tell the officials of the church about her arrival, but he is ignored.

The play ends with a true *deux ex machina*. A Greek goddess, the Adivina, comes from the Oracle of Delphi with an elixir to cure all problems. It will strengthen those who fight against injustice and those who struggle against apathy and indifference. However, the director of the play closes the curtains on her before she can offer the cure to the audience. The director claims to be out of time but the message seems to be that the authority/system has conspired to keep people in the vicious circle of crisis. The system is too overwhelming to fight. The only thing to do is acknowledge the insanity.

Conclusion

I joked with Jorge Ramírez that I was going to take the texts of his most popular satires and produce them in the United States under my name. I had just seen his most recent play, *Guatemala en pelota* [double meaning—*Guatemalan Soccer, Guatemala Stark Naked*]. Ramírez had tapped into the passion for the game of soccer in Guatemala and its twenty-year history of failure to make it to the World Cup. His show had sold out for months. I have rarely seen an audience as enthusiastic. They cheered and booed as if they were at a soccer game. Ramírez and I realized that this play could never work in the U.S. The Guatemalans have a national identity as the perpetual losing underdog. This is related to the enthusiastic reaction to the political satires, "Leave it to us Guatemalans. We manage to screw it up worse than any other country in the world!" It is a self-effacing humor that is part of the national psyche and stems from the days of conquest. Ramírez told me that a hypothetical rewrite, *Los Estados Unidos en pelota* [The United States Stark Naked], would never play because U.S. history positions its citizens as winners. The archetype of the disillusioned victim of circumstance would probably not play as humorous in the United States. Ramírez's point—and I agree—is that the effectiveness of satire depends upon local circumstances.

For this reason it is difficult for a foreigner to recognize the subtlety as well as the degree of satire in Guatemalan theater of the 1990s. For example, in William Lemus's play *Frente al Palacio Nacional* there are numerous jokes about gays and AIDS. The gays are presented as being very stereotypically effeminate. When an interviewer asks a gay man with AIDS what the chief cause for AIDS is, he replies with aplomb, *"Ir a Chimaltenango por Retalhuleu. Y en Estados Unidos—ir a Ohio por Detroit"* [Going through Chimaltenango to get to Retalhuleu or in the United States going through Ohio to get to Detroit (joke referring to anal sex)] (20). The cast of characters in the plaza wildly applauds this comment. Without knowing the country intimately, it is impossible to know if it is a gay-bashing joke or a satirical comment challenging the lack of empathy for the dying man. (I wish I had asked Lemus, but I didn't.) And of course satire is hard to pin down even if one is from the country. As mentioned earlier in the chapter, satire's amorphous nature is what makes it the safest form for representing the civil war after the repression.

Because of satire's nature and my foreign status in Guatemala, identifying plays that promote reflection on committed atrocities is therefore problematic. Facts are burlesqued in both the political satires and the analogical satires. The satires appear to make a travesty out of the victim's pain. The plays incite an emotional reaction from the audience but it is difficult to specify exactly what that emotional reaction is: recognition, relief, suppressed anger, or anxiety. It is perhaps the most subjective response since most of the plays can be interpreted as anything from a comedy to a bitter protest. Nevertheless, the Guatemalan satirical playwrights all seek to encourage laughter. Humor is the most alluring form of theater to encourage reflection on challenging and painful issues.

After interviewing the political satirists Ramírez and González and the analogical satirists Lemus and Cruz, I noted a striking difference in their perspectives. The political satirists both deny a political agenda, seeking a political "edge" only to incite laughter. Their work actively promotes a unified mainstream morality. Perhaps their "apolitical" stance is necessary in order to take on the political situation directly. Their work focuses around the fantasy of power inversions. The analogical satirists consciously cover their political references. Yet both Lemus and Cruz acknowledge the social/political critique in their work and encourage the audience to look for the message rather than spelling it out for them. The protagonists have almost no power and little to no influence on the insanity around them. Rather than the topsy-turvy model of political satires,

Lemus and Cruz focus on the political instability that in turn makes it impossible for the characters to have supportive relationships.

Peter Petro argues in *Modern Satire* that the principal aim of satire is to teach. He states that satire is the art of persuasion (Petro 1982). Satire seeks to convince the viewer that the diagnosis of the human condition points to a serious disease. Both the analogical and political plays portray a world in crisis and on the brink of collapse. This point of chaos is portrayed as a cause-and-effect relationship; the political choices of yesterday have brought the country to the point it is at today. However, the plays also offer hope that if the country turns from its previous destructive course based on indiscriminate violence, corruption, war, and fascism then the Guatemalans may move away from the brink of chaos. In this sense, the plays advocate a more peaceful, sane world. These plays are in stark contrast to the abrasive *Huelga* satires which pit the righteous disenfranchised (the artists and the spectators) against the depiction of the evil Establishment.

The major significance of the commercial satiric plays is that they tested the Establishment's willingness to accept clear—if indirect and detached—portrayals of social and political conflicts. These plays paved the way for the more explicit didactic plays dealing with the atrocities committed during the civil war.

4
Didactic Theatre

NUMEROUS DIDACTIC PLAYS ABOUT THE GUATEMALAN CIVIL WAR have sprung up between 1995 (just before the signing of the Peace Accord) and the present. Guatemalan plays written specifically about the violence and adapted foreign antiwar plays have been produced to encourage discussion and reflection on the civil war and, above all, to promote peace. The plays written by Guatemalan playwrights use factual information dealing with the war and are loosely based on real-life events. These plays focus on the victims of the conflict. The foreign plays are adapted to correlate directly to the war in Guatemala. They stress a clear social moral: there is no easy exoneration for war activities. Those characters that participated in war eventually realize they have paid a devastating price for their actions. All the plays in this chapter share a common theme which is articulated most succinctly in Margarita Kénefic and Luis Escobedo's *Nunca más: "La paz es perdón, la paz no es olvido"* [Peace is forgiving, peace is not forgetting.] (1999, 32).

The Guatemalan plays discussed in this chapter are as follows: *Mujeres de la guerra, Rapidísima historia de la paz, Alaíde,* and *Nunca más*. The adapted plays are *El monte calvo, Madre Coraje, and Frida y el Capitán*. These seven plays are performed by new groups with mostly young, enthusiastic actors and directors who tour with the plays to numerous towns and villages. They perform in various settings from town halls to high schools as well as play in traditional theater spaces in the capital, Guatemala City. The general audience for these plays tends to be the middle to lower-middle class. All of these productions receive funds from private or public institutions, which promote the Peace Accord and do not depend solely on the box office.

Patrice Pavis describes didactic theater as theater that aims to instruct its audience to "reflect on a problem, understand a situation, or adopt a certain moral or political attitude" (1998, 100). He acknowledges that there is an element of didacticism in all theater work, but he nevertheless notes a distinction in didactic theater: "What varies is the clarity and force of the message, the desire to change the audience and to subordinate art to an ethical or ideological design" (Pavis 1998, 100). Didactic theater in the strict sense is moralizing (morality plays), political (agitprop), or pedagogical (parables, thesis drama). Pavis writes that this form of theater has often been used to expose underprivileged audiences (workers, peasants, and children) "who often lacked a specific form of expression, to an often difficult art that was expected by artists and intellectuals to contribute to social change" (1998, 100). Although the moral themes in these plays are varied depending on the focus (i.e., innocent war victims, the individual perpetrators, and communal tragedies), there is a clearly delineated antiwar theme underlying them all.

The theater practitioners' goal in Guatemala is to shine a light on the inauspicious past and raise issues, which had been too dangerous, painful, or shameful to acknowledge, in a direct, emotional manner. The satires, which preceded these plays by several years, emphasize a detached, indirect approach. The didactic plays employ a variety of approaches in order to hold an audience's attention long enough for the "history lesson." Most of the plays encourage an empathetic bond between the characters and the audience. All of the plays have cathartic moments where the characters recognize they have become trapped in a cycle of violence and struggle, usually unsuccessfully, to find a way out. The plays in this chapter range from comedy with a heavy dose of gallows humor which turns on a dime and ends in death and destruction, to serious drama, depicting horrific acts of atrocity. Most of them are a mix of grotesque comic-tragedy dealing with acts of brutality, especially torture and murder. One often does not know how to react: shock, anger, tears, disgust, or laughter all seem appropriate. Although they take on these potentially inflammatory and divisive issues, most of them do it for the major purpose of encouraging the audience to reflect on and emotionally process the turbulent past.

Mujeres de la guerra

Mujeres de la guerra [*Women of the War*], written and directed by Fran Lepe, is a musical drama about the victimization of women during the war. It was performed by four actresses from the group ACSA just before the signing of the Peace Accord and won first prize in the *Festival Nacional de Teatro Popular Guatemalateco* in 1995. The play details the story of four women whose lives are tragically influenced by the armed conflict. The characters presented are loosely based on real-life people. The actresses and the director researched actual case studies in Guatemala for the four roles (therefore, in an ongoing dispute with Lepe, the actresses from ACSA claim that they co-wrote the piece).

ACSA *(Arte y Comunicaciones Sociales para la Paz)* [Art and Social Communications for Peace] is a private institution dedicated to raising consciousness about peace through the theater. The actors from ACSA stated in interviews that many people were worried for the safety of the group because of their peace activist stance (ACSA interview). ACSA began in 1994 for the purpose of mounting spectacles that offered hope for peace and national reconciliation. Members state that they are hoping to develop a spirit in the new generations that looks unblinkingly at the war. They posit that the atmosphere of fear generated by the violence perpetuated denial of the past. This denial, combined with intimidated silence, created a cycle that enabled the war to continue unabated. ACSA breaks the silence by using theater arts. They propose alternative paths to a more positive, just society that is grounded in reality. The group writes in the *Mujeres de la guerra* program:

> *El país vivía una época de conflictos y se hallaba enfrascado en el silencio. . . . Después de ser azotados por una guerra de 36 años en Guatemala, ACSA se ha propuesto llevar un mensaje de Paz y reconciliación a los países hermanos e iniciar un movimienta hacia la cultura de paz a través del Arte Teatral.*

[The country lived through a time of conflicts and found itself trapped in silence. . . . After being beaten down by the thirty-six years of war in Guatemala, ACSA has proposed to take the message of peace and reconciliation to the brother countries and initiate a movement toward the culture of peace through Theatrical Art.]

ACSA toured Guatemala extensively as well as other countries, including the United States, Puerto Rico, Mexico, Spain and France, giving almost 300 performances between 1995 and 1997. Their project, entitled "Tour for Peace," included three works: *Pinocho y la paz* [*Pinochio and Peace*] for children, *Eduquémonos para la paz* [*Let's Educate Ourselves About Peace*] for students, and *Mujeres de la guerra* for the adults. Director and playwright Fran Lepe states that a message of reconciliation and hope to Guatemalans is the plays' common theme (*Guía*, June 27, 1997, 21).

Mujeres de la guerra begins in a tone similar to an evangelical church service as the women sing about how nothing will defeat them (the actors in ACSA are all Evangelical Christians). The song's second verse is as follows:

> *El espíritu de guerra / el espíritu de muerte / y el espírtu de sangre / hoy han sido derrotados / nuestro Dios ya los venció / El amor es más fuerte.*
>
> [The spirit of war / the spirit of death / and the spirit of blood / today have been defeated / Our God has conquered them / Love is stronger!]
>
> (1)

The next verse states that although it is a struggle to see the horizon of liberty, they have faith that it is just beyond the hills. The song continues:

> *Treinta y seis años de sangrar sin poder gritar / y el cielo sigue tan azul / los montes muestran su verdor / El amor de Dios no pasa / y el dolor que sigue aquí / se lo llevara la historia.*
>
> [Thirty-six years of bleeding without being able to cry out / and the sky continues to be so blue / the mountains show their greenness / The love of God does not end / and the pain that continues here / will be carried away by the story.]
>
> (1)

The four actresses come on stage as if they are in a rehearsal and state that they must create a collective work. They are

4: DIDACTIC THEATER 117

afraid to approach the taboo topic of war. One denies she is afraid. The actress Claudia responds: *"¡No seas mentirosa! Porque aquí él que no haya sentido miedo es porque no está vivo.... Todas tenemos una historia que contar, porque ya sea de lejos, de cerca, por dentro o por fuera, todas tenemos que ver con guerra"* [Don't be a liar! Because here, the only one who is not afraid is not alive.... Everyone has a story to tell whether from far or near, inside or outside, everyone has been affected by the war] (2).

The women describe the challenges and their fears about talking of the recent past. There are spies everywhere who force them to speak quietly: *"Sólo los locos se atreven a hablar piensan ser libres"* [Only insane people dare to speak, thinking about freedom] (3). They list the social problems of the past and present including illiteracy, starvation, and exploitative landlords. Then they begin to list the names of famous people who have been killed during the war (including Alaíde Foppa, who will be discussed later in this chapter). The actresses become different characters for each of the four case studies.

The story of a female guerrilla is dramatized. She speaks as if at a protest rally, describing several massacres as well as numerous rebel victories in the 1960s. The other three actresses act as a chorus. They challenge her terrorist actions and her idealism. They accuse her of not knowing how much blood had to be spilt for the rebels' cause. The story ends with the guerrilla being killed by a military bullet. The idealism and spirit of revolution fade into meaninglessness.

The next scene takes place in the capital and notes the numerous women who died or disappeared during the war. One of the actresses argues that to disappear was not the biggest problem. Some suffered worse, such as the old indigenous widow, Marcial Atot, who witnessed her husband, children, and friends being killed in the war. The violent memories that haunt her are dramatized in scenes from the massacres.

> *Marcial. Mucho tiempo el río fue rojo y después tal vez gris, pero en cuántas noches sin luna, el río fue rojo.* [For a long time the river was red and later it was gray, but in how many nights without the moon the river was red.]
> *(entran las tres indígenas atadas, cayendo al suelo)* [enter three indiginous women tied up and falling on the ground]

Voz en Coro. Indias shucas! Cuántos guerreros les han salido de la panza?[Voice in Chorus: Dirty Indians! How many warriors have you given birth to?]

. . . .

Voz en Coro. Vos!! Vos hablas! Ni modo que soy igual a vos! [You! How dare you speak! No way are you my equal!]

Marcial. Me dijo pero no se animó a mirarme los ojos.[He spoke to me but he did not dare look me in the eyes.]

Voz en Coro. Sabemos que de aquí han salido muchos hombres a la guerra, y les vamos a meter tierra en la panza. [We know that many men have come out of your bodies to go to war and we are going to stuff dirt in your belly.]

Todas. Nuestras entrañas, sufrieron más la herida, sentíamos a la crueldad, rompiendo nuestra carne. [Our insides, they suffered the worst wound, we felt the cruelty destroying our flesh.]

(4)

The song/dialogue/chanting continues to identify the womb and the ovaries as the place where the women hold a metaphysical wound. The imagery connects the oppression passed on through 500 years of repression with the physical and psychological pain suffered by generations of families that continue to be decimated. Marcial weeps in agony and rage during this song. She remembers the scars and scabs on the navels of her children who died. She cries out for closure to the war but realizes she has to grieve the tremendous loss first. Life cannot move on until her people have taken account of the atrocities caused by the war. The scene ends as she repeats her chant: *"Mucho tiempo el río fue rojo, y después tal vez, cuando pudimos abrir los hoyos de la tierra . . . para ver los huesos de los nuestros entonces pudimos enterrar la guerra . . . y el río . . . volvió a ser azul"*. [For a long time the river was red. Later, perhaps we could open the holes in the ground in order to see the bones of our people. Then we could bury the war and the river would again be blue (4–5).] The chorus laments and shouts as the imaginary river flows on, ¡¡*"Adios Sangre!!* [Good-bye blood!].

This remarkably visceral scene is an unabashed lament, seeking to portray the primordial wound caused by genocide. It is a cathartic scene that encourages the public to grieve with the actors, to share an unfathomable communal pain.

After this scene the play highlights the more hidden, pervasive social problems caused by the war. Female leaders in the resistance movement who are also mothers are described. When they are killed, innocent children are left war orphans. Catocha, whose parents were murdered near Rabinal, came to the capital by bus. A song describes her destroyed childhood and descent into prostitution: "*¿Quién se tragó tus esperanzas y quién volvió basura tus ganas de vivir? ¿Quién tuvo ese derecho, de sacar de tu pecho, ese corazón, esa ilusión? ¿Quién te enseñó a pagar con besos y con todo tu cuerpo, la cuenta de cenar?*" [Who swallowed your hopes and who trashed your hopes for life? Who had the right to pull that illusion from the heart in your chest? Who taught you to pay the bill for dinner with kisses and your entire body?] (6).

Catocha becomes pregnant. The actresses take on the roles of young prostitutes who fight over the corner of concrete where they sleep, as well as their makeshift toys and sniffing glue. When asked how old she is, Catocha responds that she is twelve. Another prostitute states blandly that she is already too old for the life in prostitution. Her innocence is highlighted in this scene; when she gives birth, she still does not understand that she is pregnant, what the labor contractions are, or why she is in pain. After her baby is born, she leaves the life of prostitution and becomes a beggar. She pretends to be blind and begs for food with her baby. Eventually her milk dries up from malnutrition and the baby starves to death. Innocent Catocha, who has treated her baby as if it were a doll, is slow to realize that she is dead. Her response is to lie down with the baby and go to sleep, hoping that tomorrow will be better. Asked what happened, she responds that she hopes this war will end soon.

The actresses discuss the various escape routes people have used to avoid thinking of the past, including drugs and religion. One accuses another of hiding in the church praying to God while people in the streets and the mountains are being kidnapped, raped, and killed. A third actress reminds them that the church has not been immune to the violence. She points out the recent massacre when the peasants were shepherded into Catholic and Evangelical churches by the army, who then burned them all alive. This topic brings into the discussion other violent acts, including the Spanish embassy attack (discussed in chapter 2).

The last story in *Mujeres de la guerra* is about a middle-class university student who passes out fliers to the public and appears to be a subversive. She shouts slogans such as, *"¡¡Recuerden que la lucha es de todos!! ¡Hasta la victoria siempre!"* [Remember the struggle is everyone's! Keep going until the victory!] (9). The student is kidnapped off the bus in the middle of the day. Three of the actresses put on hoods, assume a masculine voice, and begin to interrogate her.

The torturers begin by threatening her with rape and a painful, slow death. When she begs for mercy they tell her, *"¡Anda decile eso a Fidel! !Por la defensa de la democracia! ¡por la conservación de nuestras instituciones sociales!! ¡Movete asquerosa zurda!"* [Go tell that to Fidel. This is for the defense of democracy! For the conservation of our social institutions!! Move it you filthy leftist!] (9). The torturers defend their action in the name of the church and list their barbarous leaders as saints: *"Por San Romeo Lucas. Por Carlos Manuel Mártir. Por sus beatos Coroneles y Generales . . . Amén"* [For Saint Romeo Lucas. For Carlos Manuel Martir. For the blessed Colonels and Generals . . . Amen (10).] They beat her and threaten to kill her parents. (This scene is very similar to the torture scene of a young woman in *Nunca más*.) However, they eventually discover that they made a mistake: she is an Evangelical Christian and the "propaganda" she was passing out on the bus was religious material. They let the woman go, but like Juana in *El corazón del espantapájaros*, she has lost her mind.

The play ends with the actresses asking the public to honor the victims of the war by supporting the peace process. Reviewer Luz Méndez de la Vega writes that the play creates powerful pathos, using a style reminiscent of Jerzy Grotowski's work. She finds Grotowskian influence in the highly stylized shouts, silences, music, choreography, rhythmic speech, and repetitive gestures, as well as the sparse set and props (*Cronica*, Jan. 24, 1997, 58).[1]

After the national success of *Mujeres de la guerra*, the actresses, musical director, and tech crew had a falling out with playwright Fran Lepe during their tour in France. Although *Mujeres de la guerra* was able to tap into a profound communal pain, the didactic themes in Lepe's later work at times fall on the side of being simplistic.[2] I sat in on a rehearsal for a new play Lepe was directing and co-writing on women's issues.

Again there were four stories of different women.[3] The third scene was from a newspaper story Lepe had read about a high-ranking female guerrilla during the war. He was intrigued by this because he had been associated with the guerrillas in the 1970s until he came to recognize that they were as infected with corruption as the army (interview with Lepe). Likewise, the female guerrilla becomes disillusioned with the movement, realizing that the rebels' corruption and immorality were equal to that of the other side. The other guerrillas kill their own comrade to set the example that people do not simply walk away from the war. In the play, the guerrilla woman tries to wake up her younger comrades from their rebel idealism to recognize that love is the only path worth following. The next day she is scheduled to be court-martialed and shot by the guerrillas.

This dramatization stands out as one of the few plays that emphasize the violence committed by the guerrillas. It was common for plays during the "Golden Age" of theater in Guatemala to side with the people against the army's brutality. The plays in the 1990s often place the responsibility for the conflict on both sides. More striking than the issue of shared responsibility is the theme of sympathy for the perpetrators or supporters of the war in plays produced around the time of the Peace Accord. This is especially pronounced in the following adapted plays: *Madre Coraje*, *El monte calvo*, and *Frida y el Capitán*. In all three plays a central character realizes (s)he has paid an exorbitant price emotionally, physically, or psychically and regrets the choice of having participated in war.

MADRE CORAJE

ACSA asked Mercedes Blanco, a Cuban director, to direct and adapt Bertolt Brecht's *Madre Coraje [Mother Courage]*. They toured Central America (Costa Rica, Panama, Nicaragua) and Cuba in support of the victims of Hurricane Mitch continuing their theme of promoting peace.

ACSA and Blanco reset *Madre Coraje* in the Guatemalan war and highlighted a theme of peace and reconciliation. They changed the end of the play to make the antiwar message more prominent, ensuring that the focus did not become the victimization of the title character. ACSA's version portrays Mother Courage's betrayal of her children as a corollary to the *ladinos'* apathy toward the genocide of the Indians. The protagonist is a *ladina* and the children she exploits for good business are indigenous. ACSA emphasizes how the mother collaborated with the war in order to gain profit. Blanco writes in the publicity release for the play:

> *De modo que esta madre, que ahora llora a su hija, no es totalmente inocente de esta muerte. Ella que vive por la guerra, ella que clamaba "¡No lograreis asquearme de la guerra,!" ella que finge perseguir la guerra sin pagarle tributo, cuando ésta la despoja sucesivamente de todos sus hijos. Ella, que no hace nada contra la guerra."*

> ["The nature of this mother, who now cries for her daughter, is not completely innocent of her death. She who lives for the war, she who cries out, "You will not succeed in making me sick of the war!," she who tries to pursue the war without paying the price, when she is successively stripped of all her children. She, that does nothing to stop the war.]

The daughter, Katrina, is not killed in the end as in Brecht's version. Katrina is "symbolically" Mother Courage's conscience, which has been speechless throughout the play (interview with director Mercedes Blanco). ACSA was seeking to critique the passivity of the traditional indigenous women as well as to make a statement about Mother Courage's lack of integrity. The play ends with Katrina finding her voice to speak out against the injustices caused by the war. She has been mute throughout the play, speaking only directly to the audience. ACSA described the choice for Katrina to be mute as the perception that the indigenous, especially the indigenous women, are passive and submissive. They hoped the play would encourage this sector of society to become more active in political decisions. In the end, Mother Courage finally listens to Katrina's last speech and repents her inadvertent support of the war. Katrina speaks directly to the audience:

> *He decidido nuevamente hablar! Y es que hay cosas que realmente son incomprensibles de que cosas como estas hallan pasado aquí en este país. Y quisiera evitar que el día mañana pasara en cualquier*

en cualquier otro. Trágico es que después de tanto tiempo no podamos siquiera poner un ramo de flores en el lugar donde talvez, descansen los seres que más queremos.

[I have decided to speak again. It's just that there are things that are truly incomprehensible, such as the things that have happened in this country. And I would like to avoid that things such as these occur someday somewhere else in the world. Nightmares like these should not be repeated. And possibly the most tragic thing is that after so much time has passed, we can't even place flowers (on the grave) where the people whom we most love lie.] (36)

Madre Coraje was not nearly as popular with the audience as *Mujeres de la guerra*. The actors from ACSA suggest that this is because of the "preachy" intellectual approach rather than the more emotional, cathartic one characteristic of the earlier play. The highly conceptual version of *Madre Coraje* and the direction of Blanco, who demanded a highly stylized performance from the actors (i.e., speaking directly to the audience throughout 90 percent of the play), left at least the three members of the audience I spoke with feeling uninvolved and "alienated." The actors reminisced that often the audience would cry during the visceral action of *Mujeres de la guerra*. In *Madre Coraje*, the concept dominated the performance and it became a well-articulated propaganda statement for intellectuals against war. However, the kind of healing ACSA aims to facilitate rarely takes place in the intellect. The antiwar/propeace message was loudly hammered in *Mujeres*, but the actresses were able to incorporate movement, song, and story into an artistic whole that carried the audience's emotions and resulted in a profound cathartic experience. I would posit that postatrocity audiences have a greater need to process the past emotionally than conceptualize it with the assistance of overt antiwar propaganda. Guatemalans heard enough propaganda from both sides during the civil war. The majority of them are seeking to go beyond the issue of right or wrong to mourn the tremendous losses incurred by the war.

The musical also emphasized a hopeful message: *"el amor es más fuerte"* [love is stronger]. Williams de León, a reviewer, states that the theme is not religious but refers to the need to search for a more human form to resolve the conflicts between people (*Siglo Veintiuno*, March 22, 1997, 36). However, Blanca argues that *Madre Coraje* is not a play about transcendence. She writes: *"En Madre Coraje se sitúa el nivel de las relaciones sociales: colocarla en el nivel de los problemas metafíscos o religiosos es tracionarla"* [Mother Courage is situated on the level of social relations: to attribute it to the level of metaphysical or religious problems is to betray it] (Publicity release). The former play offers hope. The adaptation of Brecht's play reminds people only of their shame.

EL MONTE CALVO

A young group of actors, who graduated from the National Academy of Theater Studies at the National Theater in 1998, formed an acting troupe called *Kaji' Toj'* (Mayan name), dedicated to performing contemporary work. They toured the country with Jairo Anibal Niño's antiwar play *El monte calvo* which was written in 1966 in Bogotá, Colombia. *Kaji' Toj*'s 1997 production was the Guatemalan premiere.

The setting is a city dump where two tramps are waiting for a friend who will lend them money. Canuto, an ex-clown, vividly describes their unlucky position: *"Estamos más varados que puta en Viernes Santo"* [We are more stuck than a whore on Good Friday] (93). His companion, Sebastian, is missing one leg and moves around on a small board with wheels. They are waiting for Sebastian's friend from his wartime days who will lend them money if they enact his military fantasies and pretend they are his soldiers. Sebastian is trying to hold onto his patriotic illusions and Canto, the realist, continually reminds him of the high price he and his fellow soldiers paid in following deranged orders to kill unknown, so-called enemy, soldiers. Currently, Sebastian cannot get work because employers believe that ex-military people are dangerous and partly insane. He is baffled about why the officers who convinced him to risk his life in the war have forgotten him.

Sebastian describes the calamitous cost his fellow soldiers paid for the war: *"Muchos heridos; algunos cojos como yo. Otros paralizados. Otros locos o sin brazos* [Many wounded; some crippled like me. Others paralyzed. Others crazy or without arms] (6). Sebastian states that he was defending his country when he lost his leg. He shows Canuto his medal of valor for being wounded in action. The clown figure responds: *"¿Quieres decir que te dieron este pedazo de lata por tu pierna?"* [Do you mean to say that they gave you this piece of tin for your leg?] (95). Sebastian defends his military career by stating that his commander had told them that they were the guardians of civilization. Canuto asks him what civilization means. He responds that it is something like books. His companion retorts *"¿Y por defender unos libros se mataron? No sabía que eran tan caros"* [You killed people in order to defend books? I didn't know that books were so expensive] (96). Sebastian and his fellow foot soldiers are portrayed as innocent pawns in the struggle of war:

> Canuto. *¿Y ganaron esa guerra?* [And did you win the war?]
> Sebastian. *Creo que sí.* [I think so.]
> Canuto. *No estás seguro.* [You're not sure?]
> Sebastian. *Eso lo saben los generales.* [The generals know about this.]
> Canuto. *Lo único que sabes con seguridad es que no tienes tu pierna. Tú perdiste esa maldita guerra.* [The only thing you know for sure is that you don't have your leg. You lost the damn war.]
> Sebastian. *La ganamos.* [We won it.]
> Canuto. *Ahora estás cojo, pobre y hambriento. Eres un baldado. Perdiste la guerra.* [Now you are lame, poor, and hungry. You are crippled. You lost the war.]
> Sebastian. *El presidente dijo que habíamos ganado. Lo dijo con palabras muy bonitas.* [The president said that we had won it. He said it with very beautiful words.]
> Canuto. *Bah... Palabras... palabras. Las palabras no se comen. Ellos han estado hablando desde hace mucho tiempo y no han arrreglado nada.* [Words... words. No one can eat words. They have been talking with words for a long time and that hasn't fixed anything.]
>
> (8)

Canuto reveals that he used to be a clown until one day during a performance he began to cry real tears and the people began laughing uncontrollably. He felt exploited by the people he was seeking to serve. The parallel between the two friends is clear. The difference between them is that Canuto admits his disillusionment in what he thought was an honorable career. Although they are both stuck economically, Canuto's acceptance of the situation enables him to enjoy simple pleasures such as playing the harmonica. The continued dialogue portrays him as the realist at peace with his past while Sebastian remains stuck in a cycle, needing to defend his past war activities.

In the last ten minutes of the play the insane colonel finally arrives with numerous grotesque medals hanging from his uniform. He treats the two as if they were his soldiers and Canuto and Sebastian play along in the absurd rituals. The colonel tells them they have a great responsibility and are going to write the glorious pages of history. Canuto responds that he doesn't know how to write. The colonel assures him that he doesn't need to write; he only needs to know how to shoot a gun. He orders them to march as soldiers. Their pompous strutting appears absurd in the shabby dump setting. When the soldiers complain that they are hungry, he orders them to be silent. He then asserts that Canuto is a prisoner and that he can choose how he will be killed. The colonel claims that he has been accused of distributing subversive propaganda and having communist leanings. In the mock trial, the accused is not allowed to speak. Canuto, thinking this is a game, is excited when he hears he will receive his last request: a cup of hot coffee. Sebastian is given money by the colonel to go and buy it. Canuto plays his harmonica for the last time as the colonel shoots Canuto dead and exits. After Sebastian returns and realizes what has happened, he picks up Canuto's harmonica and plays it.

The production's didactic emphasis included a questionnaire for the audience to fill out after the performance. The actors had a public talk-back session after each performance. They also did numerous performances for high school audiences and gave them the same questions. Although the play refers to the Korean War, the questions focus on the topic of the recent events in Guatemala. Some of the questions are the following:

1. Which role would you prefer to play in life?
2. If democracy is a social system that searches for equality and liberty of expression and action, would you be willing to lose a leg or an arm in exchange for this system to continue?

3. Which of the following words best defines Sebastian: fighter, friendly, ignorant, ambitious, proud.
4. Are there valid justifications for war?
5. What does Canuto symbolize and what social group does he represent in the civil war in Guatemala?
6. Do you know how long the civil war lasted in Guatemala? What was the magnitude of human losses and materials?
7. What word defines our attitude after the war: shame, forgetfulness, reconstruction, reconciliation, indifference?

While many of the questions promote discussion about the war, some of the questions are extremely leading. For example, in question no. 1, Canuto, the realist and martyr, is the only admirable character until Sebastian is awakened from his delusions of aiding his country by supporting the war.

The director of the company, Fernando Nicolás Juárez, argues that Canuto represents the first guerrilla peasants who were not afraid to say "the emperor has no clothes" (interview with Juárez). Canuto can also represent the people who become disenchanted with the self-righteousness on both sides of the conflict because of his ability to detect the manipulation beneath the propaganda. Juárez, who also played the role with a red ball on his nose, interprets the character as one who became a rebel when he felt the people laugh at his pain, the moment he opened his eyes and recognized the exploitation. Although Sebastian is depicted as unenlightened, he gains insight when he sees how he has been manipulated by the military indoctrination and seeks to follow in Canuto's example of thinking for himself.

One of the most significant contributions of this play to the didactic literature of antiwar/propeace plays is the concept that one can recognize the madness behind the military institution while affirming the pain and loss of the individual soldier. Although the colonel is still portrayed as power hungry and insane, the soldier is portrayed as an innocent pawn seeking to help his country. During their dialogue Canuto has pushed Sebastian to the painful realization of the absurdity of war. The cripple is confronted with the truth that he killed Koreans/Guatemalans who were just cannon fodder like himself. Sebastian's final choice not to pursue the colonel for the murder of his friend but rather to play Canuto's harmonica suggests the transformation that he "ain't gonna study war no more." In the following play, *Frida y el Capitán*, a middle officer is portrayed sympathetically as well; his transformation comes about when he is confronted with his own depravity.

Frida y el Capitán

Contempo Teatro [Contemporary Theater] began in early 1997 and describes itself as *"una manifestación cultural alternativa, que busca involucrar expresiones artísticas diversas en la comunicación teatral . . . que transitar en los caminos difíciles del arte guatemalteco, máxime cuando la propuesta artística es de corte eminentemente social"* [an alternative cultural manifestation that seeks to introduce diverse artistic expressions in theatrical communication . . . to travel through those difficult paths of Guatemalan art, especially when the artistic proposal is to represent social reality] (1999 Program from *Frida y el Capitán*). The company produced an adaptation of Mario Benedetti's play *Pedro y el Capitán* written in 1983 in Buenos Aires. They changed the character of Pedro, the prisoner being tortured, to a woman named Frida, retitled the play *Frida y el Capitán*, and produced it intermittently throughout 1998–99. The program states that the company chose a woman because of the crucial role women have played in bringing the country to peace:

> *[p]orque en alguna medida la participación de la mujer en la construcción de una sociedad diferente y mejor, ha sido fundamental, sin la cual hubiere sido sumamente difícil llegar a concretizar los acuerdos de paz; y esto aunque no se reconozca, pero que todos sabemos es cierto.*

> [(b)ecause in some measure women's participation in the construction of a different and better society has been fundamental, without which it would have been extremely difficult to concretize the agreements of peace; and although (their role) is not recognized, we all know it is certain.] (Program for *Frida y el Capitán*.)

The play focuses on Frida's torture and slow death, which takes place over weeks and precipitates the captain's self-reflection and self-destruction. She is accused of being a communist and of having several aliases. The captain is horrified to discover that he too has an alias. Superficially he is the righteous army man and loving husband/father, but he is also an inhuman torturer who has received sadistic pleasure from his tasks. He realizes that his righteous justification for torturing rebels in the name of national security is fraudulent.

This play is different from most "torture" plays in that it portrays the victimizer in a sympathetic way. Although Frida plays the typical suffering underdog figure of the noble rebel, the captain's role as the all-powerful perpetrator of cruelty reveals the psychic harm that the torture is inflicting on him. The play portrays reciprocal suffering; the more pain he inflicts on Frida, the more anguish he feels. Although he is seeking to get a confession about her true identity and that of the rebels, he ends up confessing to her. The power relations are reversed and he ends up begging her for help, guidance, understanding, and forgiveness.

Frida has been beaten by other soldiers. When she is close to death in the third scene she tells the captain that she has become invulnerable to his techniques of torture. She has found tranquillity in a state of grace where no one can hurt her further. She states, *"No me importa porque estoy muerta y eso da una gran serenidad, y hasta una gran alegría"* [It doesn't matter what you do because I am dead and this gives me great serenity and happiness] (52). As she becomes more and more immune to him, he becomes more dependent on her to justify his actions. Ironically, earlier in the play, he had told her that Gandhi's passive resistance ideology could never work in this day and age.

The captain desperately wants to keep Frida alive, as if his life depended on it. He confesses to her that when he was watching his soldiers raping an average-looking female prisoner, he became sexually aroused. He admits that the only time he is able to perform sexually with his spouse is when he thinks of the prisoner being raped. In the final scene, Frida states that she wants to help him create a healthy relationship with his wife and children. He claims they love him and refuses her help. She warns him that they are going to hate him when they discover who he is. *"Y nunca te perdonarán. Nunca los recuperarás"* [And they will never forgive you. You will never recover (from their rejection)] (81). She explains that this is because he has a bad conscience. When Frida is a hair's breadth away from death, the captain realizes he too is dead. He acknowledges that Frida has more peace and a greater purpose than he does because she has the capacity to love people, to suffer for people, and to die for people.

Almost all plays that relate Guatemala's political problems either through specific examples or through fiction portray the rebel in a positive light. The difference in plays of the 1990s is that their moral world is less black and white than the protest plays of the "Golden Age." The problems are no longer framed as the greedy, sadistic, power-hungry elite (which is how people who support the Establishment are inherently prone to be portrayed), versus the pious, generous, impoverished people fighting for human rights.

Werner Ramírez describes the group's artistic philosophy in the program for *Frida y el Capitán*. He states that art is a nonviolent social tool which struggles either to maintain or to transform the status quo. The artist has traditionally adopted one of the following approaches: (1) to defend the system, (2) to criticize and attempt to transform the system, or (3) to try to detach art from the social context in order to focus on form. However, the group seeks to give an unbiased perspective which includes social criticism without attacking the system. Ramírez writes:

> *En el campo artístico se da, en una forma no violenta, la lucha de las clases sociales por mantener o transformer el status quo. Inconscientemente, muchas veces el artista presenta en su obra el pensamiento del grupo social al que pertenece. Aunque algunas veces y en determinada rama del arte, la influencia de la realidad social no esté claramente manifesta. . . . Dentro de las nuevas corrientes del arte lantinoamericano, se presenta una visión crítica de la realidad que vivimos. Se trata de hacer reflexionar al público sobre lo que acontece, y motivarlo para tomar consciencia de la necesidad de construir una sociedad más justa y humana.*

[The artistic field portrays in a nonviolent form the class struggle which either maintains or transforms the status quo. Unconsciously, many times the artist presents in his/her work the ideas of the social group to which (s)he belongs. Even though sometimes in certain branches of art, the influence of the social reality is not clearly manifested. . . . Within the new trends of Latin American art, a critical vision of the reality that we live is presented. It seeks to make the audience reflect about what is happening and to motivate them to become conscious of the need to make a more just and humane society.] (1988 Program for *Frida y el Capitán*)

This group seeks to present a new critical vision of reality in which it lives by presenting both sides of the story. *Contempo Teatro* is trying to get the public to reflect on the past from numerous perspectives in order to help create a healthier society.

It is interesting to note that *Frida y el capitán* was enormously popular and was performed more than 100 times. The year before, IGA *(Instituto Guatemalteco Americano)* had put on a production of Ariel Dorfman's *La muerte y la doncella [Death and the Maiden]* for a run of three months with the best known and most talented actors, designers, and director in Guatemala. They invited VIPs from both sides of the cold war, the guerrillas and the army, to talk in a forum after several of the presentations. However, in the 400-seat theater, often only a handful of people would come out to see it. Since both plays center on torture, it raises the question of why one would be very popular while the other provoked almost no interest. There are several possibilities for the Guatemalan public's overwhelming preference for *Frida y el Capitán*. The obvious argument, which would support the thesis of this dissertation, is that *La muerte y la doncella* promotes the possibility of divisiveness.[4] Dorfman's play raises the volatile issue of impunity in an unspecified Latin American country which is trying to progress from its violent past to becoming a more stable, democratic nation. Obviously this issue is very potent in Guatemala. Many people are enraged that the army is not being held accountable for their violent actions. The public may have shied away from the divisive and dangerous issue of impunity that is overtly examined in Dorfman's play. *Frida y el Capitán* subtly suggests that the issue of impunity is irrelevant because the perpetrator of inhumane crimes is psychically punished for his actions.[5]

Contempo Teatro also wrote and produced *Rapidísima historia de la paz [Rapid Story of the Peace]*,[6] which is very similar to "living newspaper" theater in its emphasis on factual history. The introduction to this play states that it was written to support reconstruction. The play uses a novel device to create distance from the war; the story is told as if it were taking place in the future and looking back on the past conflicts.

> *Versión libre del proceso de pacificación en Guatemala, visto desde la perspectiva futurista; creación original de la Compañía Contemporánea de Teatro de Guatemala, como un aporte a la reconstrucción del proceso de recuperación de la memoria histórica, y la visión de los jóvenes de la paz.*
>
> [A loose version of the peace process in Guatemala, seen from the futurist's perspective; it is an original creation of the Contempoary Theater Company of Guatemala, as a contribution to the process of recuperation of the historical memory and of the young people's vision of peace.] (1)

The opening begins with a character in a science fiction futuristic costume. He is sitting among the audience in the seventh row of the theater. The stage directions state, *"el vestuario debe ser sencillo futurista; y su posición debe reflejar la de un espectador más"* [the costume should be simple and futuristic; and his/her position should reflect being one of the spectators] (1). The character *Personaje del Futuro* [Person of the Future] serves as a narrator, addresses the audience, and reminds them of their history. S/he begins with Spain's conquest, describing it as the destruction of a wall that had separated the paradise of Guatemala from the rest of the world. This character states that this brutal destruction left many lost in terms of their purpose in society. In the twentieth century many of the indigenous became revolutionary when they noticed the material and social injustices. S/he mourns for the idealistic young peasants who joined the failed resistance movement in order to find meaning in life:

> *Sin entender qué, pero sí para qué, blandieron la bandera de las Reformas. Claro que no hallaron multitudes victoriosas que los siguieran, pero hacían causas nobles y se aceptaba como correcto que fueran pocos los que las defendieran, hablaran o vivieran de ellas. Como los viejos hábitos no se dejan con facilidad y ya no estaban en edad de hablar en voz alta, siguieron encontrando personas que en busca de darle sentido a su vida se sentían honestamente satisfechas escribiendo los nombres de la Paz y la Libertad en las paredes de la ciudad, cargando mantas en manifestaciones cada vez*

más raquíticas, . . . *o haciéndole propaganda a un partido sin ninguna posibilidad de triunfo.*

[Without understanding what but understanding what for, they adopted the flag of reforms. Of course they did not find many victorious multitudes to follow them (the revolutionaries), but they did noble deeds and it was accepted that there were few people who defended, spoke, or lived by the deeds. Since old habits do not die easily and they were not even of the age to speak in their own voice, they kept on finding leaders who would give meaning to their life. They honestly felt satisfied writing the names of Peace and Liberty on the city walls, carrying protest signs in demonstrations that grew increasingly thin . . . and making propaganda for a party that had no possibility of victory.] (2)

After reminiscing about the past conflicts, the person from the future states that Guatemalans alone are responsible for arriving at the point where they are today. S/he asks them how they feel about what they have done as a society.

At this point the action begins in flashback. The narrator asks the audience if they remember the injustice that occurred when they were forced to leave their lives on the plantation. The next eight scenes focus on the injustice and exploitation of the worker. There are short domestic scenes with a married Indian couple, Juan and Maria, and their friend, Chepe. They complain about the bad crops and the difficulty of making a living off the land. They decide to leave the countryside to go to the shore. She eventually dies from the poor conditions and Juan complains to the boss of being treated like an animal. The boss shoots Chepe when he accuses the boss of being responsible for Maria's death. He threatens Juan that if he tells anyone, he will kill him too. This segment is the only naturalistic one in the play. The rest of the play is a rapid dramatization of the major events and ideological shifts during the civil war.

The narrator states that the people must remember that whenever anyone challenged the system, he was marked as a communist. After this scene there is a lengthy, rapid interchange between characters with a leftist perspective and ones with a rightist perspective. They cite dates of factual "victories" in the struggle on both sides. The struggle escalates as the left and right sides strategize to gain dominance over the other:

Izquierda. Es inconcebible que nuestro territorio siga siendo utilizado para preparar disidentes cubanos. Además la corrupción es el común denominador. . . . 13 de noviembre esa es la fecha que indicamos para el alzamiento que depara un mejor futuro para todos, Izabal, Cobán, Xela, Zacapa y la capital, todos estamos listos. [Leftist. It's inconceivable that our land is being used to prepare Cuban dissidents. Furthermore, corruption is the common denominator. . . . The thirteenth of November is the date that we will make the rebellion in order to offer a better future for everyone, Izabal, Cobán, Xela, Zacapa and the capital, we are all ready.]
Derecha. Cómo se atreven a atentar contra las instituciones y poner en peligro el orden constitucional. Exomulgarlos esa será la primera medida. [Rightist. How dare they go against the institutions and put the constitutional order in danger. The first step should be to excommunicate them.]
. . . .
Izquierda.: Traidores eso es lo que son, vendieron el movimiento, solamente Izabal y Zacapa respondieron, ahora debemos reagruparnos. [Leftist. (After discovering some of the towns are not going to fight) They are traitors, they have sold out the movement. Only Izabal and Zacapa responded. Now we have to regroup.]
Derecha Así había que tratarlos desde el principio, aplastarlos. La disciplina en el Ejército se respeta, se premia a los obedientes y se castiga a los rebeldes. [Rightist. We should have tried that from the beginning, smash them. The discipline in the army is respected, rewards are given to the obedient ones and punishment to the rebels.] (9)

This dialogue continues until the entire war is rapidly retold. The one on the right becomes more determined to punish the rebels, while the one on the left becomes more zealous in describing the revolution as a mission. Both sides shout their slogans, such as: Rightists:*"Desde ahora comunista visto, comunista muerto"* [From now on, a communist seen is a communist dead] (8). They dramatize a scene killing the people because they believe a communist might be living in the town. The leftists state: *"El corazón del enemigo será el incendio de la lucha revolucionaria. . . . A esta lucha popular deben unirse los estudiantes, los obreros, campesinos y los sectores populares"* [The heart of the enemy will be the fire of the revolutionary battle. . . . This popular struggle must unite the students, the workers, the peasants and the popular sectors] (10). The highlights of the "battles" continue until the person of the future comments that both sides were guilty of causing enormous suffering for the civil population. Again s/he encourages the people to reflect on whether the country has ended up where they hoped it would.

The almost documentary approach clearly seeks to suggest that both sides lost their perspective and encourages the audience to see the foolishness of polemic escalation. The use of the futuristic image encourages people to have some distance and perceive the social problems less emotionally. The play mixes naturalism and a more presentational, narrative style. The domestic scene in the first half with the overt injustice of the married couple and their friend hooks the audience emotionally. The second half describes more than dramatizes the two different strategies to dominate the political ideology. The play confronts the extensive inequality in the society while seeking to avoid the same pitfalls caused by the civil war. Whereas *Mujeres de la guerra* encourages a more emotional processing of the war, *Rapidísima historia de la paz* emphasizes logic and reason. As with *Mujeres de la guerra* and *Madre Coraje*, the visceral portrayal of *Frida y el Capitán* was much more popular than *Rapidísima historia de la paz*.

ALAÍDE

For some people, the play *The Diary of Anne Frank* is a symbolic reminder of the sorrowful waste of human potential caused by the Holocaust. Others argue that it sentimentalizes the Holocaust and does not begin to portray the catastrophic magnitude of the devastation. The one-woman play *Alaíde* has an effect similar to *The Diary of Anne Frank*. Written by Mayro De León in 1999, the play focuses on the real-life story of Alaíde Foppa. Anne Frank and Alaíde Foppa, a young girl and a grandmother, respectively, both had a passion for expressing themselves with words. Both of their lives were snuffed out because of a fascist dictatorial regime; their names have become synonymous with the horrors of war. The focus of both plays is the powerful life force within these individuals. Ominous oppressive forces threaten them, but these are never seen. Neither the Nazis nor the Guatemalan officers are portrayed on stage by actors.

Although Foppa is not known in the United States, she is widely respected in Latin America (NACLA 1981). She was raised in Guatemala and had to leave the country when her husband, the director of Social Security under President Arbenz, was exiled to Mexico. A well-known poet, writer, and art critic, Foppa was the first person in Latin America to teach a university course on women. She produced over 400 radio programs on women's liberation and co-founded and edited Mexico's most respected feminist journal, *fem*. She was branded a communist because of her argument that poverty is a social problem and not an example of God's wrath against the poor. Foppa had recently conducted a series of interviews with Quiché women and documented the genocide carried on by the Guatemalan army before she herself was kidnapped, tortured, and killed in 1981 by the military. The poet was sixty-seven years old. She had returned to Guatemala for a short Christmas visit; the decision proved fatal.

The play begins with Foppa in jail, begging for a glass of water and a pen with which to write. Both requests are to no avail. She explains to the guards outside her cell that words are her greatest joy in life and that she must write or go mad. Her description of words as swords, thorns, flowers, and paths highlights the freedom of speech issue, which she had worked tirelessly to advance her entire working life.

During the course of the play, she talks to the soldiers and torturer as if they were in the room with her. When the action calls for her to be physically punished, the actress mimes being beaten. Often during the play she recites her poetry, prays to God, or grieves for her three children involved with the guerrillas who died in the war. Throughout the play she is slowly losing her mind from the incarceration, retreating into happier times she had in Mexico.

The old woman repeatedly tries to reason with her captors. She asks them why they would want to kill her since she is sixty-seven years old and no longer biologically reproductive. She states that *"todos sabemos de la política de ustedes, mujer muerta, guerrrillos menos no nacidos"* [everyone knows your politics. A dead woman means fewer guerrillas born] (9). She pleads with her captors, saying that when a man employs violence, he loses intelligence. With her poetic language skills, she warns the soldiers that they must act honorably or be eternally damned. The play ends with her begging God to fortify her and by her reciting the 23rd Psalm.

The main theme of *Alaíde* is the main character's need to write and express her thoughts and feelings in words. She sees some newspapers and painstakingly tears the letters out as if her life depended on them, content only after she constructs her poem. When the torturer comes in to the room, he destroys the painstaking work in an instant. This effect is accomplished with pipes and a machine that blows the newspaper pieces around the stage as if someone had kicked them (interview with Mayro De León). This action is the symbolic center of the play: we see the beauty of poetry, freedom of expression, and magnificence of this woman's soul brutally wiped out of existence.

Near the end, Foppa asks the torturer why he is not wearing the mask and did not bother to remove his wedding ring. She realizes that he is going to kill her, or have her killed, and that this will be the last visit. Defiantly she asks him if the army will put her name in the file in code as usual. She remembers that when she was tortured by the guards, she sat on a stool. She asks if the numerous other stools strewn around the stage were used in the torture of others: peasants, workers, intellectuals, artists, and students.

The heroine's articulate and eloquent defiance of their inhumanity continues throughout the piece. She tries desperately to awaken her torturers to the realization of what they are doing:

> ¿Cómo es que pueden vivir así ustedes? ¿Cuántas veces se lavan las manos después de habérselas manchado de sangre? Usted cree que el agua y el jabón borran la sombra oscura de la muerte, cada vez que toca y acaricia a sus hijos, cada vez los tiñe de rojo. (Ríe sarcástica) No. No me diga que todo lo hace por ellos, por sus hijos . . . no. Todo esto lo hace usted por dinero, por placer, por descomposición social, por esa pasión de monolitos enfermiza, por ese culto a la violencia, por deshumanización que genera la industria de la guerra, lo hace por el ejercicio de un poder efímero sin sentido. No, no se acerque allí, son sólo pedazos de papel, si es un poema nada más.

[How is it that you all can live this way? How many times do you wash your hands after having stained them with blood? Do you think that soap and water can erase the dark shadow of death?

Every time you touch and caress your children, you stain them with blood. (Laughs sarcastically) No, don't tell me that you do it all for your children. No, all of this you do for money, for pleasure, for social decompression, for this passion for the unhealthy monoliths, for this cult of violence, for the dehumanization generated by the industry of war, you do it for the army, an ephemeral power without feeling. No, don't go close to that, it's only pieces of paper, it's just a poem, nothing more!] (14)

She mockingly marvels at how the soldiers pass the Christmas holiday, torturing prisoners and going home to play with their children. She tells the officer in charge of her captivity to inform his children that the presents he gives them for Christmas have been earned by torturing her. He should therefore tell his kids that the gifts come from Alaíde Foppa.

Throughout the play, she tries to break the officer's blind allegiance to the army. She tells him that his superiors will never thank him, that they are using him as they gain millions and he will be left without any glory. She asks what he will do after the war. Will he organize groups of robbers to rob banks and kidnap people? Although the officer is not given the same empathetic role as in *Frida y el Capitán*, the audience is reminded of the psychic difficulties he faces in the future. The absence of the character on stage invites the audience to imagine the role he is playing. Whereas the audience admires Foppa for her intelligence, passion, charisma, and spirit, they are encouraged to recognize the faceless officer as trapped, following orders in an impersonal, cancerous institution. Like *The Diary of Anne Frank*, *Alaíde* encourages people to lament the senseless loss of a great life. Although it inadvertently raises the issue of impunity, it does not incite the people to continue the conflict.

Elinor Fuchs, who edited an international anthology of Holocaust plays, writes that there is a surprisingly varied theatrical approach to theater of atrocity (1997, xi). In her collection is a wide range of expression of the "tragic consciousness" of the Holocaust, everything from black farce to theatrical performance-within-a-performance. Nevertheless, Fuchs posits that there are basically two types. "The first category showed catastrophic historical events as the private experience of individuals or families" (xii). These works evoked pity and sadness. *Alaíde* and many of the plays discussed in this chapter thus far would also fit into this category. Fuch's second category emphasized events as collective catastrophe where the dramatic interest was focused not on the individual but on the fate of the entire community. She writes, "[T]hese plays do not permit us to shed tears at their characters' fates (which we have escaped), but leave us with a painful sense of desolation and even culpability" (xii). The following play, *Nunca más* [*Never Again*], fits closer into this category in its scope, emotional devastation, and direct challenge to the Guatemalans that they must make sure that the atrocities committed during the thirty-six-year war never happen again.

NUNCA MÁS

Nunca más [*Never Again*] by Margarita Kénefic and Luis Escobedo (1999), was written at the request of several organizations (CALDH, PRODESA, UNESCO, and HIVOS) that support the actions of the Ministry of Education. These organizations specifically *"llevan adelante en las comunidades afectadas por el conflicto bélico que enlutó a Guatemala y para contribuir a los procesos de reforma constitucional"* [support the communities affected by the warring conflict that has saddened Guatemala and aim to contribute to the process of constitutional reform] (1).

The authors Kénefic and Escobedo are a married couple who had both secretly been part of the guerrilla movement in the 1970s and early 1980s. While living in Guatemala, they did political theater. In the late 1970s they became disciples of "the great" Hugo Carrillo and joined his acting troupe (interview with Kénefic and Escobedo).[7] They left the country in the mid-1980s because of death threats and lived in exile in El Salvador where they wrote and performed plays supporting the people and left-wing ideology.

Nunca más contains some scenes written by Carrillo before his death in 1994. The play is so remarkably similar to *El corazón del espantapájaros* (discussed in chapter 2) that it serves as its sequel. The metatheatrical plot contains a play within a play, with two characters, who act as the omnipresent Masters of Ceremony, relating the story of the war. The first part of the play begins with the same circus atmosphere as Carrillo's play:

the *Pregonera* and the *Pregonero* [male and female town criers] narrate directly to the audience, telling them of the extraordinary, magical actions they are going to see. Sounding like a barker at a circus, the *Pregonera* opens the show: *"Recorrimos mares y continentes repartiendo nuestro elíxir maravilloso de paz, amor. Curamos enfermedades, renovamos la juventud, y prolongamos la vida con nuestro espectáculo de arte. Transformará en diamantes las lágrimas y tristezas de todos los que sufren"* [We travel across oceans and continents sharing our wonderful elixir of peace, love. We cure sickness and disease, rejuvenate youth, and we prolong life with our theatrical art. The tears and sadness that we all suffer will be transformed into diamonds] (2–3). She goes on to state that the content in the play was inspired by facts of the past and the present. The *Pregoneros* describe their talents as sorcerers and conjurers who offer hope: *"Con mi vara abro el cofre de los secretos y los silencios; con ella respondo a todas las preguntas; por ella penetro al fondo de los enredos"* [With my magic wand, I open the coffers of secrets and silences; with the magic wand, I respond to all of the questions; because it penetrates into the depth of the entanglement] (3).

The play takes on a darker tone as the female town crier states that the jokes and intrigues are mixed together with stories of tortures and assassinations. Her counterpart then asks the audience in an enticing tone, *"¿Quién quiere conocer la suerte de los desaparecidos? ¿Quién el sitio donde se pudren los cadáveres? ¿ Quién las voces que dejaron olvidadas los muertos?* [Who wants to know the luck of the disappeared? Who wants to know where the corpses are rotting? Who wants to hear the voices of the forgotten dead?] (3). Although it is clear that the play is going to bring up the horrors of the war in a lighthearted, direct manner, it is with the assurance that they have *"el remedio para todos los males de la Tierra"* [the remedy for all the bad things on Earth] (3):

> *Pregonero. Transformamos la tristeza en caracajadas.* [Let's transform the sadness into cackles of laughter.]
> *Pregonera. Traemos la luz y la esperanza. [We bring light and hope.]*
>
> (3)

As in Carrillo's play, the structure is similar to *Huelga de dolores* with songs commenting on the action between scenes. The first song uses flowers to represent the people who have been killed either by the army (represented in the color green) or the guerrillas (represented in red).

Flores, de flores yo me acompaño / Cuando se mueren las lloro / y no me importa si mueren / por culpa de mano roja, por culpa de mano verde / Ay de las tiernas flores de mi campo / trochadas por mano roja, quebradas por mano verde.

[Flowers, of flowers that accompanied me / When they die, I cry for them / and it doesn't matter if they die / because of the red hand or the green hand. Ah, the tender flowers of my countryside / squashed down by the red hand, broken by the green hand.] (4)

The following scene between two pairs of lovers (again mirroring *El corazón del espantapájaros*) is set in the early 1960s. The first pair express their love for each other and hope for a future. The second pair are idealistic guerrillas who say that if the war is won, the entire exploited and oppressed town will also win. The female guerrilla describes oppression: *"Ser oprimido es como ser uno y no ser, es que otro te mande, que decida tu vida, que no te deje vivir como vos querés"* [To be oppressed is like being and not being, it is like having another control you, who decides your life, who doesn't let you live as you want] (6). The couple describe the horrible living conditions and the injustice, complaining that if one protests, the authorities will cut out the person's tongue and set him on fire.[8] They idealistically believe they will quickly be able to take over the stupid government and *"toda la gente va a vivir como Dios manda. Con justicia y dignidad . . . todo lo que le ha sido negado al pueblo por quinientos años y más"* [all the people are going to live as God demands. With justice and dignity . . . everything that has been denied to the people for five hundred years or more] (8). The guerrillas claim that they are going to demand better schools and health care. They state that the first thing to do is to stop the rich people and the gringos (who are really the bosses of the military) from abusing and exploiting the poor.

The young couple in love decide to stay behind. The woman

is afraid the soldiers will come and force the man to enlist as they have done with countless others. The pair create a fantasy of the future together. Suddenly, the play becomes surreal as spirits flit onto the stage. The spirits become the torturers who demand to know where the subversives are. The girl is forced to witness her lover being beaten by the spirits/soldiers. At the end of the scene characters sing about killing people in silence in the secret jails. The song describes the entire country as a gigantic jail of silence.

The following scene becomes even more nightmarish. Saint Sirisay, a godlike figure, is preaching to the masses about how to follow God's Word. He then rips the head off a doll dressed in indigenous clothes and throws it on the ground, accusing the figure of being a communist. A drunk stumbles in, mumbling his support of President Arévalo and the ten years of love and peace after the revolution. The inebriated man recognizes the religious fanatic as someone who burns flesh and spills blood. The man moans in pain, declaring that his toothache is pleasurable compared to the suffering all around:

> San Sirisay. ¿Qué te duele, animalito? [Where do you hurt, little animal?]
> Bolo. El alma, mi general, mi gran mariscal de muertos. Es el alma la que duele, después de ver el incendio, y las carnes arrancadas después de ver las aldeas ardiendo en fuegos de muerte, las muelas no duelen nada, es el alma la que duele. [My soul, my General, my great marshall of death. It is my soul that hurts. After seeing the fires and the flesh ripped, after seeing the burning villages in fires of death, I no longer have a toothache. It is my soul that hurts.]
> (14)

The play becomes disjointed with flashes of nightmare images. Saint Sirisay goes crazy, claiming that communists deserve to die because they do not love God. He tells the drunk that if he wants a red country, then he should go to hell and burn. The saint burns model villages while the other calls him an assassin. A pregnant woman enters who is split open with a knife. A naked child enters and is stabbed with a bayonet. Saint Sirisay, totally insane, shouts, *"Yo soy todo corazón, y me importa un pepino la constitución. Pero, hermanos, si no quieren mi compasión, pues los mando al paredón"* [I am all heart and I don't give a damn about the constitution. But, brothers, if you don't want my compassion, then I send you in front of the firing squad] (14). His supporters enter and worship their master. The man accuses Saint Sirisay of being drunk. His supporters support the godlike figure, saying he is drunk with faith and the love of liberty. They then turn and shoot the inebriated man for challenging authority. When the drunk is shot the sadistic Saint Sirisay, making sounds as if he is having a sexual orgasm, shouts: *"Oh, Dios, un comunista menos . . ."* [Oh, God, one less communist . . .]. He only laments that he cannot be president. This is the moment the audience realizes this pernicious character represents General Ríos Montt who was not allowed to run for president because of his involvement with the coup d'etat in 1982 (discussed in chapter 3). At this moment his soldiers go out in front of the audience and joyfully chant *"Al paredón los mandarán"* [They will be ordered to go in front of the firing squad] (16).

Saint Sirisay describes himself as death—the death of communism. He ordered the war in order to cleanse the land of indigenous peasants, strengthen the rule of the rich, and offer power to the military. The following song notes the numerous people Saint Sirisay/General Ríos Montt has killed:

> *El adora el paredón / la Ley Fuga y la muerte /*
> *Ay de la mala suerte del que hiera su razón /*
> *Cientos de aldeas ardieron / cuando el general rezaba /*
> *millones de ojos vieron / cómo él los mataba.*

[He adores the firing squad / the Fugitive Law of shooting a prisoner in the back when he tries to flee, and death / Woe to the ones with bad luck who go against his logic / Hundreds of villages were burned / when the General praised God / thousands of eyes saw / how he killed them.][9]

Again both the *Pregoneros* break into the action and claim to have the ability to make the people's prejudice dissipate. The male says some magic words in another language in order to evoke the people killed in the war. The *Pregonera* states that she cannot translate what he has just said because it is politically dangerous . . . still.

The following scene takes place in a store. The neighbors come in to share news about the most recent deaths. One person disappeared when they put him in a white van with three guys wearing sunglasses. Another complains that a journalist was kidnapped in the middle of the night. They talk about people who have been tortured and tied up with barbed wire. Young children have been found with their brains smashed. The group continues to gossip about the various actual atrocities. For example, one character describes a school where all the children were burned alive by the army. Those that survived went to the hospital where they were *rematados* [killed again] (22). All of the atrocities described in the play are factual and public knowledge.

As the neighbors continue to gossip, they notice that the clerk has been writing down what has been said. The atmosphere in the room turns to one of distrust. Spies are felt to be everywhere. After the scene, the *Pregoneros* ask whether the clerk was a spy for the army or the guerrillas. The *Pregonero* segues into the issue of impunity: *"Nos hemos quedado sin jurado, sin testigos y sin jueces. No hay pruebas, no hay quién acuse, no hay delito. . . . Quién alza la voz contra Terror y Espanto y la mano macabra que los hace bailar"* [We have been left without a jury, without witnesses and without judges. There is no evidence, no one who accuses, no crimes. . . . Who would ever raise a voice against Terror and Fright and the macabre hand that makes you all dance?] (23). Then the actors enter and cry out a litany of names of famous people in Guatemala who have been killed (including Alaíde Foppa). While the shouts continue, some of the actors go into the audience with *"gestos grotescos de oreja y asesina"* [grotesque gestures of spies and assassins]. The energy of fear and distrust grows until the auditorium becomes chaotic and delirious.

In the following scene two actions occur simultaneously. The army is on one side of the stage and the guerrillas are on the other. The army tortures a woman to get her to betray her boyfriend, a teacher who argued for the rights of the poor. Intercut with this action is one in which guerrillas decide that they must kill a group of innocent peasants who stumbled upon their path by mistake. The peasants must be killed to protect the secret position of the camp. The commander states, *"En México están esperando buenas noticias nuestras. Qué va a decir el comandante que si por salvarale la vida un puño de vaqueros se pone en risego la revolución. La guerra es cruel, compañera"* [In Mexico they are awaiting our good news. What will the commander say (when we tell him) that by saving the life of a bunch of cow herds, the revolution was put at risk] (27). They decide to kill the peasants. Throughout this scene, Llorona, a legendary figure who wanders the night crying for having killed her own children, enters as a ghost. She dances between the two camps and exclaims her feelings of loss and anguish.

The last scene begins with the question, *"¿Qué falta, qué delito, qué violación quedó sin cometerse, en el tintero de esta guerra cruel?"* [What is missing, what crime, what violation has not occurred in the ink well of this cruel war?] (31). In the last scene Monseñor Gerardi enters and is described as the voice crying in the desert.[10] In this scene he states that Guatemalans must open the tombs. He begins to pray. The *Pregoneros* state that peace always has a price and that it must be paid with blood. Gerardi states, *"La paz es perdón, la paz no es olvido. La paz es la palabra de Dios"* [Peace is forgiving, peace is not forgetting. Peace is the Word of God] (32). After saying this, he is bludgeoned to death on stage. The cast comes out singing, *"paz en la tierra a los hombres de buena voluntad"* [peace on earth to men of good will]. The *Pregoneros* enter asking if the signing of the Peace Accord was an illusion or a reality. The play ends with the *Pregonera* stating that only the people of Guatemala can make it a reality.

Perhaps this play stands more as a response to Carrillo's *El corazon del espantapájaros* than as a sequel. Although the structure, tone, and action seem to be taken from Carrillo's 1962 text, the central message has changed (they give Carrillo partial credit for some unspecified scenes in the text). Carrillo's play sought to incite anger about social injustice and the impotence of the little man against tyranny. The play focused on blaming rather than forgiving. Kénefic and Escobedo's play *Nunca más* still protests the tremendous injustice, but almost forty years later, it now holds both sides accountable. Written in the postwar era, it categorically supports the peace effort. However, in the words of Bishop Gerardi, peace does not mean forgetting. It does mean the monumental task of forgiving.

Conclusion

The didactic nature of these plays teaches (whether factual or simply possible events caused by the violence) about the cost of the Guatemalan civil war. The docudrama styles of *Mujeres de la guerra*, *Alaíde*, *Rapidísima historia de la paz* and *Nunca más* pay homage to the victims of the war, using actual names and often portraying their heroic lives. The foreign plays have been specifically adapted to fit scenarios that could have occurred during the civil war. These plays reflect the wide ramifications of social upheaval caused during and after the war. Both styles of plays lament the deaths of innocent people caused by the violence. The works by foreign authors raise the provocative issue of whether the perpetrator is a victim of war as well. The rampant brutality created in the armed conflict has deadened the humanity of Madre Coraje, Sebastian, and the captain and entrapped them in the vicious circle of perpetuating the violence. The sympathetic depiction of these characters creates understanding, thereby fostering an atmosphere of forgiveness. However, the national plays do not portray specific perpetrators of the violence in a sympathetic light. Although there is a myriad of plays noted in the previous chapter depicting General Ríos Montt, none of them are sympathetic. There are no sympathetic biographical depictions of specific guerrilla leaders either. Perhaps this suggests that four years after the peace agreement is too soon to deal with specific war figures. Generalized forgiveness is the first step in promoting healing; perhaps more time is needed before plays appear portraying the leaders in the political strife sympathetically.

As noted in the chapter, the plays that created an emotional response (rather than the intellectual history lesson of *Rapidísima historia de la paz* or the highly conceptualized production of *Madre Coraje*) were most popular and, therefore, most widely attended. The emotional range in these plays goes from deep grief over the loss of lives to the grotesque horrors of the madness of war. The moral questions raised are numerous: society's duty to protect the powerless from victimization, decisions based on ethics rather than patriotic duty, the attempt to survive by profiteering from the war, the use of torture for national security. However, the most central moral question raised by these plays is how to forgive by remembering the past without resparking the cycle of vengeance.

Szanto describes this dynamic as "theater of agitation propaganda" which raises the audiences' consciousness to own the immediacy of social problems. These plays unapologetically agitate the audience in order to break through their apathy and fear. The plays frame the topic of peace as an ultimatum: it is not only the desired path, but the single viable option. The alternative is to be condemned to repeat history.

5
Symbolic Theater

IN THIS CHAPTER I FOCUS ON THE WORKS OF MANUEL CORLETO, JOSÉ Osorio, and Rubén Nájera and their self-identified connection with postwar European theatrical movements: Theater of the Absurd, Dadaism, and Existentialism. These movements range from the irrational and nihilistic to optimistic philosophies determined to wrench order out of chaos.[1] However, the common denominator in these three movements is their iconoclastic challenge to the concept of a divinely ordered universe. In the context of the civil war and postwar period, Corleto, Osorio, and Nájera portray a world that is devastated by ideology and conflict. A common stylistic element in all of the works is the appropriating, contrasting, and distorting of symbols to portray a godless world. They challenge all social convention in order to liberate the individual. Martin Esslin writes that the underlying purpose of Theater of the Absurd is to get the spectator to "face up to the human condition as it really is, to free him [/her] from illusions that are bound to cause constant maladjustment and disappointment" (Esslin 1961, 377). This aim is equally true for Corleto, Osorio, and Nájera as they seek to confront society with the trauma caused by the civil war.

These three artists all express the moral and philosophical collapse caused by the catastrophe of war. Corleto uses poetic symbolism to lament the repression of the artist. He also uses Theater of the Absurd to portray the nightmarish world caught in a cycle of oppression. There is a subversive edge in this style of theater which encourages the spectator to laugh at one's fears in order not to be cowed by societal pressures. His work condemns the war but does not promote the idea of hope or unity. Osorio uses Dadaism to break through people's apathy toward the horrors of the war. His work is on the outermost fringe of *mestizo* theater and is very reminiscent of protest plays from the "Golden Age" of Theater. Nájera is a great admirer of Albert Camus and emphasizes an Existentialist perspective to liberate people from the cycle of violence and oppression. Nájera's work reminds the spectator that the community is completely responsible for the world it has created. Out of the three he is the most optimistic that there is a path out of the nightmare.

Whereas the didactic plays tend to use simulated violence on stage and to ground the work in factual history and psychological realism, these works use more metaphors, rituals, and symbols to express the irrational, pervasive violence.[2] The artists discussed in this chapter create complex and contrasting perspectives on political/social thought and even metaphysical matters with denser, less clearly delineated morals. Osorio's and Corleto's ambivalent images contain elements of uncontained protest and rage that challenge and even contradict my theory that atrocity is being portrayed for communal reconciliation. Nevertheless I include them to reveal the diversity of approaches to reflecting on the civil war as well as to reveal that the protest theater did not die although it is no longer the model appropriated by the mainstream middle class.[3]

All of these symbolic works are ambiguous and open to interpretation because of the spectator's interpretive role in decoding the images. While all theater uses symbols to create the world of the play, the use of images in the following works is central and takes precedence over any realistic/naturalistic expression in the plays. Whereas all the plays thus far in the study emphasize colloquial speech and mimetic reality, these artists consciously use symbols "to invent a self-sufficient language" (Pavis 1998, 374) which is less interested in offering an objective account of social reality. Theater scholar B. Dort describes the metaphysical reality in the symbolist representation: "the attempt to organize, on stage, a (closed or open) universe that borrows some elements from apparent reality but which, through the actor, refers the spectators to another reality that he must discover" (quoted in Pavis 1998, 177).

Symbolic theater works on numerous levels of the spectator's psyche. On a conscious level the audience is challenged to decode the complex symbols in order to unlock the abstract themes and ideas. More profoundly, however, symbolic theater seeks to engage the viewer metaphysically on a spiritual/subconscious plane. It invests material objects and actors with meaning in order to express the invisible or intangible. These works tend to be more accessible to a European/North American than the didactic or satiric plays, for three reasons: (1) the plays are more open to interpretation; (2) the plays focus less on specific historical events in Guatemala and use fewer topical references than the didactic or satiric plays; and (3) the artists identify themselves with the canonized European theatrical movements of Theater of the Absurd, Dadaism, and Existentialism. Ironically, however, in Guatemala these three artists have the smallest following and appeal mostly to a highly educated, middle to upper middle class audience. Corleto's and Osorio's avant-garde, anti-Establishment emphasis has a limited audience draw. Nájera is called "Guatemala's Shakespeare," but this is because of his great command of language and his reputation as the most talented playwright rather than his popularity. His highly intellectual, literary plays are not greatly appreciated by Guatemala's majority of semiliterate people. His plays are often produced at festivals rather than in the commercial theater.

Manuel Corleto

Manuel Corleto began writing plays in the late 1960s and is both a novelist and one of the most prolific playwrights in his generation. He had four volumes of plays published in the 1970s and 1980s. Many of these works have the recurring theme that (wo)man is an inept clown in an absurd universe. His most popular play, *El animal vertical* [*The Vertical Animal*] (1973), centers on a president's impossible struggle to find a balance to ruling with "a cross and a sword." His plays are mostly abstract pieces which have become progressively more absurd and difficult for audiences to interpret throughout the years (interview with René Molino).[4]

Nevertheless, Corleto has written several more realistic plays since the repression. His first realistic script, *La profecía* [*The Prophecy*],[5] was produced in 1989. It was a huge historical production with music and choreography that centered on the conquest of Guatemala by Spain and the colliding of the two civilizations. This was a joint production of the Ministry of

Arts in Guatemala and a French organization, *Association Française D'Action Artistique,* and toured Central America extensively.

In 1992 he wrote *La café,* a fictional story set in Guatemala during the violence. The play is a blending of naturalism with surrealistic interludes of poetry. It begins with a long monologue by the poet Miguelito (who has recently been killed but does not seem to know it) who tells an obscure story of a death in which he cannot distinguish between reality and fiction. During his monologue, nine people fearfully huddle together in a café. They are mourning the loss of a local poet and trying to make sense out of their small, frightened lives. It is revealed that the police cut off the poet Miguelito's hands and threw them to the dogs in the street. After they cut off his hands, they killed him, confiscated his writings, burned them in the Central Plaza, and even changed the name of the street that had been named after him. The violence continues to rage outside in the streets as the play begins and sounds of explosions and shouts of fear are heard intermittently throughout the drama.

The people in the café have no sense of purpose without the poet to lead them. Despairingly, they discuss the violence, destruction, tortures, and death that surround them. Corleto's characters describe a hopeless, bleak world:

Dondequiera que el hombre pone su huella, la tierra se contamina. El agua se ensucia y los bosques y montañas son liquidados. Dondequiera que el hombre se establece, hay basura, ruido, plagas, promiscuidad, vicio, desequilibrio.

[Wherever man makes his mark, the earth becomes contaminated. The water becomes polluted and the forests and mountains are destroyed. Wherever man establishes himself, there is trash, noise, plagues, promiscuity, vice, and lack of balance.] (47)

Another character states it more succinctly: *"Guatemala es la bullshit capital del mundo. Siempre lo he afirmado"* [Guatemala is the bullshit capital of the world. I've always said that] (29).

The only one who offered them hope in this dismal world was the poet. One character tries to inspire the others by commenting on Miguelito's valiant approach to life. She suggests that one can either contract and retreat with fear from the violence or expand and speak one's truth in spite of repression as the poet had done, even though it cost him his life. She reminds the people that liberty is a state of mind that is better than the meaningless limbo people are left in:

> *El Poeta fue libre porque no quiso ser ave ni viento. Fue bandera y consigna, sable y rugido. Para él la libertad se manifestaba primordialmente en la existencia misma. "Se puede ser libre entre cadenas/ prisionero de pasiones." En el momento mismo que suele, paradójicamente, coincidir con el de la muerte, fue libre para regar la tierra con su sangre, para ser alimento de rapiña, para ser separado de los vivos . . . Esas manos-mariposas volaron a los confines del país de nunca jamás y se perdieron para siempre."*

[The Poet was free because he wanted to be neither a bird nor the wind. He was a role model, sabre and roar. For him liberty manifested primordially in existence. "One can be free in chains/a prisoner of passions." Paradoxically, at the same moment that it coincides with his death, he was free to water the earth with his blood, to be nourishment for the scavengers, to be separated from the living. . . . Those hands like butterflies flew to the confines of never never land and were lost to us forever.] (52)

The poet (whose name interestingly enough is the same as the playwright's, *Miguelito*—little Miguel) moves among the people as a spirit and makes metaphysical comments about his life, though it is not made explicit that he is the dead poet until his last monologue. He responds to their comments, but they do not know he is present. Throughout the play he speaks in lengthy monologues about metaphysical concepts and human limitations, describing "the poet" (himself) in the third person:

> *El Poeta fue un soñador, porque aún sabiendo que el sol terminaría por derretir sus alas de cera, tentó al sol con un dedo y se quemó las manos. Tal vez por eso nunca aparecieron, tal vez se hicieron ceniza y nadie reparó en ello. Fue un místico, porque aún habiendo renunciado a la promesa de lo eterno, tocó a Dios con las manos sucias de tinta y Dios, en venganza, hizo que ángeles, arcángeles y querubines se las cortaran.*

[The Poet was a dreamer, because even knowing that the sun would end up burning his wings of wax, he touched the sun with his finger and burned his hands. Perhaps, therefore, his hands never reappeared again, perhaps they were turned into ashes and nobody noticed it. He was a mystic because although he had renounced the promise of the eternal, he touched God with his dirty hands of ink and God, in revenge, made the angels and archangels and cherubim cut them off.] (53)

The play laments the loss of artistic voice in a violent, repressive society. Only the poet has the ability to rise above the momentary political crisis and lead people to metaphysical insight, into the mysterious beauty of life. The people have been cut off and left in the bleak world. When he is killed, it is as if their connection to spirituality is severed as well. The world is pathetically absurd without a reason to continue.

This play serves as a reminder of the loss of the artistic voice in the 1980s and the consequences of the social chaos caused by the civil war. Although the dominating theme in the play is lament for a country that represses its artists, the fact that the play exists, that the national voice is again finding expression, suggests a message of hope. The reality that Guatemala can artistically lament the repression of the artists in the 1980s is a healing affirmation that times have become more open. The play can be interpreted as protest against censorship and repression; however, that excludes it from the context of the 1990s as a time of reflection on the dark years. The play has a self-referential aspect that freely comments on censored poetry. Through the use of poetry it seeks to capture the metaphysical anguish of a time of chaos, with the hope that Guatemala will never return to such a time.

In 1996 Corleto returned to his earlier work in Theater of the Absurd in *La Crónica fidedigna* [*The Trustworthy News Chronicle*]. His anarchist, anti-establishment philosophy is more easily hidden in this style of theater (interview with Corleto). The play depicts the violence and insanity of the war. The characters change periods, social positions, and identities without rational explanation. The three central characters are Juan, Manuel, and Timoteo. They begin as Indian janitors; other times they represent powerful figures such as the president and his advisors; in some moments they are only playing at being these powerful figures; and in later scenes they play rulers from an unspecified time in the Mayan past who are buying and selling female slaves. Their wives names correspond to their names and they never change identities: Juana, Manuela, and Timotea. The auto-defense patrol (community members in support of the government who police local areas) known as PAC has five "clown" types named PAC, PUC, PEC, PIC, and POC. They change from being the vulgar civil defense patrol trying to capture subversive Indians to becoming secret spies and assassins for President Juan. In the beginning of Act Three they play vultures in a dump where bodies of peasants are buried.[6] In one scene each is dressed as half man/half horse, representing the conquerors (and their horses). The play fluidly moves between the seeming naturalism of Guatemalan rural life and domestic squabbles between the husbands and wives to surrealism and back again.

The play fits into Deborah B. Gaensbauer's "textbook" description of French Theater of the Absurd which she theorizes is a phenomenon of the postwar years (1991, xvi). She describes the Theater of the Absurd as antirealistic and antipsychological:

> Plots, individual identities, comprehensible human relationships, plausible settings and rational language are bafflingly, sometimes even terrifyingly, absent. In their place are ambiguous, repetitive, nightmarish situations involving alienated, mechanical characters whose clowning nullity is emphasized by childish, vague or punning names. The language in these plays is pointedly unrealistic, a derisive combination of poetry and profanity. (Gaensbauer 1991, xvi)

The misuse of power is a major theme in this play. There are recurring images of the president's chair throughout the play. One of the wheels is broken in the beginning but eventually gets poorly repaired. At first it seems that Juan, the janitor, is only playing at being the president. Manuel asks Juan why he didn't kill the man who wanted to sit in Juan's presidential chair. Juan responds: *"Porque ésta es una democracia primero y no se puede o no se debe más bien andar matando gente por cualquier cosa además los ojos del mundo están puestos sobre nosotros en estos momentos difícles"* [Because this is a democracy first and one cannot or, better, should not go around killing people for just any reason. Furthermore, the eyes of the world are upon us in these difficult moments] (7).⁷ The spectator is never sure if these peasants are pretending to be powerful figures or if the play is making the comment that Guatemalan officials are uncouth, untrained peasants who approach their work as if it were a game.

The scenes have a semblance of chronological order in the broad comedy of PAC, PIC, PUC, PEC, and POC waiting to ambush and murder Manuel and Timoteo. Interspliced with these scenes are domestic situations as well as the surrealistic, dreamlike moments. Juan has betrayed his friends Manuel and Timoteo for unexplained reasons. PAC has an affair with/rapes Juan's wife and she becomes pregnant with his child. Preposterous images, such as Juan commanding a battalion of vultures, are pervasive in Acts Two and Three. President Juan tells the vultures: *"Van a ser recompensados por sus servicios recibirán la más alta condecoración todo sea por la concordia (harmony) y la paz"* [You will be rewarded for your services and you will receive the highest medal of all for the peace and harmony] (58). These disturbing images of pregnancy/rape and vultures/soldiers depict a disturbing world with no resolution. War has caused the sacred to be profaned, and men to lose their humanity and prey on weak and dying flesh.

The violence caused by the civil war and the Spanish Conquest are contrasted, implying a repetitive cycle of exploitation and injustice. Surrealistic images of murder, dead bodies moving in the dump yard, and burning towns are spliced together with images of the Spanish conquerors. This is followed by slaves asking if the bargaining has begun, mixing images of the treaty that the conquerors made with the 1996 Peace Accord. PAC's army is suggestive of the Spanish conquerors when they speak of the seas they crossed. They rape the women, explaining that they have come to write the history. The women accuse them of writing the future on top of the millions of widows and orphans.

The absurdity in the text enables Corleto to reveal an irrational, chaotic world. The most clearly pronounced theme is the abuse of power and how it begets betrayal and ends up destroying one's own family. The connection between the conquerors and current postcolonialism and exploitation suggests that humanity is caught in a trap of dominance and repression. The playwright indicates the future Peace Accord will not bring about a positive transformation. His theater strips away the pretense of justice and encourages people to recognize the greed, betrayal, and deceit inherent in human nature.

Non-realistic dialogue with rhymes and word games, and repetition in chorus, occurs throughout the play. A typical example of the word play occurs in the scene when Juana explains to Juan that she is going to have a baby:

> Juana. *Fui* [I went]
> Manuela. *al* [to]
> Timotea. *dispensario.* [the dispensary.]
> Juan. *¿Qué?* [What?]
> Manuel. *¿Qué?* [What?]
> Timoteo. *¿Qué?* [What?]
> *(Los zopilotes se asustan con los gritos y revolotean inquietos alejándose.)* [The vultures become scared, squawk and flutter anxiously as they leave.]
> Juan. *Barajámelo* [Explain it to me]
> Manuel. *más* [more]
> Timoteo. *despacio!* [slowly.]
> Juana. *El doctor dice que va ser para octubre.* [The doctor says that I'm going to give birth in October.]
> Manuela. *Tubre.* [ober.]
> Timotea. *Ubre.* [er.]
> Juan. *¡Puta (se pone a contar dificultosamente con los dedos).* [Whore! (he starts to count with difficulty on his fingers)]
> Manuel. *¡Uta!* [ore]
> Timoteao. *¡Ta!* [re] (43)

This type of word play comes in intermittently throughout the scenes. Martin Esslin writes in *Theater of the Absurd* that the absurd works are often noted for their word play and devaluation of language, which reflects "the senselessness of the human condition and the inadequacy of the rational approach by the open abandonment of rational devices and discursive thought" (196, 6).

Esslin acknowledges that there is an element of social criticism against an inauthentic society in these plays. However, he states that the more pronounced purpose is to face up to the deeper layer of the absurdity of the human condition:

> The Alienation effect in the Brechtian theater is intended to activate the audience's critical, intellectual attitude. The Theatre of

the Absurd speaks to a deeper level of the audience's mind. It activates psychological forces, releases and liberates hidden fears and repressed aggressions, and, above all, by confronting the audience with a picture of disintegration, it sets in motion an active process of integrative forces in the mind of each individual spectator. (362)

Esslin argues that when the spectator recognizes his anxieties formulated on stage, he can liberate himself from them. "It is the unease caused by the presence of illusions that are obviously out of tune with reality that is dissolved and discharged through liberating laughter at the recognition of the fundamental absurdity of the universe" (364). Theater of the Absurd is very similar to the satire paradigm in chapter 3 in provoking laughter at one's deeper fears in order to liberate oneself. Esslin states that Theater of the Absurd is the latest example of gallows humor, which enables the spectator to free him/herself from internal, inarticulate fears (364). However, there is an integration of the irrationality in the form with the absurdity of the content that separates it from the category of satire. "The Theater of the Absurd has renounced arguing about the absurdity of the human condition; it merely *presents* it in being" (6). Esslin describes this as the difference between Theater of the Absurd and Existentialist theater. Satire parallels this distinction in that it presents an irrational world rationally in terms of a linear plot, understandable (albeit exaggerated) behavior, and ideas. The spectator is in on the joke. However, Esslin describes Theater of the Absurd as emphasizing metaphysical anguish, puzzling images, and devaluation of language. The audience is often in a combative relationship with the concepts of the play where the darkness threatens to overshadow the humor.

Corleto's disturbingly absurd world with its nightmarish symbols leans more toward processing the violence than protesting it. He intends to enable people to process the disintegrating effects of war on a deeper level than the more cerebral, didactic approach of preaching a direct antiwar message. However, being an example of Theater of the Absurd, it is open to interpretation. This play can be interpreted nihilistically or as a critique of the perpetuation of the cycle of the dominant hegemony exploiting the weak.

Theater of the Absurd does not offer easy answers and does

not suggest that there is a communal way out of the nightmare. Nevertheless, it can be liberating for the individual to be confronted with absurdity in order to process the tremendous change the society is undergoing at the end of a war. The plays enable the spectator to recognize the metaphysical anguish and uncertainty pervading the culture during the years of the Peace Accord and brings him/her to the acceptance that the path to peace is going to be fraught with uncertainty.

José Osorio and the *Casa Bizarra* [Magnanimous/ Courageous Spirit House]

During my second interview with José Osorio he gave me a souvenir poster from the 1999 Urban Arts Festival which he helped produce through the Municipality. The picture of the poster was a single open hand with outstretched fingers. Being a foreigner I missed the symbolic meaning. He told me not to feel too bad since many Guatemalans also thought it was just a "catchy" picture of a hand. Others recognized the intentionally offensive meaning of the picture: this hand gesture with outstretched fingers is a more forceful expression of "giving someone the bird."[8] The poster was for the Second Annual Arts Festival which included performance and visual art. In 1999 Osorio's group helped sponsor ninety-five events/performances, up from forty-five the year before. He describes the 300 artists involved in the 1999 event as seeking an outlet for their creativity. However, the provocative work included nude dance and vulgar poetry, which challenged the boundaries of censorship and has led to a break in the relationship between the Municipality and the artists. Osorio's group decided not to accept financial support for the Urban Arts Festival 2000. Rather than accept the censorship regulations of the Municipality, they produced it themselves. The group of loosely linked artists espouses the anarchical concept of Dadaism and its most central principle of breaking rules and challenging the boundaries of social convention. Osorio explained to me that the picture of the hand on the poster is representative of his group's intent: to offend and assault the audience.

Dadaism began in Germany in 1914 and flourished in Paris from 1918 to 1922. It began as a protest against institutions and ideologies that brought Europe to the brink of destruction in World War I. Dadaism rejects reason and emphasizes spontaneity and visceral expression. The staging of theatrical events in Paris was done in an unrealistic and provocative style; the content was full of nonsense and scatology. Dada events were often staged on street corners "where outraged passersby would be drawn into 'happenings' in which spectacular impropriety was generally the key note" (Gaensbauer 1991, 9). J. H. Matthews describes Dadaism as the anti-art form which casts down sacrosanct forms, repudiates established esthetic principles, and is "wary of all rules in deference to the spirit of revolt and iconoclasm" (1974, 7). Likewise, Osorio and his group of artists attempt to move outside the traditional confines of theatres, provoking the observer to participate in the happening, often mocking the audience, and leaving the message open-ended for spectators to interpret for themselves.

Osorio describes his group as being from "Generation X," the first wave of artists after the war. Osorio states that most of the intellectuals and artists had been killed or persecuted during the late 1970s and early 1980s, leaving a gap of ten years with little to no art being produced. The artists, musicians, and actors in his group are mostly under twenty-three years of age, middle class, disenchanted, and claiming to be apolitical (which means they are not aligned with either side in the conflict). They grew up in the conflict with sadness and fear, viewing the war as something to avoid or forget. Osorio and his group of painters and musicians opened an artist commune in 1997 called *Casa Bizarra* in the central district of Guatemala City. The house was built in 1930 in a neighborhood where much violence has taken place over the years and the political swings have been keenly felt. Osorio explains that this area, where numerous students had been killed during the height of the war, is fitting for a renaissance led by young artists. Osorio describes the commune as having created "a surrealist world which is an alternative to the Establishment" (interview). They would put on performances of absurd theater with rock music and poetry readings, and offer workshops in various forms of visual art to help support the commune.

The group sought to create a rupture with the past and start from zero, reinventing the arts. Their "Dada philosophy" is to break rules that govern the institutional forms of art. Therefore, their experimental, absurd theater work prides itself on having no relation to traditional theater. Osorio explains: "This generation has nothing to inspire them. They have nothing to build on or to challenge. We want to dig into our creativity. To encourage people to say things and identify social problems. But we are not wanting to align ourselves with different parties" (interview). This generation of artists was raised on MTV and was not interested in being drawn into the polemics of the civil war.[9] Completely disassociating themselves from responsibility for the war, their attitude toward both the guerrillas and the army is one of condemnation.

Osorio described to me numerous performances the group had given in different settings. One event was dealing with a sadomasochistic poet who read his graphic work. The microphone was eventually turned off by the sponsors and he was asked to leave the auditorium. For another event, the group rented a pornographic movie theater for an antifashion show with drag queens. Osorio described one fashion outfit as having a picture of Marilyn Monroe and Rigoberta Menchú on the back. He described "Bus Theater," in which the audience sat inside a bus while it was driven around the city. The actors would enter and play roles such as a prostitute or a beggar talking about social problems.[10] The actors dressed as if they were in the military and took everyone out of the bus, frisked them, and asked for their I.D.s. Osorio noted that the audience always laughed during this point in the performance because it was a common situation, especially during the war. At the end the actors gave audience members little mirrors to encourage them to reflect upon themselves and their society.

Another event featured a woman who hung herself in a harness from the outdoor arch of the Post Office on a Friday afternoon in the busy downtown district of Guatemala City. She wore a long white dress and screamed her feminist poetry into the wind. The people could not understand what she was saying because she was too high up. As she finished one poem she would throw it into the crowd. Osorio thought it was ironic that the men were actually fighting with each other to get the pieces of paper filled with feminist poetry. Osorio describes her act as "seeking to reconstruct the 'moral equilibrium.'" However, he states that each audience member interprets the act in his/her own way. Many people said they thought it was justice hanging herself. There was a political cartoon the following day about a drunk who was upset because he thought justice had hanged herself over the issue of impunity for the army involved in the atrocities during the 1970s and 1980s.

One of the most provocative events took place in the Central Plaza in front of the Palace. In 1999 there was a ballot to change the Constitution to adopt the Peace Accord doctrine of giving the indigenous respect and acknowledging them as equals. Osorio and his young group of artists were appalled that 80 percent of the voters abstained on the question, which resulted in the measure being defeated. His group created a happening to protest the apathy. They put fifty small, preschool chairs in a circle in the Central Plaza. Twenty barefoot people dressed in white robes entered the circle and stood like statues. A woman dressed as a politician in a suit and beard walked with two chairs tied around her feet and talked about political atrocities committed during the war. When she began preaching her political perspective, the twenty people took their individual pieces of string and started balling them up, trying to ignore her as well as the other robed actors. She took out buckets of cow blood and threw the blood at their feet on the cement. Unfazed by the blood, the twenty barefoot people stood up on top of the chairs and continued focusing on their string. They portrayed the survival method of avoiding a terrible reality by ignoring it, that is, "I can ignore the blood all around by simply focusing my attention elsewhere." During this happening, several preachers who were sermonizing in the park came over and shouted out that the group was being satanic. Although Osorio and others passed out flyers stating that this was performance art that portrayed "the evasion of political reality" to protest the apathy and the small turnout of voters, many people were baffled by the ritual. However, Osorio considers the "happenings" successful if they leave a deep impression on the audience and create a disturbance.

Although Osorio claims to follow Dadaist principles of trying to insult the moral law and to break the rules of art in terms of structure, there is not the nihilistic focus that Gaensbauer sees in the original movement (1991, 10). Events arranged by residents of *Casa Bizarra* are more like the happenings in the 1960s sponsored by the Living Theater than the original Dadaist movements in Europe. Osorio describes this generation as having been closed down emotionally and artistically because of fear. The mission of *Casa Bizarra*, as he sees it, is to encourage people to accept the past, confront their fears, express their anger, and wake up from the culturally pervasive apathy. He describes his position as producer of the happenings as the person who empowers the performers, musicians, and painters, and "gets people to feel they can do something" (interview). Osorio states that they have lived with so much violence they are all filled with rage and violence within themselves. They are all desperately seeking an alternative lifestyle. The bohemian lifestyle they embrace he describes as "human, gentle, and unmacho";[11] they are people fighting sexism, racism, and homophobism and classism to make a better world. Yet, ironically, much of their work is filled with rage and anger as if they use it as an outlet for years of repression and anger against society.

Rubén E. Nájera

Rubén E. Nájera is the foremost playwright in Guatemala and his large body of theatrical work merits a study unto itself. His writing, which is poetic, intelligent, and highly stylized, profoundly dissects the root of the issues of conflict in Guatemala. He impartially condemns the violence without writing agitprop plays. His dramas focus on language and debate; therefore, he is often criticized for the lack of action.[12] (During my first interview with Nájera he acknowledged his preference for playwright Jean Racine over Molière.) He works fluently in English, French, Portuguese, and Spanish.

Many of Nájera's plays are period pieces that argue contemporary issues. *El huésped de Longinos [The Guest of Longinos]* centers around a debate between Caifás [Caiphas] and the political prisoner Jesus. They argue over issues of peace, the challenges of racism, and Judea's right to govern itself apart from the influence of Imperial Rome. Nájera wrote *Sacra conversación* [Sacred Conversation] about the life of Sister Juana de Maldonado. It is set in the seventeenth century and deals with issues of sexism. This play is taught in a feminist theater class in the State University of Rio Grande do Sul, Brazil. The professor, Márcia Hoppe Navarro, told him it was the only feminist play written by a man in Latin America that she has ever found (interview with Nájera).

Most of his early playwriting, beginning in the 1980s, is reminiscent of French playwrights around the time of World War II, such as Giraudoux, Anouilh, Cocteau, and Camus, and their expression of the fundamental absurdity of existence, death, violence, and horror. These common themes in French theater in the 1940s were often expressed using the classic Greek tragedies and myths "to give meaning and form to the shapeless mass of despair and confusion which was their common lot at this time" (Freeman 1971, 11). The canonized playwright most like Nájera is probably Albert Camus. Both focus on the violence, repression, and absurdity of the human condition, as well as on how individuals are haunted by their obsessions. E. Freeman claims that Camus's philosophical theater mirrors the metaphysical anguish of the age but avoids nihilism (164), which is applicable to Nájera's writing as well. He argues that Camus's plays are more authentically classical in form than those of his contemporaries because of his emphasis on the universal and symbolic implications. Freeman lists the qualities of Camus's plays: "elevated and unified tone, purity of language, minimization of physical detail and concentration upon theme to the exclusion of superfluous humour" (160). All of these qualities are trademarks of Nájera's work as well. However, Nájera's later works follow the French fashion of using "modernized" classical myths as a means of introducing a tragic metaphysic into the contemporary theater which Camus's theatre never did (Cruickshank 1970).

Nájera's *Clitemnestra ha muerto [Clytemnestra has died]* won first prize at the *Juegos Florales Centroamericanos* in Quetzaltenango (1991). He dedicated the play to Myrna Mack Chang, a British-educated anthropologist who conducted research on Guatemalans displaced by the counterinsurgency campaigns of the late 1970s and early 1980s. She had been under surveillance by the army because of the political nature of her work. In September 1990 Mack was stabbed to death with more than twenty-five wounds. The failure of the authorities to investigate her death drew outrage from the international community, many members of which believe the army was responsible for her murder. She has become an internationally known martyr and was used by the resistance movement as a symbol of the army's brutality.

Nájera knew Mack and describes the strong impact her death has had on his life. He dedicates the play to her memory because of her violent death. He writes, "*Mi principal preocupación, el sentimiento que me hizo redactar las primeras líneas de Clitemnestra . . . era la muerte violenta y la secuela de absurdo dolor que la sigue*" [My first preoccupation, the feeling that made me write the first lines of Clitemnestra . . . was the violent death with the result of absurd pain that follows] (87). But he rejects the idea of trying to make her a symbol in the war. He writes in his introduction:

> *El "amor que sigue doliendo después de la muerte" es un dolor personal, no colectivo, que se rehusa a ser parte de causas y movimientos. Más aún, no existe manisfestación artística que reivindique la memoria de una víctima de la violencia, política o no.*
>
> [The "love that keeps hurting after death" (quote from *Clitemnestra ha muerto*) is a personal pain, not a collective one, that refuses to be part of causes and movements. Moreover, there does not exist an artistic manifestation that recovers the memory of a victim of violence, political or not] (87).

Therefore, the play is neither a metaphor nor an allegory of the death of Mack in spite of the obvious correlation between her brutal stabbing death and that of Clitemnestra [*sic*]. Nájera's retelling of the tragedy of the Oresteia and the retribution of Clitemnestra's murder centers on the absurdity of the endless cycle of violence.

Nájera's Existentialist argument is central in the play: God is a construction that is manipulated by those in power in order to hide their obsessions. All values descend from humanity itself. War and vengeance are also human-made constructions that arise from muddled thinking. Humanity is caught in a cycle of violence because it cannot wake itself from the perception that it has suffered grave injustices, been cheated and abused. Nájera suggests that individuals have constructed a victim identity. This "false" identity holds that s/he (or one of the tribe) has been mistreated. Therefore, to honor the identity, s/he must extract vengeance. The other side responds in the same manner and the construction of the mistreatment continues to expand until the two sides can no longer see the common humanity of the others, but only the generic mask of the enemy. Forgiveness is anathema when the list of offenses has become the sacred canon by which the victim lives; one cannot forgive without sacrificing his/her identity. This cycle of violence is broken when (1) one recognizes the construction of the victim identity, or (2) one recognizes that s/he is as culpable for the cycle as the enemy. Nájera takes these abstract arguments to retell the story of the Oresteia. He tries to explain the absurd trap of violence into which Guatemala has fallen and to provide a potential road map for breaking the cycle.

In Nájera's version, the real Orestes died when he was a child. A *Pseudorestes* [Pseudo-Orestes] has been created by Electra. She has convinced a young boy named Lysias that he is Orestes and that he must fulfill his destiny of honoring their father. The entire play is a ritual "eternally repeated" which takes place *"en el mundo de las sombras; todos los personajes están muertos y se convocan cíclicamente para representar de nuevo sus vidas para ver si esta vez, al fin, Pílades convence a Orestes de que no es Orestes"* [in the world of the shadows; all of the characters are dead and cyclically are called together to represent again their lives in order to see if this time, finally, Pílades convinces Orestes that he is not Orestes] (90). The only possibility of ending this cycle of violence is if Pílades is successful in convincing Lysias that he is not Orestes. Pílades is the only one with clean hands and the objective perspective necessary to stop the cycle.

Nájera emphasizes that this tragedy takes place without gods and without the impositions of destiny. In this, he follows Camus who holds that all values come from humanity itself. Nájera does not believe that the crimes have a divine cause and states that the play is

> una metáfora extensa, dolorosa, oscura, de Guatemala. Su propósito no es aclarar sino proyectar la confusión. Al final importan poco las causas.... Lo único que permanece es el absurdo y la falta de sentido, el asqueo, el baño de sangre del que ninguno se salva. Las manos de Pílades, limpias, son una necesidad de romper el ciclo, de establecer que la única posibilidad de sobrevivir es no matar.

an extensive metaphor, painful and dark, about Guatemala. Its purpose is not to clarify but project the confusion. In the end the causes do not matter much.... The only thing that remains permanently is the absurdity and the lack of feeling, the disgust, the blood bath from which no one is saved. Pílades' clean hands are a necessity to break the cycle and to establish that the only possibility of survival is not to kill.] (88)

The play begins with the ritual murder of Clitemnestra. The chorus members, Eumenides 1, 2, and 3, state that destiny does not exist. They philosophize and comment on the action throughout, as well as grieve the cycle of violence. They state that in the depth of the cave of humanity an ambition is revealed that conspires against the light. This ambition invents its own logic, creating elaborate stories of torture/victimization in order to justify its crimes. The chorus laments the repetitive ritual killing of Clitemnestra which they explain occurs again and again: *"Muero con su muerte, muero por el odio y la ceguera que guían el puñal, muero por los universos de terror y de oscuridad que el hombre inventa"* [I die with her death, I die because of the hate and the blindness that guides the dagger, I die for the universes of terror and darkness that man invents] (95).

Orestes argues with Pílades that Clitemnestra's death was preordained and that he does not exist except as a puppet of destiny. Pílades tries to convince him that destiny does not exist, stating that the heavens are empty except for the grim intentions that people write on them. He argues that anyone who claims to speak in the name of the gods is really speaking in his own selfishness. Orestes lists Clitemnestra's numerous offenses and why the gods demand that she die. Pílades counters that the list was created by Electra. She transformed a young boy named Lysias into Orestes because she required an executioner. Orestes tells him to shut up, unable to admit his own voluntary involvement in the violence: *"Si yo no soy yo, si éste no es un acto de justicia, si ningún espíritu se mueve detrás del puñal, entonces pertenezco a las sombras para siempre y el crimen no tiene perdón"* [If I am not who I think I am, if this is not an act of justice, if no spirit moves behind the dagger, then I belong to the darkness forever and the crime does not have an excuse] (100). Pílades tries to absolve Orestes by making him realize that Electra has manipulated him and left him with the blame. He reminds the boy that both are guilty of the crime, but that she alone enjoys the victory. Orestes is the equivalent of the numerous foot soldiers who have been manipulated by their commanding officers on both sides of the struggle to wage the officers' battles.

Like Pílades, the chorus tries to get to the root cause of the conflict. They state that Helen is an absurd pretext for Menelao's [Menelaus's] war against Troy. Heroism is a false construction; it is "an invention by the poets" (104). The chorus elaborates the Existentialist argument to include murder and war: *"La causa de toda muerte es siempre un equívoco: el asesino acaba con un enemigo imaginario que otros le han inventado"* [The cause of all murder is always a mistake: the assassin ends the life of an imaginary enemy that others have invented] (105). The chorus concludes: *"El absurdo de la guerra es hijo del absurdo de la razón. Es en medio de la colectiva demencia que los dioses hablan"* (105). [The absurdity of war is the child of the absurdity of reason. It is the measure of the collective dementia that the gods speak of] (105).

Calkas convinces Agamemnon to sacrifice his daughter. He agrees to do so because of his own lust for Helen and his desire to keep his army occupied. Agamemnon complains about the lack of wind affecting the morale of his troops. *"El reposo es el peor enemigo del soldado; por eso, aun en tiempo de paz, los generales inventan enemigos inexistentes"* [Idleness is the worst enemy of the soldier; because of that, even in times of peace, the generals invent enemies that don't exist] (106).[13] Agamemnon is convinced by the high priest to sacrifice his daughter in order to invigorate his troops, even though he knows the gods are a construction. He states: *"Los dioses no existen, son fruto de la necesidad de suprimir la voluntad de los pueblos"* [The gods don't exist, they are the fruit of necessity to suppress the will of the people] (107).

Clitemnestra and Agamemnon's union is one of open hatred and distrust. She knows about Agamemnon's desire for Helen. Their extreme ruthlessness is expressed in their struggle over which daughter should be sacrificed. Clitemnestra is not willing to let her favorite daughter die and asks him to sacrifice Electra in her place. Agamemnon does not want his devoted daughter Electra to die because he wants her to honor his memory after he is gone. The children take on their parents' hatred. Electra has grown to hate Ifigenia [Iphigenia], Clitemnestra's favorite daughter, out of loyalty to Agamemnon who hates Clitemnestra. Obsessions of passion and power are presented as the root cause of hatred and conflict:

> *Clitemnestra. El odio es la inevitable secuela de toda pasión.* [Hatred is the inevitable result of all passion.]
> *Euménides 2 and 3. El odio es el hijo bastardo del poder.* [Hatred is the bastard son of power.]
>
> (116)

The Euménides are split on their reaction to the violence. One is excited about the spectacularly grand vengeance and the excitement and determination in the eyes of those that want to kill. Euménides 2 and 3 are appalled, arguing that the new death brings no new insights; the vengeance extracted will only bring more conflict. *Euménide 3: "La muerte sólo alimenta a la muerte, la conspiración se reproduce a sí misma"* [Death only feeds death, conspiracy reproduces itself] (120).

Pílades tries again to convince Orestes that the cycle of violence has all been a bad dream: *"Sueñas, eres el sueño de una torcida ambición de venganza que no era la tuya"* [Dream, you are the dream of a twisted ambition of vengeance that wasn't yours] (122). Pílades notes that even Agamemnon's soldiers are sick of the "erratic and monotonous" repetition of the parents using the children and the children killing the parents. He then changes his attack when Electra enters. She won't listen to Pílades when he confronts her with the truth that Orestes died years ago. She tells him that only her hatred is truthful. He accuses Electra of letting her desire for vengeance become pleasurable in itself. Electra states, *"¡Qué sabes tú de las convulsiones del placer! Sólo el poder las produce, no el amor"* [What do you know about the convulsions of pleasure! Only power produces it, not love] (124). Pílades confronts Electra with a mirror to see herself. She is shocked to recognize her mother's face in the mirror, the face she has learned to despise. She becomes hysterical, shouting that Clitemnestra has died. Pílades responds:

> *¡Clitemnestra no ha muerto, Clitemnestra no muere mientras Electra viva! ¡Ah! Tanto tiempo amamantando tu odio y olvidaste que Clitemnestra era tu madre, no sólo la asesina de tu padre. Aprendiste a abominar de cada rasgo, de cada expresión, de cada gesto,*

de cada mirada de Clitemnestra. Te concentraste tanto, Electra, que no reparaste en cuán parecida a ella te tornabas. . . . Ahora Electra es Clitemnestra, porque toda obsesión nos transforma en el objeto de la obsesión.

[Clitemnestra has not died, Clitemnestra won't die while Electra lives! Ah! So much time nursing your hatred, you forgot that Clitemnestra was not only your father's assassin, she was your mother. You learned to hate each of her features, each expression, each gesture, each look of Clitemnestra. You concentrated so hard, Electra, that you didn't notice when you became her. . . . Now Electra is Clitemnestra, because total obsession transforms us into the object of the obsession.] (126)

Electra realizes that Clitemnestra cannot die until her assassin has died. She proceeds to stab herself to death, releasing Orestes/Lysias from the imposed construction of his identity.

The epilogue by the chorus states that all of those who have died on both sides appear to have the same face in the end:

Euménide 1. Y el que odia se transforma en el objeto odiado. [He that hates is transformed into the object of hatred.]
Euménide 2. Todo homicidio es ilusorio . . . [All homicide is illusory. . . .]
Euménide 1. Nada soluciona la muerte. . . . Una muerte engendra la otra y la muerte es más fértil que la vida. [Death does not solve anything. . . . One death engenders another and death is more fertile than life.]
Euménides 2 and 3. El ciclo se rompe el día que el asesino se asesina a sí mismo. Los fantasmas se exorcizan con ese gesto banal, las sombras se disipan. [The cycle is broken the day the assassin kills himself. The phantoms are exorcised with this banal gesture, the shadows dissipate.] (127–28).

The Euménides state that the world will have to be reinvented and that the memory of men will have to be erased because all pain comes from memory. The spirits are worn out by the atrocities and long for a day when they might be over.

Euménide 3. Me he cansado de contemplar el paso de tantas sombras que emigran de la vida a la extinción, no por azar, sino por el equívoco temor de los hombres. ¿Es que esta especie nunca terminará de atormentarse a sí misma? [I am exhausted from contem-

plating the past of so many shadows that emigrated from life to extinction, not by chance but because of the mistaken fears of men. Will this species never stop tormenting itself?]
Euménide 1. Cuando sólo queden sobrevivientes, cuando los asesinos terminen de matarse entre sí. [Only when the survivors remain, when the assassins end by killing each other.] (128)

After I read the play, I asked Nájera questions about his work:

John: When you wrote the play in 1991 did you have any concerns about repercussions? Was the choice not to write "political plays" made because of not wanting to fall into the limited "protest" model? Was it an artistic choice to stay away from openly inflammatory material?
Rubén: No, repercussions were never in my mind with *Clitemnestra*. ... The play was presented in 1993. Even shortly after Myrna's [Mack] murder my major concern was with my other AVANCSO friends, who had been more related to her. By 1993, however, we were already living our second elect government and we were seven years away from the military—in a way, at least. At that time I was more disturbed by the fact that most people had appropriated Myrna's death in a way I had not always liked; a new Myrna had been invented by alleged friends and by people who, by pretending to pay homage to her, were only after some notoriety. I didn't want this to be my case, so I lowered the profile of the dedication of the play. My directors and actors, however, were fully aware of this and they even used some elements of her murder to develop their characters—but that was only a method, not propaganda.

Since my university years I became intoxicated with political and protest art. In the seventies that was the "official canon" of university students. I realized soon that, while pretending to defy, teach, criticize, mock, denounce the "enemy," this model, as you call it, was far from producing change, reflection, repentance, or even converts—it is designed for the consumption of those already convinced and, under the disguise of an "ideological" attack, it only serves purposes of catharsis, and self-delusion.

My conviction was that art is powerless to produce any change unless it becomes, in some way, universal—that is, unless it addresses more substantial issues. Contribution to social change, however, must be sought somewhere else. In my own limited way, I think my other activities have more to do with it than literature.

John: What is the significance of "Orestes" waking at the end as Lysias?
Rubén: Liberation, I suppose. Mine, I suppose.... It may be a metaphor of my coming into being, but also a sort of invitation for others to become themselves beyond social and religious machinations.
John: Could you explain to me the concept *"Todo homicidio es ilusorio. Cuando el cuerpo inerme exhala el último hálito y se desploma, es como si el objeto del homicidio estuviera ya en otra parte?"* [All homicide is illusory. When the inert body exhales its last breath and crumbles, it is as if the object of the homicide was already in another part] (127).
Rubén: Now, this is the atheist in me speaking. It may sound formulaic at the beginning—if there is no soul, then, the moment you kill the body everything in it stops existing and the murderer's object is no longer there. This may reflect my feeling that no matter how many deaths were accumulated throughout those years, nothing seemed to change, nothing seemed to have purpose, no ideological position seemed justified at all.

I have always had the idea that the human spirit has only two ways of surviving—through its works (e.g., art works) and through its reproduction in others' spirits. Therefore, once the murderer kills, the only thing that he achieves is the illusion of the killing. The spirit is, indeed, already elsewhere or nowhere—and the spirit being what defines man as human then the paradox is complete.
John: Do you see yourself in the position of Pílades in that there is no blood on your hands and your work may help break the cycle of violence as well—or what has been your journey/role through the years of violence?
Rubén: No, I am not that messianic. But I think that the only hope of breaking the cycle is people trying to go beyond violence as a solution. I think I am one of the survivors, like my Euménides—witnesses full of painful memories, walking among the corpses, between love and death. I do not think I have been an actor—though this is only accidental, a matter of chance, perhaps. Just a part of the audience—which does not mean I have not been involved by the suffering and the absurdities of the actors and the situations going on around me.

Clitemnestra ha muerto was written five years before the official end of the war. At this point, despite the atrocities and thirst for revenge, Nájera broadly portrays a powerful argument that the cycle of violence must end. His dramatization of the war as a humanly constructed enterprise deconstructs arguments justifying the continued struggle. He is one of the first to suggest the provocative concept that both sides have found a perverse pleasure in the violence which has helped to continue the insanity. Nájera highlights the depravity of the vampirish obsession for blood with contrasting attitudes toward violence. Most of the characters do not find the violence abhorrent, only tedious. The drama, written in 1991, reflects a country worn out, eager to pursue negotiation at any cost. Nájera bypasses the issue of who is right or wrong, who has the most blood on his/her hands. He avoids this topic because the issue of impunity involving past crimes in Guatemala threatened to bring the peace talks to a standstill. However, the issue arises again in Nájera's more recent work.

Nájera wrote a trilogy of loosely connected one-act plays entitled *Los dioses ausentes* [*The Absent Gods*] (1997–98) which he describes as three metaphors about Guatemala (1998, 51). The first one is entitled *Antígona* and centers on the relationship between two sisters. One sister, Romelia, represents Guatemala's past and Emilia, the other sister, represents the future. Emilia has returned home to find her sister in the house. Their father, who had molested them both, is dead and rotting inside the house.

Romelia continually accuses her sister of having abandoned her and their father and tries to get her to stay home with her. Emilia insists that they bury their dead father or the sickness will spread. Romelia would rather just seal up his room and try to forget the past. She says, *"Es importante olvidar el pasado, para que no se convierta en una pesadilla"* [It is important to forget the past so that it doesn't turn into a nightmare] (4). Emilia responds, *"No basta con enterrarlo para olvidarlo, no basta con cerrar las habitaciones para silenciar las voces del pasado. El pasado está aquí, adentro de nosotras"* [It's not enough to bury it in order to forget it, it's not enough to close the rooms in order to silence the voices of the past. The past is here, inside of us] (4). Romelia remains determined to keep things closed, such as the gate which opens to the outside or a trunk where the father kept all the "answers." The sisters' struggle over whether to keep things buried or to uncover them is symbolic of the struggle over the Truth Commission's decision to make public a list of atrocities committed during the war. After the Peace Accord, the commission had to decide what crimes to reveal and what cases to investigate, which has created great turmoil for the country.[14] Some argue that it created more conflict and that it would be better to forget the past and move on. Others argue that the only way to advance and begin to heal the communal trauma is to make specific atrocities public knowledge.

Romelia says that she often looks out into the orchard where they had buried other family members and tries to guess who is under each unmarked tomb.[15] There are numerous unmarked graves in the play, which suggests, of course, the many unmarked graves in Guatemala because of the violence.[16]

Emilia demands that they open the trunk: *"El encerró nuestras vidas ahí adentro, en ese pedazo de papel. Luego nos abandonó aqui, para siempre"* [He buried our lives inside, on that piece of paper. Then he abandoned us here forever] (5). Romelia refuses to accept this idea, declaring instead that the father protected them. Emilia realizes that through his tyrannical control of their lives, he had constructed their identities, fear of the outside world, and morbid obsession with death. She says: *"El nos inventó. Estuvo bien mientras creímos en él. Pero tú dudaste, por un instante dudaste, Romelia, y todo terminó para él"* [He invented us. It was fine while we believed in him. But you doubted, for only an instant you doubted, Romelia, and everything ended for him] (10). Nájera explains this line: "The tyrant remains alive as long as there is at least one who still believes in him. With Emilia far away, the tyrant's life was terribly fragile—one doubt could kill him" (interview).

When Emilia finally opens the trunk, it is filled only with dust. She states, *"Tu cofre está vacío y no hay motivo para que permanezcamos aquí"* [Your treasure chest is empty and there is no reason for us to stay here] (12). She tells her sister to stay if she wants to but that she is going to go outside the family compound. She invites Romelia to come with her but she is frozen with fear. Romelia describes her nightmare of leaving the home filled with horrible worms, slugs, and rats. She cannot bring herself to open up to the outside world. In the last scene Emilia returns with a lover. The lover is uneasy about Romelia watching them make love, but Emilia, dominating the situation, assures him that she is just a shadow, that they are alone. She continues to seduce him. The ending image of Romelia watching her sister have sex with a stranger suggests that her sister is going to continue to haunt Emilia, an ever present shadow over her life. There is no clear indication that the lover, possibly a one-night-stand, is going to permanently improve the situation. He may be pulled down into the mire of this home. However, the ending with the couple making love in the bed that had held the corpse of the father is a regenerative image. Emilia actively takes control of her life and is determined to shape her destiny in spite of Romelia's comatose state.

The following is an excerpt from an interview with Nájera about *Los dioses ausentes*:

John: In what ways are the images metaphors for Guatemala?
Rubén: Almost immediately the image flashed in my mind: two women, one old, one young, disputing around a body. I thought that was the allegory of Guatemala (that was happening just before the Peace Agreements), torn between past and future, unable to bury the dead.... They would have Greek titles and they would refer to things "absent" or denied in the Guatemalan social landscape. *Antígona* was the denial of death; *Orpheus* would be a descent into hell signifying the denial of identity; *Endimión*, referred to, as I told you, Goethe's Endimión in *Faust's* second part, [which] was to be the denial of violence.

John: Why the image of making love mixed with images of death? Outside the gates seem to be filled with images of worms and rats as if the inside of the house is a coffin. Romelia is afraid to go outside—why?
Rubén: Everything within this house without windows is promiscuous. That is my perception of Guatemala's forty and so years of violence. Relations are at the same time hate and love; death and life are difficult to tell apart—and then outside is the unknown, the perception of a death worse than the immediate obvious death inside. It is a delusion, indeed. Out of habit we have learned to live with dead bodies, with hidden tombs in the garden. It is not that we are afraid of dying, we just deny the fear every other moment because that's the only way to survive. And then, to justify our remaining inside, we have to invent a darker world outside.

John: Why does Romelia think all of the answers will be found after the father died? Emilia tries to break into the coffin to dig up the past for justification—why?
Rubén: Romelia may have thought that while he was alive, but now that he is dead she has contradictory feelings about wanting to know because she already knows but knows she won't be able to

live with the truth (the truth being something like there is another better world and there is a future). Emilia wants to understand but is not willing to do it by herself—she needs something or someone to tell her. I don't think they really expect or fear to find the truth—they are tormenting each other in order not to learn the truth, to remain the same.

The second play of the trilogy, *Orfeo [Orpheus]*, details the life of a man in higher academia who has been cut off from his ancestral roots. He is forced to write books to "jump through the hoops" and keep his position in the never-ending intellectual mill. He is devastated to discover that his modern life is empty and cut off from meaningful communication compared to the tribal way of life he has recently studied.

The third one-act is entitled *Endimión*. The play takes place on an empty shore with a broken-down group of circus entertainers. Their beloved friend and leader Endimión has disappeared. Etan, a lion tamer, is mourning the loss of his friend while the couple Blondel and Eno dance and play the violin in order to forget the past. Eno states that he longs to fly. Etan tells him, *"Para volar, para volar de verdad, tienes que estar más allá de los engaños"* [In order to fly, to really fly, you have to be far from the lies] (2). Etan believes that Endimión knew how to fly before he disappeared. Etan wishes that he had the ability to forget like Eno and Blondel. Eno offers to forget for him. Etan responds:

Gracias, Eno. Hay cosas que no puedes hacer por los demás. La expiación es un mito. Pero tal vez Blondel tiene razón y basta con quedarse y callar o cantar o bailar. Cada uno en su mundo. La impresión de que lo compartimos es mera ilusión. Solo compartimos nuestro temor de Golo."

[Thanks, Eno. But there are things you can't do for others. Atonement is a myth. But perhaps Blondel is right and it's enough to stay here and to be silent, or to sing, or to dance. Each one in his own world. The impression that we share is a mere illusion. We only share our fear of Golo.] (4)

Golo is a tyrant who has terrorized them, destroyed the circus, and led them to this beach. He has been sleeping during the first half of the play. When he wakes from his drunken slumber he terrorizes the small band of players, making them call him Lord. He beats them with a whip and threatens to rape Blondel. Etan finally stands up to him: *"Nos has aterrorizado desde siempre. . . . Tu terror era tolerable. Pero poco a poco creció y destruiste a los niños y ahuyentaste a los payasos y quemaste las jaulas y esto es todo lo que nos queda. Un desierto. Un mar que no tiene naves"* [You have always terrorized us. . . . Your terror used to be tolerable. But little by little it grew and you destroyed the children and scared away the clowns and burned the cages and this is all that is left for us. A desert. A sea without ships] (10). Etan forces a confession out of Golo that he killed Endimión. Envious of Endimión, Golo shot him the moment he started to rise off the ground to fly. Etan assures the group that he is not dead: *"Cuando sabes volar, las balas son inútiles"* [When you know how to fly, bullets are useless] (15). Etan tells the group that Endimión is waiting for them on the other side and that there is hope.

John: *Endimon* seems consciously reminiscent of Samuel Beckett's *Waiting for Godot* although much more optimistic. There are similar themes of grotesque characters from a circus without a circus tent on the edge of the shore, the strong hierarchy, the oppressive relationships, the sense that time used to have meaning but now Etan says *"Es bueno tener corta la memoria cuando los días son tan largos y tan parecidos y tan vacíos."* [It's good to have to cut the memory when the days are so long and so similar and so empty.] This band of misfits without a purpose, and in this case, an audience. This makes me wonder after this country has gone through tremendous trauma similar to that of Europe after the wars, if there is a parallel to be drawn in terms of the existential message of God being absent? Yet, in your writing, hope and faith are underneath the despair and confusion, as if the ugliest dictator, the most tragic path a country could take, would never be able to kill the inherent beauty of life forever. It's as if the hope/desire for a better life is eternal and continues within us, but when we lose sight of that a crippling fear takes over us.

Rubén: Beckett is not a part of my culture at all. . . . It is also, you are right, my own feeling with regard to this country—I was born in an age of violence, I have lived through it, I am a survivor, I love life. I am very rational, anyway, and have always considered myself a "not militant atheist." Gods are absent in all my writings except as a man-made creation . . . all values come from man/woman and there are no values superior to him/her.

John: Etan does not respect or fear authority for himself and is looking for leverage to force a confession out of Golo. Why was Golo determined to kill the light—was it out of envy of Endimión?
Rubén: Golo is perhaps the best allegory/metaphor for most people I have known throughout my life. He summarizes them—spiritual sloths, personifications of ugliness. They are the real murderers of our society, for no other reason than their inability to be otherwise. It reflects my own pessimism. Etan knows the truth from the beginning of course. He is denying it, too. . . . The truth? Saint Exupery has been a great influence on me and he would have answered something like "the truth is that we all can fly but more often than not get shot for trying to."

Conclusion

Clearly, Osorio's protest-oriented work does not fit easily into the concept of reconciliation. Yet, some of it, such as the happening in the Central Plaza with the cow blood, is theater of atrocity in terms of its representation of atrocities committed during the war. His work pays homage to victims of the war, seeks to educate, and raises moral questions. Osorio and Corleto's provocative works suggest that the anti-Establishment protest model is capable of encouraging people to reflect upon the war even though it does not follow the trend of reconciliation.

Both Osorio's group and Corleto's Theater of the Absurd seem to enjoy perplexing, provoking, and offending the spectators' sensibilities. They are on the edge of the *mestizo* theater and use their avant-garde position as nonconformists to challenge the status quo. Reconciliation and support of the community is not their primary goal. They seek to break through the layers of fear and hypocrisy to expose the facades and power struggles that are the root cause of the war. They both focus on the individual and on the fragmentation caused by the war. Osorio's group creates an us/them model to protest the apathy of mainline society, which permitted the civil war in the first place and created such an intolerable situation for the individual. Corleto's work encourages the individual to confront his/her fears. Nevertheless, Osorio's group is seeking to help individuals process the devastating effects of the war and to empower new artists to express it; Corleto's writing encourages reflection on the war. This suggests that the healing potential of the arts is much more vast and complex than the trend of mainline theater this study identifies.

Nájera also writes of individual liberation and challenges the tyrannical societal pressure to conform. However, Nájera's primary purpose is to teach conflict resolution and offer hope. His plays use metaphors to portray the violence, yet his optimistic perspective suggests that healing is possible; reconciliation is attainable. Corleto's play *La Café* reminds society of the vital contribution of artists as social critics as well as creators of beauty and integrity in society. His work in the Theater of the Absurd raises moral questions through its images of recurring exploitation. Both Nájera and Corleto use their symbolism to portray the vicious circle of war. However, Nájera's writing inspires the community with the possibility of ending the violence. Corleto's work uses pessimistic humor to portray a bleak, ridiculous world that only liberates the individual. He raises issues of the war through the via-negativa, expecting the individual to draw conclusions about the absurdity of war and the challenge of developing a nonviolent, nonrepressive environment in a twisted world.

The symbolic works in this chapter reflect myriad expressions about the war. They range from highly intellectual to irrational, hopeful to pessimistic, volatile and provocative to melancholic and wistful. One of the few common elements in these pieces is the fact that they use powerful images to evoke a reaction from the spectator and confront her/him with the innumerable psychological, emotional, and spiritual challenges a long civil war raises.

6
Conclusion

THE THEATER IS AS RESILIENT AS THE HUMAN SPIRIT IT REFLECTS. The resiliency is especially striking in Guatemalan theater. It has survived various waves of openness and repression, but continues to portray Guatemalans' journey, mirroring the hopes, fears, and traumas of a people. The theater artists have persevered in depicting Guatemalan reality in spite of the numerous political and social obstacles. Tyrannical forces have never been able to permanently silence the creative force. Like the phoenix, it has arisen twice in the twentieth century from the ashes of repression. Humanity's need for unity, reconciliation, and identity in a shared past has ensured theater's survival.

When a communal traumatic event such as a war occurs, there is an emotional, intellectual, and spiritual wound that begs (often subconsciously) to be healed. If it is not addressed, it will continue to fester and drain the energy of the body politic. Lawrence Langer posits that the theater artist in the aftermath of unmitigated violence has the unsolicited responsibility to confront the people with the catastrophe. Langer argues that the theater of atrocity shifts the "focus from renewal to decay" (1978, 4) where a community must fight a rearguard action rather than speculate about the future. In Guatemala, however, the theater in the 1990s reflects on the decay and past wounds in order to create the future. Ariel Dorfman's question, "How do we keep the past alive without becoming its prisoner?" (1992, 78), can only be answered when one's overreaching goal is a healthier future. The theater expresses Guatemalans' hope for renewal by looking at the past. Rather than being haunted by their traumatic history, their theater pushes the painful issues forward to center stage in order that the vicious circle of old hatreds and grudges not hold them prisoner.

Every play in this study, from satire to tragedy, suggests breaking free from the bars that entrapped the country in violence and warns about repeating the past. The key to release from the cycle of violence is portrayed as remembering without blaming.

In Dorfman's question, "How to confront these issues without destroying the national consensus, which creates democratic stability?" (1992, 78), one recognizes the motive of the playwrights in the 1990s testing the political waters tenuously yet persistently. The transformation of the kind of plays written and produced since the 1980s suggests the theater artists' attempt to walk the fine line: to confront without polarizing the national consensus. The plays written and presented during the 1980s, such as Jorge Godínez's *Electro show* and *La consigna*, emphasized powerlessness to stop the escalating violence and to escape pain. The cure Godínez suggested was to confront reality and feel the pain. The introduction of the commercial satires in the early 1990s confronted the public with the harsh reality in a humorous manner. The political and analogical satires brought up painful and often taboo subjects, encouraging the healing energy of laughter. Dick Smith comments on how the people left the theater healthier and happier after watching the imitation of Ríos Montt. Likewise, the healing impact of the following commercial satires encouraged people to move beyond the tyranny of the armed conflict. If the satiric movement is going to stay as spirited, the satirists will have to continue pushing the envelope and unearth sensitive topics. One wonders, will the satirists continue to capitalize on provocative topics in a detached, intellectual manner as they have in the 1990s? Satires have much more edge during periods of mild repression according to Griffin. It will be interesting to see whether the satires retain their immense popularity if more political stability is attained. Humor not only is an acceptable outlet for hostility, it also has a healing impact on the psyche of the audience which changes the tension and reduces anxiety. According to Robin Haig, humor enables one to accept his/her situation. Therefore, a communal experience, such as theater, enables a people to accept their situation collectively. The theater offers the comfort that they are not alone in facing the horrors of the past and creating a safe place for healing. This type of theater does not suggest that the people can actively change the system. It simply suggests that they are not alone as they attempt to confront the crisis.

The humorous critiques opened the door for more emotionally engaging material in the didactic and symbolic plays. The didactic plays continued to dig deeper into the painful factual history of the war. The popular didactic theater has shone a light on the past, enabling a tremendous cathartic release. The plays force the audience to grapple with different layers of pain and grief concerning the war. The audience empathizes with both perpetrators and victims as the protagonists struggle to get out of the vicious circle of violence. The postatrocity audience's profound need to process the past emotionally and grieve the losses is addressed most profoundly in the didactic theater.

The symbolic plays confronted the issues of the war in contrasting images, rituals, and symbols. They pushed beyond intellectual and emotional reflection and encouraged metaphysical contemplation. Through Theater of the Absurd, Dadaism, and Existentialism, these works confront the individual with the nightmare of a chaotic world in order to get them to accept the depth of the moral and philosophical collapse.

Using theater to process horrific events is not unique to Guatemala. Last month I went to the Denver Center Theater to see *The Laramie Project*, dealing with the aftermath of Matthew Shepherd's torture and eventual death. Two young men took Shepherd in their car, tied him to a fence post, severely beat him (allegedly because he was gay), robbed him, and left him to die on the back roads of Laramie. As I was in the audience, I realized this was an example of the didactic docu-theater I speak about in chapter 4. The purpose of *The Laramie Project* is to heal a community and nation shocked, angered, and saddened over an atrocious murder. Hate crimes such as this one stir up communal outrage that festers and has little outlet. Seeing the men responsible for Shepherd's death sentenced does not enable us to comprehend and process the systemic hatred and violence which is complicit in their hideous act. Nor does the jury's verdict alone allow us to recognize our own individual role in perpetuating hate crimes. Like the Guatemalan theater I have discussed, the purpose of *The Laramie Project* is to help us make meaning: make sense of our culture, grieve over our losses, and laugh at our shortsightedness; and to inspire us to grow in our humanity.

The Laramie Project was created from interviews with people living in Laramie, Wyoming, where Shepherd had been living and going to college. The actors impersonated the people they had interviewed in order to portray how the entire town had grappled with the communal responsibility of Shepherd's death. I found this didactic docudrama, which emphasized the change this young man's death had on a community, to be personally healing. I came to the play still angered over the senseless death and left feeling Shepherd had not died in vain. It gave me renewed hope that we were moving forward as a nation as we grapple with our pain, anger, and prejudices. The constructed ideology of the play offered hope that his death has served as a catalyst for communal reflection in the town as well as for the public the play reaches. Through describing in detail Shepherd's last hours of life and impersonating the remorse and grief of a town, a new sense of harmony and balance was achieved. The audience stood on its feet and cheered not only for the brilliant performances and ingenious construction of the text, but for the gift the actors were offering: confronting us with our unresolved emotions toward this incident. The blending perspectives from the actors as well as the people from the town enabled us to process the incident in a larger national context.

I bring up this lengthy description of my experience with "healing didactic theater" in order to highlight the relevance of the plays in this study. As I was reading the Guatemalan plays with numerous topical references, I often found myself judging some of them as lacking "universality." I would judge the satires as "too broad" or the didactic plays as "melodramatic," favoring the symbolic pieces. I often forgot the purpose the theater was serving in offering hope and regeneration. I had to remind myself of the courage it took to mount the political satires in a country where artists have routinely been silenced, threatened, and killed. In chapter 4 I found myself calling "manipulative" some of the melodramatic "flaws" in the plays that brought a cathartic experience to many Guatemalans' hearts because I did not have the same emotional need to process the atrocities. Therefore, I could not appreciate the play's emotional style. I begin to understand the significance

6: CONCLUSION

only when I engage my imagination to use analogies from my own life, such as the play about the death of Matthew Shepherd. Admittedly, as my opening analogy was unable to portray the level of violence Guatemala had experienced, so too my attempt to parallel *The Laramie Project* and the plays dealing with Guatemala's civil war is inadequate. Clearly, the need for solace and understanding must be multiplied exponentially after a war that has ravaged one's country. One man's death cannot begin to capture the fear and chaos of the conflict in Guatemala.

If I want to begin to understand the healing purpose these plays have served for Guatemala, then perhaps my "objective" esthetic judgment needs to be put into check. This study has challenged me to think about the criteria I use to judge plays. I tend to set the artistic structure higher than the social function of the work, valuing "universality" over topical references. Some of the plays in this study have an inherently short life span. Most will not be deemed worthy to be translated into other languages or ever play outside of Guatemala. Yet, I believe they are significant. They document a transitional time in the life of a country as the people strive to cope and find meaning. The symbolic plays challenge us to recognize the complexity of war, reconciliation, and human culpability in a godless universe. The satiric plays are shocking in their blunt treatment of the violence, yet noble and daring for broaching the topic. The didactic plays offer the perspective of communal hope that life still has meaning in spite of the atrocity.

Solórzano writes that the post–World War II Latin American drama signals a return to universal ideas from local and national ones. After the horrors of the war, there is a search for a new moral order; the theater serves to regenerate humankind. In post–civil war Guatemala, theater seeks to create a national identity rather than universal insight. It is a theater that unifies the people in their struggle to find a more harmonious nation, encourages reflection on the violent past, and promotes the possibility of healing. It is an era that seeks yet again to identify "a new moral order and to use theater to regenerate humankind" (Solórzano 73).

Westlake argues that Galich set the action of the play *El tren amarillo* in the 1920s so that the audience would understand the inevitable outcome of the events of the revolution of 1944. She writes:

> The performance strives to resolve the tension between the ruptures of history, most notably ruptures of national revolution, and the continuity required for legitimization. The cure is to create a sense that the past was inevitable in order to reach where we are today. (1997, 228)

Likewise, the emphasis on the past horrors of the civil war is necessary to resolve the tension and fear as authorities and peasants, military men and students, indigenous and *ladino*, embark on a more peaceful coexistence. As I have shown, theater in the 1990s suggests that the end of the war was either inevitable or highly preferable to the past indiscriminate violence. Sacrifice and suffering is not meaningless in this construction; it has served a purpose. From this perspective, the victims did not die in vain. This perspective (constructed to offer security and solace) is "manipulative," as was *The Laramie Project*. The underlying ideology has been constructed to offer hope to a people who are wrestling with difficult issues. This perspective suggests that even the worst atrocity has a silver lining.

One can perceive this period of reconciliation in the theater of the 1990s either as healing or as an illusion, an "opiate of the people" to coerce the masses. The illusion argument states that the theater has been co-opted by the government to support the hegemonic ideology. Therefore, the playwrights who write plays that promote peace to audiences longing for a silver lining are choosing the easy nonconfrontative path of "selling out." (This is an especially complex argument in *mestizo* theater which claims to incorporate the voice of the oppressed indigenous groups while having vested interest in the dominant ideology.) The underlying drive in this argument is anger at the perceived injustice.

I favor the healing argument which acknowledges that the manipulation of history is inevitable; the sense of security suggested in the construction of hope or manipulation of the silver lining may foster a more positive reflection on the past. It constructs the idea that the war was not in vain because it has forced the nation to confront its racial and class prejudices.

6: CONCLUSION

This argument offers the possibility that if the citizens act wisely and learn from the past, the future may be less fraught with conflict. Therefore, the question posed in the plays is how to encourage confrontation of the past that will not simply repeat the stalemate. The underlying drive is hope for a more harmonious existence in a wounded country.

As stated earlier, I disagree with the premise that a theater supported by the state cannot also represent the people. Clearly, it is restrictive to be doing the balancing act of reconciliation/atrocity. This tightrope walk of keeping one eye on the past atrocities and the other on the present reconciliation is risky. Admittedly, the people's voice is more restrained and censored now than during the "Golden Age" of theater of the 1960s and the 1970s when there was great freedom of rage. However, Rubén Nájera, Dick Smith, and Adolofo Hernández Sol point out that the "Golden Age" of denouncing the Establishment was a form of self-delusion and not effective in terms of political-social transformation. The agitprop works were only preaching to the converted. I believe the current mainstream theater seeks to be more fairly balanced and therefore more inclusive. It promotes healing as well as the possibility for dialogue. Yet this is speculative. Only time will tell. The devastation of the war will continue to unfold slowly as Guatemalans continue to reflect on their individual role in the war through the mirror of reality on the stage.

This book has several implications for further study in Latin American theater studies. One is to learn if the attempt to create a nationalist theater by reconciliation/atrocity has occurred in other countries as well. Has the revolutionary zeal identified in Latin American theater studies which demands a radical social transformation reached its end? Or is this study simply identifying a hiatus in Guatemalan politics as the democratic government becomes stabilized? Clearly, the protest model prevalent in the "Golden Age" of Guatemalan theater continues in Dadaist-inspired works by José Osorio and his troupe of actors. Ten years from now it will be interesting to discover whether or not the dominant trend remains, that is, reflecting on the atrocities committed during the war. More than fifty years have passed since World War II and Holocaust plays are still being written. Plays, movies, and musicals are still being written on the Civil War in the U.S. more than a century later. If the civil war in Guatemala has had the impact these other events in history have had, one would expect this theme to be played out for generations.

This study may also encourage further documentation of unpublished works in other Central American countries, including studies on indigenous theater. More in-depth studies will enrich future Latin American theater studies as they reveal similarities and differences among the different nations. In Guatemala, more in-depth studies on the volumes of works by Hugo Carrillo, Víctor Hugo Cruz, Manuel Corleto, and Manuel José Arce would also provide insights for cross-cultural studies with Guatemala. I wanted to write a study on Rubén Nájera's work, but decided a more general overview of Guatemalan theater in the 1990s needed to be written first. I will be interested in following Nájera's career. His talent seems to be undervalued in his own country. His work merits international attention and could play dramatically in numerous different locations because of his emphasis on universal issues.

Although Latin American theater studies is a relatively small field, I think it would be helpful to focus on the smaller countries as well and their contribution to the theatrical field. These studies may encourage more cross-pollination of theater artists from various countries as the Latin American theater festivals have done since the early 1960s. Some of the plays in this study could easily be translated into English and performed successfully in the United States. It is very common for plays from the United States to be translated into Spanish and performed in Guatemala. It would be beneficial for both countries if this exchange were a two-way street where we might begin to hear the Guatemalan voice.

Writing this study has forced me to grapple with my own anger and sadness over my country's involvement in the war. Clinton's apology in March 1999 for the role the U.S. played in their violence and widespread repression was a breakthrough. However, it is only a first step in the long road of healing the international relationship. I went to a lecture last month on the "Holocausts of Central America." Ironically, I still found myself feeling defensive when the speaker (a Maryknoll priest who was forced to leave Guatemala in the 1960s because of his political solidarity with the poor) stated that the U.S. has a de facto army in Guatemala. I wanted to argue with him that just because we overthrew their elected government, taught them techniques in torture and war, knew about the acts of genocide and torture committed by the army, and have continued to support their military financially does not mean that the atrocities committed were done by our army. I was surprised by my defensive attitude (not to mention my weak logic). It made me wonder if the plays that I have argued are so distant from my North American perspective are really that foreign. My ethnocentric bias (read provincial defensiveness) may have made the plays seem more foreign than they really are. Why do Guatemalans continually adapt our plays but we never (or very rarely) adapt theirs? Why are they able to adapt to our cosmological perspective and we cannot adapt to theirs? A two-way street of artistic exchange would benefit the U.S. greatly in recognizing how our vested interests have perpetuated atrocities. But perhaps the U.S. would rather ignore the Guatemalan's reality. If so, it will be to our great impoverishment.

Notes

1. Introduction

1. I owe a large debt to my sister, Sandra Shillington Lopez, who has a master's degree in Spanish translation, and to her native Spanish husband, Toni Lopez, for their editing assistance.

2. Two days after Clinton's apology the Guatemalan National Revolutionary Unity, the leftist rebels who had fought the government, also issued a statement asking for forgiveness from the victims, their families, and communities. As of this writing the army has yet to apologize.

3. The dramatic works in chapter 3 mirror the European existentialism movement in postwar theater and suggest that the war in Guatemala may have shifted the perspective from the social-political inequalities Albuquerque cites to a belief in a world governed by irrationality. Yet I am wary of this analogy because it may be misconstrued to suggest that postwar Central America is following in Europe's "more advanced" footsteps.

4. Taylor posits that all theater of atrocity is a theater of crisis but not vice versa. Theater of crisis deals with all types of violence such as the subtlety of racial and sexual violence. She understands Langer's "aesthetics of atrocity" to express only the unmitigated horror of overt violence (1991, 54). The Guatemalan plays in this study all deal with the overt violence of the civil war. Her definition becomes muddled when she states that the theater of the Holocaust has a strong sense of direction which should exclude it (as a subgroup of the theater of atrocity). I define theater of atrocity as encompassing expressions of profound chaos and uncertainty. However, Guatemalan theater portrays atrocity to incite communal shock, outrage, and condemnation of violence in order to suggest that the only sane path to take is toward stability.

5. The *mestizo* theater is the voice of the *ladino* and should not be confused with the indigenous theater. The plays in this study often claim to side with the indigenous and portray their plight sympathetically. Therefore, the perspective of the war is portrayed by the dominant class and not by the group of people most profoundly affected by the war. Often theater artists described their frustration in not being able to reach an indigenous audience or find indigenous actors because of social and cultural barriers.

6. These actors perform Sophocles and Shakespeare as well as Ionesco.

2. History of Twentieth-Century Guatemalan Theater

1. This law, which enabled an officer to shoot a prisoner in the back, has been portrayed in numerous plays in Guatemala, including Manuel José

Arce's *Arbenz: El Coronel de la primavera*, Jorge Ramírez and Douglas González Dubón's *El General no tiene quien lo inscriba*, J. Orellana's *En los cerros de ilóm*, and Huelga de dolores's *El Paabanc*. The plays portray this law as a ploy to kill prisoners with impunity. When an officer wants to kill a prisoner, he tells him he is free to go and then shoots him in the back.

2. Perera argues that this law was responsible for planting the seeds of Mayan resistance and led to the formation of the first peasant unions under President Arévalo and Arbenz after the revolution of 1944.

3. I write "liberation" in quotes because most of the playwrights I interviewed referred to it as anything but liberation. Two of them referred to it as the time the U.S. shat on Guatemala. However, "shat on" is still not the official version of the coup. Cerezo's government in the early 1990s was the first to publicly acknowledge the positive accomplishments of President Arbenz. For the first time since his overthrow in 1954, the press portrayed Arbenz as patriotic rather than "communist sympathizer" as all regimes had done since liberation. Perera writes, "The ten-year 'Guatemalan Spring' of 1944–1954 returned to haunt the country with visions of what might have been if Arbenz's agrarian revolution had been permitted to run its course" (1993, 294).

4. There are numerous examples of family members being beaten, raped, and killed in front of other members by the army in order to intimidate or get information. One unforgettable story is of soldiers cutting open a pregnant woman and playing "ball" with the fetus in front of her family (Perera 1993, 112).

5. The stereotype of a "stupid, stubborn Indian" is very common in numerous plays, including Maria Eugenia Gallardo's *El jurado de las cuatro grandes* and Douglas González Dubón's *Vida, pasión y muerte de un pueblo* and *Romeyo Subuyey and Julieta Piri*.

6. Arce also wrote and produced *Arbenz: El Coronel de la primavera* while in exile in France, mirroring Galich's experience of writing and producing *El Tren amarillo* while in exile. Arce's play is a long historical epic drama focusing on General Ubico's misuse of power and the United States support of his bloody regime, Arbenz's brief but significant contribution to the people, and the United States staging of the 1954 coup. I obtained the script through his friend Roberto Díaz Gomar who helped stage the production while also living in exile. Díaz Gomar was in the original production of *Delito, condena y ejecución de una gallina* in the unforgettable role of Chicken Number Two (interview).

7. Originally from Oklahoma, Dick Smith began his career in community theater in Guatemala in the early 1960s, directing and acting in mostly foreign plays. He later became a leading figure in the theater movement directing apolitical foreign plays in Spanish, such as bedroom farces and musicals.

8. Hugo Carrillo wrote *Las orgias sagradas de Maximon* [*The Sacred Orgies of Maximon*] in 1992 and produced the play in Argentina under the direction of Guatemalan Xavier Pacheco. Carrillo felt the play was too strong to produce in Guatemala (Dreyer 1994, 186). Pacheco plans to produce the play in Guatemala in 2000 (interview). This play suggests that the conflict between Christianity and an indigenous cult religion is representative of the conflicts in society, and that they are eternally incompatible. According to

this indigenous religion, a leader who desires unrestricted power needs to have his genitals bathed in the blood of a fetus from a virgin. The play draws the parallel between the abusive power of Spanish conqueror Don Pedro de Alvarado, a current fictional president who hides his ruthlessness behind the facade of benevolence, and the dark god Maximon. The president seeks to embody Maximon's dark power through this bathing ritual. He arranges for a pregnant Indian to be sacrificed secretly and have her body disappear without a trace so that he can maintain the image of the government respecting democracy and human rights. *"Debo mantener la imagen que en mi gobierno se respetan la democracia y los derechos humanos"* ["I must maintain the image that my government respects democracy and human rights"] (19). He sells the remaining body parts of the pregnant Indian to a North American businessman. This disturbing pessimistic play critiques the abuse of power which has become embedded in the culture and has continued unabated for five hundred years.

3. Satiric Theater

1. The sociopolitical upheaval experience is unique and is represented in "nonuniversal" satires. It is difficult to imagine satires in the U.S. trying to satirize atrocities such as the massacre in Littleton, Colorado. This is a complex issue which may suggest it is a different cultural sense of humor. I would argue that Guatemala's satiric portrayal of the atrocities such as the massacres suggests a level of institutional violence which has profoundly affected the psyche of a nation.

2. Ramírez, after his ten years of unprecedented financial success in the theater, has decided to move his theater group to a new location in a neighborhood more affluent and safe. Here they plan to run *La Epopeya de las Indias Españolas* with other revivals in repertory. He took me to the new theater which is a converted movie theater in Zone 11 in the capital. I do not think this space will work for him as well as the National Theater and IGA's theater had worked for his plays. The new theater is long and narrow. I saw several of his productions during the 1990s. The communion between the masterful comic timing of the actors and the ecstatic audience was extraordinary. The theater structure felt intimate and supported the close interaction of the audience in the 400-seat house with the actors. The gales of laughter from the audience and their sense of unity as they recognized their unstable political reality being lampooned on stage was an unforgettable experience in the theater for me.

3. I remember reading the national newspaper *Siglo XXI (21st Century)* which changed its title to *Siglo XIV (14th Century)* the following morning after President Serrano's auto-coup suggesting that the country had reverted back to the dark ages. Nothing was printed on the first page in protest of his censorship of the news.

4. When I spoke with González, he was running for political office. I asked him his opinion about the infamous General Ríos Montt (discussed at length later in this chapter) who had not been allowed to run for president.

My jaw dropped when he told me the general was a good friend of his. Somehow I had never imagined the larger-than-life figure of Ríos Montt as having friends.

5. All the black and white "harsh reality" photography in this book of Guatemalans—from a fourteen-year-old male prostitute to the children called *basurero ratóns [trash rats]* scavenging at the municipal dump—are taken by professional photographer Daniel Chauche. He was my next-door neighbor in Antigua, Guatemala, and took color publicity photos for my productions of Neil Simon and Oscar Wilde comedies. It is a shocking contrast.

6. Ramírez is a brilliant comic and a very warm, fun-loving individual. He states that he does not have a political agenda to push; he simply loves to make people laugh. His theory is that anything can be humorous depending on the execution.

7. Ramírez plays with the prefix for death (necropolis) rather than metropolis.

8. President Arbenz's land reforms in the early 1950s is the central issue that led to the U.S. overthrowing the government.

9. Víctor Hugo Cruz was disappointed in this huge production with a cast of about a hundred people. Whereas the original production and various revivals used more North American cowboy music, this glitsy production used popular country and western tunes with flashy costumes. The aim was to attract a large audience, but the result overshadowed the play (interview with Cruz).

10. This theme Cruz used in his first play, *Dos y dos son cinco [Two plus Two are Five]*. This play was a great success in 1971 and has been revived at least twice since then. The play is a study on dominance and mind control through humiliation. It is about a teacher–student relationship in which the authority relationship is eventually inverted. However, the student does not continue the cycle. He does not abuse the teacher but must forcibly remove her from his new school because she will not acknowledge that two plus two are four.

11. Lemus's adult plays are so irreverent and satirically absurd one would expect him to have an outrageous Joe Orton-esque personality. However, he is deeply pensive and serious. He writes in this form to communicate his concern for the social condition, a concern he directly expresses in his children's theater.

4. Didactic Theater

1. Grotowski's plays often focused on human suffering (*Towards a Poor Theatre*. New York: Simon and Schuster, 1968). He argues that the purpose of the theater is to heal the audience. One of his most famous works, *Akropolis*, focused on the atrocity of the Holocaust. Both Grotowski's theater and ACSA suggest that actors need to take on the role of the courageous priest who takes people into their darkness for the purpose of healing.

2. He started another theater group and performed Carrillo's adaptation of *El Señor Presidente* and *Bajo la luna de Xelajú [Under the Moon of Xel-*

ajú], a play similar in plot to *Romeo and Juliet* denouncing racism. In 1999 the issue of racism was a close second to the civil war in thematic representation in the theater.

3. Lepe's direction and writing in this piece is very melodramatic, preachy, and simplistic. This weakness is especially obvious in the second scene of that play in progress which focuses on sexual child abuse. A little girl who is molested by her uncles grows up to be promiscuous and eventually becomes a prostitute. The didactic purpose of this scene is clearly denunciation of child abuse. However, the simplicity of the message was highlighted by one of the actresses during the rehearsal. She broke down crying, saying that the stereotype is not always true. She openly revealed that she had been sexually molested as an adolescent and that she was not promiscuous. Lepe understood her perspective, yet insisted that this was the only way to educate the masses about the social evils of child abuse.

4. I write "possibility" because of the ambiguity in the play; whether or not she killed the man she accuses of torturing her is the linchpin in the piece.

5. There are numerous other possibilities for the public's different reaction, such as: (1) The publicity for *Frida y el Capitán* showed a woman tied and tortured in a chair with the captain full of remorse and his face in his hands. This image possibly elicits pity. It also may be sexually provocative. Perhaps this image is more comfortable for a macho country than the image from *La muerte y la doncella* of a woman who had been abused turning the tables and currently retaining all the power over her alleged torturer; (2) the public is drawn to the remorse shown by the captain but dislikes the ambiguity in Dorfman's play since the audience is never sure whether the man is guilty of the past crimes or not; and (3) the date of the performances may have been a factor as well with IGA's production in 1986, the year of the signing of the Peace Accord, and *Contempo Teatro* in 1998–99.

6. The director of *Contempo Teatro,* Jorge Alberto Ramírez, gave me a copy of his script *Cicatrices [Scars].* It is a moralistic play about the familial problems that occur when a father is an alcoholic. The father eventually discovers the pain he has inflicted on his children and changes his ways. The play is similar to Lepe's work in its simplicity and overt didactic message, i.e., the father is drunk and accidentally leaves his daughter in the hands of his brother who happens to be a child molester. When the father realizes his mistake, he decides to never drink again. The text states that it is to help prevent and eradicate domestic violence based on Guatemalan decree number 97–96. This play is another example of how *Contempo Teatro* seeks to work within the system to address social issues.

7. Kénefic wrote the English translation of Carrillo's adaptation of *El Señor Presidente* for the aborted production with Joseph Papp.

8. The massacres were becoming public knowledge as more witnesses recounted the details. Rigoberta Menchú, Nobel Peace Prize winner in 1992, describes in detail a massacre in Chajul. The army selected the church plaza to torture prisoners for the purpose of intimidating the peasants. Most prisoners were unrecognizable to their relatives: "A number of them had been partially scalped and had one or both eyes gouged out. Others were missing

ears or fingernails, and their tongues had been cleft in two.... A young woman's breast had been entirely cut off" (quoted in Perera 1993, 105). The captain described in detail their methods of torture, including electricity and castration. They then set them on fire as the soldiers chanted, "Long live the army! Long live President Lucas!"

9. Ríos Montt's regime was a time of total chaos. In *Nunca más,* art mirrors reality; the play captures the nightmarish surrealism of his fanaticism and ruthlessness.

10. In April 1998, Bishop Gerardi had issued his report on human rights violations committed during the war. He stated that the army was responsible for most of the violence. Forty-eight hours later he was found bludgeoned to death in his garage. The judge in his case resigned after receiving numerous death threats (Harbury 2000, 334).

5. Symbolic Theater

1. An example of this determination is Albert Camus's statement, "[W]e must invent reason; we must create beauty out of nothingness" (quoted in Langer 1995, 30).

2. There is some overlap with some of the aforementioned didactic plays, such as the surrealistic scenes in *Nunca más.* However, the surrealism is used to portray a nightmarish situation rather than challenge the dominant metaphysical ideology.

3. There are always contradictions in describing theatrical movements such as my observation of a reconciliation model that reflects on the atrocities. Osorio's and Corleto's fringe work presents the violence, yet is categorically anti-Establishment theater. To illustrate this point of contradiction, I include one of my favorite anecdotes of theater during the Spanish Conquest. After Spain's invasion of 1524, Dominican and Franciscan monks brought religious plays which they implanted into the folk theater of the country. The use of theater by the church was an effective way to enslave the conquered. One of the most popular plots was of the Conquest, with a triumphant Christian baptism of the savages taking place at the end (Carrillo 1971, 41). However, the theater was not, and has never been, completely dictated by the Establishment.

Some sources claim that the theater was strongly controlled by the Spanish church and that theater was never outside the church until independence in 1821. However, Father Fray Antonio de Molina in his 1640 memoirs cites theatrical activities outside the church. In one of the stories, he describes two Mexican actresses, Teresa and Catrina, who were performing in Guatemala (Jones 1966, 446). The town official, Ignacio de Guzmán, flirted with "Cata," which enraged the actresses' Mexican boyfriends who had come to Guatemala after them. The four Mexicans tried to intimidate de Guzmán and inadvertently killed him. They were imprisoned and condemned to death. De Molina states that while the boyfriends were being hanged, Catalina was reading a playscript (probably not sanctioned by the church). She was later pardoned because of her beauty and, instead of death, was exiled. However, de Molina noted that he saw her again in Guatemala performing shortly thereafter.

4. Numerous theater artists claim they do not understand Corleto's avant-garde work. Corleto acknowledges this reaction from his colleagues. He told me that students who understand his work are able to enter into it fully. He states that it is ironic in the 1990s that only the young people understand his work. Two years ago he decided to retire from the theater to dedicate his time to writing more novels and editing. He is disgusted with the current theater and how difficult it is to make a living as an artist.

5. The script is not very inventive, but it gave work to numerous actors, musicians, and technicians and was one of the biggest and most technically advanced productions ever produced in Guatemala. The pictures that are included in the published version of the script are stunning in their depiction of two different cultures. The most talented theater artists in the country were gathered together for this production. Although the play was directed by French director Jean-Yves Peñafiel, the two most prominent directors in Guatemala served as designers: Joam Solo designed the set and Xavier Pacheco designed the costumes. Pacheco concurs that the "play is not very good, but it was a great event for Guatemalan theater" (interview).

6. When I lived in Guatemala in the early 1990s I would often pass a public dump site on the outskirts of a town called Pastores. There were always vultures flying around this particular dump which was about two miles from an army post. Every time I passed it I would think of the numerous tortured corpses that were discovered there during the years of the violence.

7. Trudeau, Simon, and Landau all argue that the major reason the human rights image has improved is international pressure monitoring the government's and army's actions.

8. They also have the vulgar gesture of the middle finger; however, five fingers spread out is the same message times five.

9. Osorio notes the irony that cable television, which brought MTV values from the States to Guatemala in the 1980s, had a much more profound impact on diverting the young from joining the idealistic rebel guerrillas and seducing them with "capitalist values" than all the money the U.S. poured into the military to fight communism. Apparently, rock-'n-roll is more enticing than the idealism offered by the guerrillas or the patriotism called for by the government.

10. Osorio told me the story of one memorable performance during which in one of the scenes an actor entered the bus with a galactic machine gun to rob the people. The police saw the bus but did not read the signs that said it was a theatrical presentation. The bus was pulled over and the police had drawn their guns as the audience screamed, "It's just a performance!" Osorio told me the actor playing the thief was in tears from his fear.

11. I went to see a very traditional foreign (Spanish) melodrama at the National Theater about El Cid's widow who wants to get remarried. There were about twenty people in the 400-seat house on a Friday night. I later interviewed the Director of the National Theater, Roberto Oliva Alonzo, who also played the role of El Cid's father-in-law. I asked him why they chose this production that had nothing to do with Guatemala. I didn't realize he had

been instrumental in choosing this play. He explained to me that "they" chose it because it was "good" theater. He then graciously offered me a book he had helped write about the National Theater which was hot off the press. The book describes the strong artistic movement in the 1970s which protested the violence and worked to promote social justice by artists such as Manuel José Arce, Víctor Hugo Cruz, and the Director of the National Theater himself, Roberto Oliva (*Teatro Nacional*, 14). It was interesting to see that Oliva included himself along with the prolific playwrights Arce and Cruz (and left out Carrillo). History is made by those in powerful positions! After the play I went with my friend to a bar in Zone 1 called *Cien Puertas* [One Hundred Doors]. I felt like I had walked into a totally different world. The bohemian atmosphere filled with artists and musicians had an energy I had never felt in Guatemala before. The men kissed each other on the cheek and embraced each other, the people sat around tables discussing art and beauty rather than money and sex, and the women were open and assertive in the conversation as well. *Cien Puertas* was filled with people from *Casa Bizarra* (Osorio's artist colony in Zone 1 of Guatemala City, discussed on earlier in the chapter).

12. My experience with Guatemalan drama is that Guatemalan artists lean toward emotional extremes (my North American perspective calls it melodrama) in their productions which Nájera does not do. The theater I worked at in Guatemala had invited a Spanish production of Harvey Fierstein's *Un final perfecto* [On Tidy Endings] from the capital which had won numerous awards for Best Production, Best Actress, and Best Direction that year. Xavier Pacheco directed this play dealing with the meeting between a gay lover and the ex-wife of a man who died of AIDS. The theater producers asked me to direct a workshop production to encourage the numerous English-speaking Spanish students in Antigua to attend my work so they would understand the Spanish production better. I was surprised to see the choices they made in the version from the capital. They either did not understand the New York, Jewish humor which runs throughout the play or they chose to ignore it. They focused on the grieving aspect in the piece and milked it for all it was worth. There wasn't a dry eye on the stage. I've seen several of Pacheco's productions and this seems to be a trademark of his work. From my North American lens I perceive the melodramatic emphasis as a flaw, but this issue of expressing emotion is clearly a cultural issue as well. This may be partly why I am drawn to Nájera's work, whom Guatemalans criticize harshly for being too intellectual and not dramatic enough.

13. During the 1980s and early 1990s people argued that the army in Guatemala would not completely destroy the guerrillas because their presence justified continued high appropriations and other benefits for the military (Woodward 1996, 122).

14. The Truth Commission findings have no judicial implications. They have no mandate to accuse individuals. However, the detailing of killings and the years most of the atrocities took place have focused attention on Ríos Montt. He claimed, on February 28, 1999, that he was never "informed of any act of that nature. I never fired a shot" (quoted in *The Economist*, March 13, 1999). The report identified American assistance in unlawful executions, kidnapping, and torture, which Bill Clinton verified.

15. North American Jennifer Harbury created an international scandal during her search for her missing husband during the war in Guatemala in the early 1990s. The Guatemalan army told her that her Guatemalan husband, Mayan Indian resistance leader Everardo Bámaca Velásquez had been killed in battle. She demanded the body be exhumed to discover if indeed he had been killed or if he was being held captive illegally and tortured. On more than one occasion, with loads of media attention, she had graves publicly disinterred to prove that Bámaca was not in the various plots the army had claimed. This courageous woman writes in her book *Searching for Everardo* that she was convinced he was alive and being detained. She knew that "in thirty years of war, not a single prisoner survived in army hands" (Harbury 2000, 12), but she was convinced that he was being tortured and thought she could save him. She held two hunger strikes in front of the major army base in Guatemala City. The media (including "Sixty Minutes") that covered her case led to the suspension of U.S. funding to the Guatemalan military. She later discovered devastating evidence that the Guatemalan army and the United States government knew that her husband had been held and tortured. By the time she discovered the information, her husband had been killed.

16. According to Guatemalan law, corpses must be buried within twenty-four hours after death. Bodies that are unidentified for over a day are buried as XX (anonymous) in the cemeteries. Sometimes when families later determine where their relatives may have been recovered, they pay the morgue to dig up a corpse. The relatives make regular visits to the morgues and often will leave photos on the walls with instructions on how to contact the family in the event of a positive identification (Simon 1987, 207). Human-rights groups and state prosecutors are collecting evidence of the 200,000 deaths during the war in an attempt to bring some of those responsible to justice. From 1997 to 1999 groups have been reopening mass graves around the country. The director of the Myrna Mack Foundation revealed the findings in March 1999: "These were no random attacks on alleged supporters of the guerrillas, but elements of a strategy co-ordinated in its aims and even its methods of death: bullets were seldom wasted on children, the killers just swung them against walls" (quoted in *The Economist*, March 13, 1999).

Bibliography

Acuña, René. "Una década de teatro guatemalteco, 1962–1973." *Latin American Theatre Review* 8.2 (1975): 59–73.

Albizúrez Palma, Francisco, and Catalina Barrios y Barrios. *Historia de la literatura Guatemalteca.* Guatemala City: University of San Carlos, 1982.

Albuquerque, Severino João. *Violent Acts: A Study of Contemporary Latin American Theatre.* Detroit: Wayne State University, 1991.

Arce, Manuel José. "Arbenz: El Coronel de la primavera." Unpublished script, 1986.

———. *Delito, condena y ejecución de una gallina: Y otras piezas de teatro grotesco.* Guatemala City: Editorial Universitaria Centroamericana, 1971.

Armírez, Olga. "Alma para una reina sin esperanza." Unpublished script, 1989.

———. "Domingo." Unpublished script, 1988.

———. "Mala noche buena." Unpublished script, 1988.

Bakhtin, Michael. *Rabelais and His World.* Trans. Helene Iswolsky. Cambridge, Mass.: MIT Press, 1968.

Bell, Peter D. *Guatemala: Getting Away with Murder.* New York: Human Rights Watch, 1991.

Benedetti, Mario. *Pedro y el Capitán.* Buenos Aires: Editorial Nueva Imagen, 1985.

Bentley, Eric. *Theatre of War.* New York: Viking Press, 1972.

Blau, Herbert. *Take Up the Bodies: Theatre at the Vanishing Point.* Urbana: University of Illinois Press, 1982.

Boal, Augusto. *Theatre of the Oppressed.* Trans. Charles A. and Maria-Odilia Leal McBride. New York: Theatre Communications Group, 1985.

Boudet, Rosa Ileana. *Teatro Nuevo: Una Respuesta.* Havana: Editorial Letras Cubanas, 1983.

Bravo-Elizondo, Pedro. "Guatemala: VII temporada de teatro departamental, May 21, 1989." *Latin American Theatre Review* 23 (Spring 1990): 111–114.

———. "II Taller centroamericano y del caribe: Guatemala." *Latin American Theatre Review* 25 (Fall 1991): 151–152.

Brenneman, Bob. "Ludicrous by Design." *Siglo News* (Guatemala), May 12, 1999, 4.

Brodie, Ian. "Clinton 'sorry for death squads': Makes apology many Guatemalans never thought they would hear." *The Gazette* (Montreal), March 12, 1999. Online Lexis-Nexis, Dec. 3, 1999.

Bruckner, Pascal. *The Tears of the White Man: Compassion as Contempt.* Trans. William R. Beer. New York: Collier Macmillan, 1983.

Carrera, Mario Alberto. *Ideas políticas en el teatro de Manuel Galich.* Guatemala City: Facultad de Humanidades, University of San Carlos, 1966.

Carrillo, Hugo. *La Calle del sexo verde y El Corazón del espantapájaros.* Guatemala City: Editorial de la Municipalidad, 1973.

———. "Cuando las putas se vestían de papel creppe." Unpublished script, 1990.

———. *The World Encyclopedia of Contemporary Theatre.* Ed. Don Rubin. "Guatemala," vol. 2 "The Americas." New York: Routledge, 1996, 286–296.

———. "Las Orgías sagradas de Maximon." Unpublished script, 1992b.

———. "El Teatro de los ochentas en Guatemala." *Latin American Theatre Review* 25.2 (1992a): 93–106.

———. "Orígenes y desarrollo del teatro guatemalteco." *Latin American Theatre Review* 5.3 (1971): 39–49.

"Celebran Centenario de Tradicional 'Huelga de Dolores' en Guatemala." *InfoLatina* S. A., Mexico, April 3, 1998. Online Lexis-Nexis, Nov. 30, 1999.

Chavarría Paredes, Miguel Angel. *Los Herejes.* Guatemala City: Comisión Municipal de Teatro, 1995.

Chesney Lawrence, Luis S. "El Teatro popular contemporáneo en America Latina." Diss., University of Southampton (United Kingdom), 1987.

Corleto, Manuel. "La café." Unpublished script, 1992.

———. *Cinco Piezas Teatro: Teatro 3.* Guatemala City: Departamento de Actividades Literarias de la Dirección General de Cultura y Bellas Artes de Guatemala, 1984.

———. "La Crónica fidedigna." Unpublished script, 1996.

———. *Cuatro Piezas Teatro: Teatro 1.* Guatemala City: Departamento de Actividades Literarias de la Dirección General de Cultura y Bellas Artes de Guatemala, 1974.

———. *La Profecía: Teatro coreográfico y musical.* Guatemala City: Manuel Corleto, 1989.

Cruickshank, John. *Albert Camus and the Literature of Revolt.* London: Oxford University Press, 1970.

Cruz, Victor Hugo. *El Benemérito Pueblo de Villa Buena and Smog.* Guatemala City: Serviprensa Centroaméricana, 1976.

———. *Dos y dos son cinco.* Guatemala City: Serviprensa Centroaméricana, 1971.

———. "El teatro en Guatemala en el marco de la represión y la violencia: El Teatro de los 70's y los 80's." Program for *Celcit en el VIIII Festival de Teatro de Cadiz,* Oct. 19–30, 1993, 10–11.

———. "En la rueda sin fin de los 'katunes.'" *Escenarios de dos mundos: In-*

ventario teatral de iberoamérica. Gen. ed. Moises Pérez Coterillo. Vol. 3. Madrid: Centro de Documentación Teatral, 1988, 15–16.

———. *Obra dramática de Manuel Galich*. Guatemala City: University of San Carlos, 1991.

———. *La pastelería*. Guatemala City: Serviprensa Centroaméricana, 1977.

———. "Vicente Nario"—*O cómo la Revolución puede ser un juego*. Guatemala City: Editorial Universitaria Colección Creación Literaria, 1994.

Dauster, Frank N. "The drama of Carlos Solórzano." *Modern Drama* 7 (May 1964): 89–100.

Delli Sante, Angela. *Nightmare or Reality: Guatemala in the 1980s*. Amsterdam: Thela Publishers, 1996.

"*Disappearances*": *A Workbook*. New York: Amnesty International, USA, 1981.

Dorfman, Ariel. *Death and the Maiden*. New York: Penguin Books, 1992.

Dreyer, Kevin. "Hugo Carrillo: 1928–1994." *Latin American Theatre Review* 18.1 (1994): 185–186.

Durán-Cogan, Mercedes F. "Hugo Carrillo's Dramaturgy as a Dialogue about Power." Diss., Simon Fraser University, 1993.

———. "Instancias de poder en *El Corazón del espantapájaros* de Hugo Carrillo." *Gestos* 22 (Nov. 11, 1996): 87–104.

Elsom, John. *Cold War Theatre*. New York: Routledge, 1992.

Espinosa, Carlos. "El Salvador y Guatemala: El Teatro peleador de Centroamérica." *Conjunto* 52 (April–June 1982): 122–128.

Esslin, Martin. *The Theatre of the Absurd*. Garden City, N.Y.: Doubleday, 1961.

Feinberg, Leonard. *Introduction to Satire*. Ames: Iowa State University Press, 1967.

Fernández Molina, Manuel. *Dos estudios históricos sobre el teatro en Guatemala*. Guatemala City: Tipografía Nacional, 1982.

———. "La Actividad teatral en Guatemala en la primera mitad del siglo XX." *Latin American Theatre Review* (Spring 1996): 131–145.

———. "1944–1988: Un Desarrollo lento pero continuado." *Escenarios de dos mundos: Inventario teatral de iberoamerica*. Gen. ed. Moises Perez Coterillo. Vol. 3. Madrid: Centro de Documentacion Teatral, 1988, 25–37.

Freeman, E. *The Theatre of Albert Camus: A Critical Study*. London: Methuen, 1971.

Fuchs, Elinor, ed. *Plays of the Holocaust: An International Anthology*. New York: Theatre Communications Group, 1997.

Gaensbauer, Deborah B. *The French Theatre of the Absurd*. Boston: Twayne Publishers, 1991.

Galich, Franz. "El Teatro como arma de lucha: De las tablas a los escenarios de la guerra popular revolucionaria." *Conjunto* 60 (1984): 107–111.

Gallardo, Maria Eugenia. "El jurado de las cuatro grandes" Unpublished script, 1999.

García Mejía, René. *Raíces del teatro guatemalteco*. Guatemala City: Tipografía Nacional, 1972.

———. "Teatro guatemalteco: Epoca indígena." *Conjunto* 29 (July–Sept. 76): 11–24.

Godínez, Jorge. *Qué lindo ser feo: Tres comedias*. Guatemala City: Editorial Óscar de León Palacios, 1993.

González Dubón, Douglas. "El Hombre sin mancha." *Cien años de Huelgas de dolores*. Guatemala City: University of San Carlos, 1998, 98–106.

———. "Romeyo Subuyuj and Julieta Pirir." Unpublished script, 1997.

———. "Vida, pasión y muerte de un pueblo." *Cien años de Huelgas de dolores*. Guatemala City: University of San Carlos, 1998.

Green, Duncan. *Guatemala: Burden of Paradise*. London: Association of Artists for Guatemala and the Latin American Bureau Ltd., 1992.

Green, Linda. *Fear as a Way of Life: Mayan Widows in Rural Guatemala*. New York: Columbia University Press, 1999.

Griffin, Dustin. *Satire: A Critical Reintroduction*. Lexington: University Press of Kentucky, 1993.

"Guatemala: Pending Justice." *The Economist Newspaper*, March 13, 1999. Online Lexis-Nexis, Dec. 3, 1999.

"Guatemala truth commission accuses military of 'genocide.' " *Agence France Presse*, Feb. 26, 1999. Online Lexis-Nexis, Dec. 3, 1999.

Haig, Robin Andrew. *The Anatomy of Humor*. Springfield, Ill.: Charles C. Thomas Publisher, 1988.

Harbury, Jennifer K. *Searching for Everardo: A Story of Love, War, and the CIA in Guatemala*. New York: Warner Books, 2000.

Hernández Solís, Adolfo. "Entrevista exclusiva: Maestro y Director Rubén Morales Monroy." *Arteatro* 3 (Feb—Mar 1991) 2–5.

———. "Política teatral, modos de producción infraestructura, festivales." *Escenarios de dos mundos: Inventario teatral de iberoamérica*. Gen. ed. Moises Pérez Coterillo. Vol. 3. Madrid: Centro de Documentación Teatral, 1988, 47–49.

Herrera, Ubico, and Ana Sivia. *"La Escenificación teatral en Guatemala en la segunda mitad del siglo XX: Dos décadas de teatro 1950–70."* Guatemala City: Serviprensa Centroamericana, 1980.

Huelga de dolores. Guatemala City: University of San Carlos, 1999.

Jonas, Suzanne, Ed McCaughan, and Elizabeth Sutherland Martínez, eds. *Guatemala: Tyranny on Trial*. San Francisco: Synthesis Publications, 1984.

Jones, Willis Knapp. *Behind Spanish American Footlights*. Austin: University of Texas Press, 1966.

Kénefic, Margarita, and Luis Escobedo. "Nunca más." Unpublished script, 1999.

Klein, Maxine. "A Country of Cruelty and Its Theatre." *Drama Survey* 71-72 (Winter 1968–Spring 1969): 164–70.

Landau, Saul. *The Guerilla Wars of Central America*. New York: St. Martin's Press, 1993.

Langer, Lawrence L. *The Age of Atrocity*. Toronto: Beacon Press, 1978.

———. *The Holocaust and the Literary Imagination*. New Haven, Conn.: Yale University Press, 1995.

Leinaweaver, Richard E. "*Rabinal Achi*: Commentary." *Latin American Theatre Review* 2 (Spring 1968): 3–15.

Lemus, William. " Frente el Palacio Nacional." Unpublished script, 1993.

———. *El Gran Titi: Teatro para niños*. Guatemala City: Tercer premio, 1982.

———. "Pánico en la cocina." Unpublished script, 1983.

Lenski, B. A. *Jean Anouilh: Stages in Rebellion*. Atlantic Highlands, N.J.: Humanities Press, 1975.

León, Mayro. "Alaíde." Unpublished script, 1999.

———. "La Esperanza y el fantasma." Guatemala City: University of San Carlos, 1995.

Lepe, Fran. "Mujeres de la guerra." Unpublished musical script of compañía ACSA, 1997.

Levenson, Deborah. "The Murder of an Actor and a Theatre." *NACLA Report on the Americas* 23 (March 1989): 4–5.

Lobe, Jim. "Guatemala: Military Logbooks Hold Gruesome Revelations." *Inter Press Service*, Guatemala City, May 20, 1999. Lexis-Nexis, Dec. 3, 1999.

Lyday, Leon F., and George W. Woodyard. *Dramatists in Revolt: The New Latin American Theatre*. Austin: University of Texas Press, 1976.

Márceles Daconte, Eduardo. "La Identidad del teatro latinoamericano." *Conjunto* 63 (Jan.–March 1985): 13–23.

Matthews, J. H. *Theatre in Dada and Surrealism*. Syracuse, N.Y.: Syracuse University Press, 1974.

McCaffrey, Donald W. *Assault on Society: Satirical Literature to Film*. London: Scarecrow Press, 1992.

McIntyre, H. G. *The Theatre of Jean Anouilh*. Totowa, N.J.: Barnes and Noble Books, 1981.

McMurray, George R. *Spanish American Writing Since 1941: A Critical Survey*. New York: Ungar, 1987.

Meléndez de Alonzo, María del Carmen. "Crónica de un grupo teatral guatemalateco: El Teatro de arte universitario." Guatemala City: University de San Carlos, 1996.

———. "Importancia del grupo diez en el teatro guatemalteco contemporáneo. Diss., University of San Carlos, Guatemala, 1985.

Méndez D'Avila, L. "El Teatro de dolores: Conversación de R. Díaz Gomar." *Cien años de Huelgas de dolores*. Guatemala City: University of San Carlos, 1998, 125–128.

Morán, Manuel. "Alaíde Foppa: El Rostro que nos falta." *Mexico*, June 16, 1977. Online Lexis-Nexis, Dec 4, 1999.

NACLA Report on the Americas. "Alaíde Foppa." 15 (Jan.–Feb. 1981): 41–42.

Nájera, Rubén E. "Laberintos." Unpublished script, 1998.

———. *WoO: Seis piezas dramáticas sin número de opus.* Guatemala City: Byrsa Ltda, 1996.

Natalia Carrillo, Norma. "Vigencia del teatro indígena." *Escenarios de dos mundos: Inventario teatral de iberoamérica.* Gen. ed. Moises Pérez Coterillo.Vol. 3. Madrid: Centro de Documentación Teatral, 1988, 38–40.

Niño, Jairo Anibal. *El Monte Calvo, antología colombiana del teatro de vanguardia.* Bogotá: Instituto Colombiano de Cultura, 1975.

O'Connell, David, ed. *The French Theatre of the Absurd.* Boston: Twayne Publishers, 1991.

Oliva, Roberto, Miguel Angel Vasquez, and Efrain Recinos. *Teatro nacional: Centro cultural Miguel Angel Asturias.* Guatemala City: Ministerio de Cultura y Deportes, 1999.

Oliver, William I., ed. *Voices of Change in the Spanish American Theater.* Austin: University of Texas Press, 1971.

Orellana, J. "En los cerros de ilóm." Unpublished opera, 1992.

Pavis, Patrice. *Dictionary of the Theatre: Terms, Concepts, and Analysis.* Trans. Christine Shantz. Toronto: University of Toronto Press, 1998.

Peña Mancilla, Roberto. "1900–1944: Primeras expresiones de un teatro nacional." *Escenarios de dos mundos: Inventario teatral de Iberoamérica.* Gen. ed. Moises Pérez Coterillo. Vol. 3. Madrid: Centro de Documentación Teatral, 1988, 17–24.

Perera, Víctor. *Unifishished Conquest: The Guatemalan Tragedy.* Berkeley: University of California Press, 1993.

Pérez, Corterillo, ed. "Once espectáculos para la memoria." Vol. 3. Madrid: Centro de Documentación Teatral, 1988, 42–43.

Petro, Peter. *Modern Satire: Four Studies.* New York: Mouton Publishers, 1982.

Pronko, Leonard Cabell. *The World of Jean Anouilh.* Berkeley: University of California Press, 1961.

Ramírez, Jorge, and Douglas González Dubón. "La Epopeya de las indias españolas." Unpublished script, 1991.

———. "El General no tiene quien lo inscriba." Unpublished script, 1995.

———. "Guatemala en pelota." Unpublished script, 1999.

Ramírez, Jorge Alberto. "La Violencia intrafamiliar." Unpublished script, sponsored by Compañía Contemporánea de Teatro, 1999.

———. "Rapidísima historia de la paz." Unpublished script, sponsored by Compañía Contemporánea de Teatro, 1998.

Risk, Beatriz J. *El Nuevo Teatro latinoamericano.* Mexico: Impresos Anáhuac, 1987.

Rosenheim, Edward W., Jr. *Swift and the Satirist's Art.* Chicago: University of Chicago Press, 1963.

Schaeffer, Neil. *The Art of Laughter.* New York: Columbia University Press, 1981.

Simon, Jean-Marie. *Guatemala: Eternal Spring—Eternal Tyranny*. New York: W.W. Norton, Inc, 1987.

Skloot, Robert, ed. *The Theatre of the Holocaust*. Madison: The University of Wisconsin Press, 1982.

Smith, Dick. "Hawks and Handsaws: A Personal History of Guatemalan Amateur Theatre and Related Civil Wars." Unpublished manuscript, 1992.

———. "Rubén Morales Monroy." *Siglo News*, Sept. 9, 1997, 2.

Smith, Jeffrey. "Massive Effort to Cover Up Facts of American's Death Despite U.S. Protests." *The Washington Post*, May 5, 1996. Online Lexis-Nexis, Dec. 13, 1999.

Solórzano, Carlos, ed. *Teatro guatemalteco contemporáneo*. Madrid: Aguilar, 1973.

———. *Teatro latinoamericano del siglo XX*. Buenos Aires: Nueva Visión, 1961.

Stoll, David. *Between Two Armies in the Ixil Towns of Guatemala*. New York: Columbia University Press, 1993.

———. *Rigoberta Menchú and the Story of All Poor Guatemalans*. Boulder, CO: Westview Press, 1999.

Szanto, George H. *Theater and Propaganda*. Austin: University of Texas, 1978.

Taylor, Diana. *Theatre of Crisis: Drama and Politics in Latin America*. Lexington: University Press of Kentucky, 1991.

"A teatro testimonio de la guerrilla." *Conjunto* 59 (Jan.–March 1984): 43–45.

Trudeau, Robert H. *Guatemalan Politics: The Popular Struggle for Democracy*. Boulder, CO: Lynne Rienner, 1993.

Versényi, Adam. *Theatre in Latin America: Religion, Politics, and Culture from Cortés to the 1980s*. New York: Cambridge University Press, 1993.

Weiner, Tim. "Guatemalans Covered Up Killing of an American, U.S. Aides Say." *The New York Times*, March 24, 1996. Online Lexis-Nexis, Dec. 13, 1999.

Weiss, Judith A. *Latin American Popular Theatre: The First Five Centuries*. Albuquerque: University of New Mexico Press, 1993.

Westlake, E. J. "Performing the Nation in Manuel Galich's *El tren amarillo*." *Latin American Theatre Review* 31 (Spring 1998): 107–117.

———. "*Tierra Libre*: Revisions of the Nation in Latin American Drama." Diss., University Of Wisconsin, 1997.

Woodward, Ralph Lee, Jr. "Guatemala." *Encyclopedia of Latin American History and Culture*. 6 vols. Ed. Barbara A. Tenenbeum. New York: Simon and Schuster, 1996.

Worcester, David. *The Art of Satire*. New York: Russell and Russell, 1960.

Zubieta, Celina. "Guatemala: A War to Exterminate the Mayan Indians." *Inter Press Service*, Guatemala City, Feb. 26, 1999. Online Lexis-Nexis, Dec. 3, 1999.

———. "Women of War." Review of play written by Fran Lepe. *Inter Press Service*, Guatemala City, May 30, 1997. Online Lexis-Nexis, Oct. 5, 1998.

INTERVIEWS

All interviews were conducted in person and audio aped during the months of September and November 1999.

ACSA (Arte y Comunicaciones Sociales) *Theatre group of five actors from Quetzaltenango,* Debora García, Yolanda Gramajo, Claudia Arreaga and Cristina Marroquín.

Armírez, Olga. *Playwright.*

Blanco, Mercedes. *Director, actress from Cuba.*

Corleto, Manuel. *Playwright, director, actor.*

Cruz, Victor Hugo. *Playwright, director, actor.*

De Leon, Myro. *Playwright, stage designer.*

Díaz Gomar, Roberto. *Director, actor, friend of Manuel José Arce.*

Escobedo, Luis, and Margarita Kénefic. *Playwrights and actors.*

Gallardo, Maria Eugenia. *Playwright, actress.*

Gonzáles Dubón, Douglas. *Playwright, director.*

Hernández Solís, Adolfo. *Theater professor and scholar, director.*

Juárez, Nicolás. *Director of Kaji' Toj', Teatro Contemporáneo.*

Lemus, William. *Playwright.*

Lepe, Fran. *Playwright, director.*

Lorka, Raul. *Actor, designer*

Molino, René. *Director.*

Nájera, Rubén E. *Playwright.*

Oliva Alonzo, Roberto. *Director of Teatro National, actor, director.*

Orantes, Patricia. *Actress.*

Osorio, Jose. *Performance artist, director of Arte Urbano.*

Panchenco, Xiviar. *Director.*

Porras, Alfredo. *Director of Teatro Centro, actor.*

Ramirez, Jorge Alberto. *Playwright, actor, director.*

Ramírez, Jorge Fuentes. *Playwright, actor.*

Smith, Dick. *Director, actor, writer.*

Valenzuela, Felipe. *Playwright.*

Index

ACSA (Arte y Comunicaciones Sociales para la Paz), 115–24
Acuña, René, 57–58, 61
Albuquerque, Severino, 23–24
Alaíde, 135–39, 146
Arbenz, Jacobo, 22, 45–46
Arce, Manuel José, 45–47, 54, 57, 64, 71, 80, 102, 186, 188–89, 195
Arevalo, Juan José, 40, 142
Armírez, Olga, 72
Asturias, Miguel Angel, 47, 55–57, 80

benemérito pueblo de Villanueva, El, 72, 102
Blanco, Mercedes, 121, 124–34
Bruckner, Pascal, 20–21

Café, La, 151–53, 178
calle del sexo verde, La, 48–49
Carrera, Mario Alberto, 37, 45
Carrillo, Hugo, 26–27, 32, 36, 41, 42, 45, 47–57, 71–72, 102, 139, 141, 145, 186, 189, 191–92
Casa Bizarra, 158–59, 161, 195
Castillo Armas, Carlos, 46–47
cerros de ilóm, En los, 91
Civil war figures, 12, 14
Clinton, Bill, 22, 188, 195
Clitemnestra ha muerto, 163–72
consigma, La, 69–70, 180
Contempo Teatro, 128, 131, 192
Contraes, Hugo, 30
corazón del espantapájaros, El, 45, 49–54, 58, 63, 139, 141, 145
Corelto, Manuel, 32, 80, 148–158, 177–78, 186, 193
costumbrista, 35, 37
criollo [Europeans born in Latin America], 44

Crónica fidedigna, La, 153–58
Cruz, Victor Hugo, 27–28, 32, 54, 65, 75, 78, 80, 101–6, 112, 186, 191, 195
Cuando las putas se vestian de papel crepe, 72–73

Dadaism, 34, 148, 150, 159–62, 181, 185
Díaz Goman, Roberto, 62
Dioses ausentes, Los, 172–77
Dos Que Tres, 73–74
Durán-Cogan, Mercedes, 53
Delito, condena y ejecución de una gallina, 45, 58–60
DeVine, Carol and Michael, 29–30
"disappearances," 12
Domingo, 72
Dorfman, Ariel, 18–19, 131, 179–80

Electro show, 69–71, 180
epopeya de las Indias españolas, La, 83–85
Escobedo, Luis, 11, 80, 113, 139

Fernández Molina, Manuel, 40, 41, 54
Foppa, Alaíde, 135–36, 144. See also *Alaíde*
Frente al Palacio Nacional, 108–10
Frida y el Capitán, 113, 121, 128–31, 139
Fusiles y frijoles, 88

Galich, Manuel, 36, 42–45, 66, 71
Gambaro, Grieselda, 26
García Mejía, René, 39
García Muñoz, Francisco, 62
General no tiene quien lo inscriba, El, 86, 92
Gerardi, Monseñor, 145, 193

Golden Age of Theatre, 31–32, 44, 54, 56, 66–67, 75–76, 121, 128, 149, 185
González, Douglas, 83–86, 90, 96–100, 111, 189, 190
gran tití, El, 106–7
Grupo Diez, 69
Grupo Teatral Fantasía, 83

Haig, Robin Andrew, 90
Harbury, Jennifer, 196
Herejes, Los, 92
Huelga de dolores, 38, 77–78, 80–86, 90–91, 112, 141
huésped de Longinos, El, 162

Ida y vuelta, 42
IGA, 11

Juárez, Fernando Nicolás, 127

Kénefic, Margarita, 55, 113, 139, 192
Klein, Maxine, 20–21

Landau, Saul, 64
Langer, Lawrence, 15, 16, 179
Laramie Project, The, 181–84
Lemus, William, 78, 101, 106–12, 191
León, Mayro, 135
Lepe, Fran, 32, 116, 120–21, 191–92
"liberation," 46
Lucas García, Romeo, 63–64, 87, 193; parody of, 93–94

Mack, Myrna, 163–64, 196
Madre Corage, 113, 121–24, 146
Mano Blanco, 54
Martínez Bernaldo, Alberto, 39
massacres, 12
Mejía Victores, Huberto, 68
Menchú, Rigoberta, 192
Méndez de la Vega, Luz, 120
Mendizábal, Ricardo, 68
mestizo [mixed European and native ancestry], 13, 19, 37, 54–55, 75, 77, 82, 184, 188
Monroy, Rubén Morales, 71, 74–75
monte calvo, El, 117, 121, 124
muerte y la doncella, La, 131, 192
Mugre, La, 43
Mujeres de la guerra, 113, 115–20, 146

Nájera, Rubén, 11, 34, 148–50, 162–78, 185–86
national theatre, 14, 40; National Theatre, 194; nationalist plays, 35
Nunca más, 113, 139–46, 193

Orellana, J., 91
Osorio, José, 32, 148–50, 158–62, 177, 185, 193–94

Pánico en la cocina, 107–8
Papá Natas, 42–43
Papp, Joseph, 55–56, 192
Patrullas de autodefensa civil (PAC), 88
Peace Accord, 13, 17, 37, 97, 99
Perera, Victor, 87

Rabinal Achí, 26–27, 41
Raíces del Teatro Guatemalteco, 26
Ramírez, Jorge, 83–86, 90, 92, 110–11, 190–91
Rapidísima historia de la paz, 113, 131–35, 146
Reagan, Ronald, 88
REHMI (the reconstruction of the historical memory), 97
Revolution of 1944, 31, 40
Rios Montt, Efraín, 67–68, 77, 79, 86–89, 180, 193; parodies on, 89–95, 142–43
Rolando, José, 73–74
Romeo Subuyj and Julieta Pirir, 96–100

Sacra conversación, 162–63
Señor Presidente, El, 47, 55–57
Skloot, Robert, 17–18
Smith, Dick, 56, 59–63, 67–68, 75, 86, 89–91, 180, 185, 190
Solórzano, Carlos, 37, 183
Sopa de cebollas, 84–85
Spanish embassy massacre, 64–65, 104

Taylor, Diana, 23–26, 188
Teatro Centro, 63, 68

Teatro Vivo, El, 62
Theatre of the Absurd, 34, 148, 154–57, 181
theatre of atrocity, 14, 17–18
theatre of the Holocaust, 15, 17–18
tren amarillo, El, 43, 44, 71–72
Truth Commission, 14, 195

Ubico, Jorge, 36, 38, 76, 80
United Fruit Company, 43–46

Valdez, Sergio, 20
Vincente Nario—O óomo la Revolución puede ser un juego, 103

Wheeler, Dennis, 29
Weiss, Judith, 14, 25
Westlake, Jane, 19, 40, 183

XX, 62

Ydígoras, Fuentes Miguel, 48–49